WOMEN IN KHAKI

Frontispiece

HRH The Duchess of Kent, Controller Commandant of the WRAC, inspecting the first WRAC officer cadets to take part in The Sovereign's Parade at the Royal Military Academy Sandhurst in April 1984. On the left is Captain Pepi Hollingsworth (now Major Pepi Simpson).

WOMEN IN KHAKI

The story of the British woman soldier

ROY TERRY

Columbus Books
London

First published in Great Britain in 1988 by
Columbus Books Limited
19-23 Ludgate Hill
London, EC4M 7PD

Designed by Ronald Clark

British Library Cataloguing in Publication Data
Terry, Roy
Women in khaki: the story of the British
woman soldier.
1. Great Britain. Army. Women's Royal Army
Corps, to 1988
I. Title
355.2'2'088042

ISBN 0–86287–321–5

Set in Linotron Palatino
by Falcon Graphic Art Ltd
Wallington, Surrey

Printed and bound in Great Britain by
Butler and Tanner Limited, Frome, Somerset

CONTENTS

ILLUSTRATIONS

Unless otherwise indicated, photographs are reproduced courtesy of the Imperial War Museum

Brigadier Eileen Nolan on her appointment as chairman of the Senior Service Women Officers of the [NATO] Alliance committee in 1976.

AUTHOR'S NOTE

This book is the culmination of three years of research that began in 1985 in the sitting-room of Brigadier Eileen Nolan CB, a former director of the Women's Royal Army Corps.

The previous year she had finally laid aside her uniform after serving seven years as deputy controller commandant, but her retirement in fact marked the end of 42 years' service in the British Army, a remarkable achievement by any standards made more notable because she had enlisted originally as a private in the wartime Auxiliary Territorial Service.

Initially my intention had been to write a biography of a woman general, but Brigadier Nolan gradually steered me away from her life story towards what she considered a far more worthy subject – the WRAC, which in 1988 celebrates its Golden Jubilee. This was typical of a woman who sees herself not as someone out of the ordinary, which undoubtedly she is, but merely as one person who made a small contribution to an organization far greater than any individual. She conveyed the enormous pride which everyone in the ATS felt, and in the WRAC today feels, about being in the British Army. Her enthusiasm was so infectious and convincing that I found myself growing more and more intrigued with the origins of a corps which pioneered women's service in the United Kingdom and, indeed, in the Western world. My interest was further aroused by reading Controller J. M. Cowper's excellent review of the ATS published by the War Office in 1949, and Brigadier Shelford Bidwell's *The Women's Royal Army Corps*, published by Leo Cooper in 1977. To both these authors I owe a tremendous debt because they stimulated further research.

Nevertheless, truly can it be said that without Eileen Nolan this book could not and would not have been written. She not only inspired it but watched over it from conception to realization. Having said that, let me at once make it clear that I am responsible for its contents and that where there are comments on military policy which are not directly attributed, these represent my own opinions. Despite any doubts she entertained, Brigadier Nolan continued to open doors which enabled me to meet a host of her fellow officers, many of them her lifelong friends, and her help throughout was invaluable. Any errors of fact or interpretation in the finished typescript are mine alone.

Perhaps it is prudent to define what I hoped to achieve in writing this book. Usually the story of any army regiment is read only by those who have a specific interest in military subjects. Being a civilian and a journalist, I could take a more objective view of the WRAC, and in researching its history I was naturally drawn to episodes which would have a wide general interest. A regiment consists of people and, wherever possible, I have tried to tell the story as they lived it rather than relate a series of events in strict chronological order. This required selectivity of a kind which may bring severe censure from those who feel that their contribution has been ignored or that other important episodes have been overlooked.

This book has received the support of the WRAC directorate and I wish to record my special thanks to Brigadier Anne Field CB, deputy controller commandant and a former director; to Brigadier Shirley Nield ADC, the director; and to her predecessor, Brigadier Helen Meechie CBE, the first former director of the WRAC to be appointed to the general staff of the Army. Despite their busy schedules they found time to grant me several interviews and cleared the way for me to interview serving officers and other ranks. My very special thanks to Colonel Gael Ramsay MBE, deputy director, who could not have been more helpful in obtaining information I required. The directorate also enabled me to visit the WRAC Centre in Guildford where the then commandant, Colonel Audrey Smith, and her deputy, Major Mary Harwood, went out of their way to co-operate. Captain Janice Robinson was also exceptionally co-operative in searching out photographs and the names of retired officers who were able to assist with certain details.

My research led me to Edinburgh and Miss Betty Vetch, a former chief commander in the ATS, who also went out of her way to assist me, even to the extent of insisting that I borrow her Mini during my stay. She took me to the home of Keith Chalmers Watson, grandson of Dr Mona Chalmers Watson CBE, the first director of the Women's Army Auxiliary Corps. He and his wife Kirsteen loaned me the press cuttings which his grandmother so meticulously kept during the First World War, thus saving me hours of research in libraries. In Edinburgh I also met Miss Bunty Craig, formerly of the Queen Alexandra's Royal Army Nursing Corps, Major Betty Crawford and Brigadier Sheila Heaney CB, MBE, TD, a former director of the WRAC. Brigadier Heaney's incisive views were of considerable help and I am grateful not only for her candour but also for introducing me to one of the few surviving members of the Queen Mary's Army Auxiliary Corps, Miss Georgina Baxter, who had kept all her badges and papers in such immaculate order that they were snapped up immediately by the Corps Museum in Guildford.

I heard last year with great sadness of the death of Dame Leslie Whateley, a former director of the ATS. Some months earlier she had given me what was to be her last interview; despite her 88 years, she was able to remember her wartime days with remarkable clarity. She was a great lady and it is distressing to all that she will miss the celebrations of the founding of the ATS in 1938. I am grateful for her generosity in allowing me to quote extensively from her book *As Thoughts Survive*, published by Hutchinson in 1948.

Another great lady, Brigadier Dame Mary Tyrwhitt TD, welcomed me to her home and revealed much about the behind-the-scenes manoeuvring in the post-war years which led to the establishment of the present-day WRAC.

Others I would like to thank are Colonel Dorothy Humphery CBE; Colonel Lucy Davies CBE; Colonel Betty Macfie; Colonel Anne Clissitt; and Lieutenant-Colonel Hugh Conroy MC. Miss Irene Ludlow BEM, who was a batwoman with the rank of corporal in the WRAC for many years, was also particularly helpful. My thanks also to Colonel Daphne Clark MBE, Lieutenant-Colonel Audrey Purton OBE, Lieutenant-Colonel Elaine Anton MBE, and Major Rowena Patrick for supplying information about their tours abroad.

I thank also former members of the Women's Army Corps in the United States for their assistance and co-operation: Brigadier-General Elizabeth P. Hoisington, Brigadier-General Mildred C. Bailey, Brigadier-General Evelyn P. (Pat) Foote, Lieutenant-Colonel Catherine Coll and Colonel Bettie Jane Morden.

I must also record my thanks to Major Dionne Parker, who until last year was curator of the Corps Museum at Guildford. Without her assistance I would certainly have missed much valuable material – for instance, it was she who put me in touch with Mrs Ruth Hicks of Farnham, Surrey, who commanded a company of bakers in the ATS. Captain Kate McGregor, who succeeded Major Parker as curator of the museum, gave me invaluable assistance in selecting photographs from the museum's extensive archives. I also thank Lieutenant-Colonel David Dunn, general secretary of the WRAC Association, for his co-operation.

If I have any regret, it is that I was never able to meet Dame Helen Gwynne-Vaughan, who became a legend in her lifetime and whose name today, nearly twenty years after her death, is still revered by all who serve in the WRAC. My knowledge of her is partly due to the superb biography by Molly Izzard, to whom I must also acknowledge my indebtedness. Fortunately Dame Helen recorded her own reminiscences in her book *Service With the Army* (Hutchinson 1942) and I have borrowed liberally from her writings. Molly Izzard called her book *A Heroine in Her Time* (Macmillan 1969) but I believe Dame Helen will remain a heroine for all time.

I am grateful to my literary agent, Christopher Little, for introducing me to my editor, Gill Gibbins of Columbus Books, who from the moment the idea of this book was put to her expressed enthusiastic interest. There are many others too numerous to mention, who helped along the way. I trust they will accept my thanks for their invaluable assistance.

Roy Terry, Berkshire, 1988

Outdoor obstacle course for potential WRAC officers at the Regular Commissions Board, Westbury.

PROLOGUE

In 1917 women for the first time officially donned the soldier's traditional khaki and proudly marched to war as members of the Women's Army Auxiliary Corps. In the excitement at being given the opportunity to serve King and Country, they probably paid little heed to the possibility that they were taking the first positive steps along a road leading towards a social revolution in Britain and the Western world. These early pioneers might have been armed only with pots and pans – 'ladies of the frying pan' as they were dubbed – but they started a war of their own against entrenched male prejudice which governed the role of women in society. The British Army had been exclusively masculine for the 256 years of its history and there seemed small chance that it would really change.

The success of the WAAC campaign can be measured today by the progress that the daughters, granddaughters and great-granddaughters of those pioneers have made in the Women's Royal Army Corps. Khaki has long since been discarded in favour of the lovat green uniforms the public sees when the Corps is on parade; but during army exercises these female soldiers wear combat kit like the men, and, like the men, will carry arms and use them when duty demands.

There is a common belief that the modern soldier is nothing like as tough as his predecessor who served Queen Victoria. The girls who braved the mud and bitter cold of France in the First World War, and even their Second World War successors in the Auxiliary Territorial Service, would envy the comparative luxury of the centrally-heated bedroom which a private in the WRAC shares with only three colleagues, but they would blanch at the training the modern soldier must undergo. 'When you join the Army, you belong to it twenty-four hours a day, seven days a week,' the recruiting brochure warns. The Army demands high standards of all who serve, and a woman has to be fit, intelligent and dedicated if she is to pass the rigid tests required to earn the coveted badge of the WRAC.

It has been said, doubtless by the less charitably minded, that men such as the Duke of Wellington, Gordon of Khartoum, even Montgomery of Alamein, might not have become officers had they faced a modern selection board. The Iron Duke – a dreary, shy lad who shunned playground games, preferring instead to lounge against a tree – would certainly have found it difficult to convince the Army in 1988 that he had the 'qualities specially belonging to a leader'. And the Army needs a lot of convincing before granting a commission. The onus is placed squarely on the shoulders of applicants to demonstrate that they possess leadership quality, what General Sir John Hackett describes as that innate 'ability to get people to do things *willingly*'.

The testing ground for future army officers, man or woman, is a country house near Westbury in Wiltshire. For centuries Leighton House was the home of the Phipps family but today it is the headquarters of the Regular Commissions Board, presided over by a brigadier, assisted by three vice-presidents who are colonels, one of whom will be a woman when there are officer candidates for the WRAC. Every candidate for a commission has to spend three and a half days here undergoing a series of tests devised by army psychologists to sort out the 'foxes', or failures, from the 'dogs', or passes. No 'fox' will ever receive the Queen's commission but the 'dogs' go on to the Royal Military Academy at Sandhurst. The course for women is almost exactly the same as for men, the only difference being that the more arduous physical exercises are slightly – and the Army stresses it is very slightly – modified to suit the smaller dimensions of the female form. So the challenge facing future officers in the WRAC is as great initially as that confronting men who might wish to join the SAS.

For WRAC officer candidates the route to Westbury lies via the Corps Centre in Guildford, where they attend a 'pre-RCB' under the watchful and critical eye of a lieutenant-colonel. 'Candidates are told that we can judge only what we see, so it is up to them to demonstrate the qualities of leadership,' she says. And if asked to clarify those qualities, she is likely to quote the recruiting brochure: 'The Army is no more able than anyone else to define leadership absolutely, other than to throw at you words like common sense, integrity, initiative, determination, responsibility, kindliness, and a concern for others.' The 48-hour course at Guildford is intended primarily to help the WRAC decide which candidates should be recommended for the RCB, but it is stressed that even if a girl fails here she still has the right to attend the board. From the candidates' point of view, Guildford helps them to familiarize themselves with the type of exercises encountered at Westbury and so confront the RCB in a more relaxed frame of mind.

The course at Westbury is designed to create conditions of stress – the sort of stress which might be faced on the battlefield where decisions can mean the difference between life and death. However, the intelligence tests are fairly standard, so by the time the would-be officer reaches Westbury she has already demonstrated that her IQ is above average. She will have to answer questions on general knowledge, service knowledge and current affairs.

It is the planning project which calls for real application. Ultimately the Army exists to fight battles, and combat requires officers to make decisions – sometimes without adequate information about the deployment of the enemy or basic details of the type of terrain ahead, or the strength and weaknesses of the firepower which may be encountered. Officers must think quickly under great stress making judicious use of people, equipment, time and distance; lives depend on their judgment. For this reason problems are set which will state a situation facing an individual but which will be deliberately vague on other points, thus leaving the candidate to make assumptions and devise a plan of action using common sense and logic. A time limit is imposed in an attempt to simulate stress conditions.

Imagine you are one of a party of four girls stranded without food or adequate clothing in the most inhospitable part of the Welsh countryside. One of your colleagues is injured and unconscious, and it is imperative to obtain medical aid as soon as possible. After heavy rain, a dam upstream is likely to burst its banks and flood the area. It is getting dark, there is no transport, emergency equipment is virtually non-existent. However, a short distance away there is a farmhouse and much further away in the opposite direction there is a power station. You are in command. What do you do? Think, think, think – in the examination room you are up against a time barrier which makes the four-minute mile look like an easy jog round a parade ground. Do you devise a stretcher and take it in turns to carry the injured girl over rough terrain without a light or a compass? If so, in which direction do you go? The farmhouse perhaps, but what is the significance of the power station? You are giving the orders . . . but you must start writing now or you will not finish in time.

This example of the sort of problem Westbury will pose has been amended so that future candidates do not gain an unfair advantage, and it might be some consolation to know that there is no correct answer. What the Army requires is evidence that candidates can think clearly and practically in an emergency, that they have a concern for the safety of others and that they can give reasons for their decisions. The problem contains complications which require the sacrifice of lesser priorities for more urgent and pressing considerations, and gives the group leader, a major who will assess the answers, an insight into the minds of the candidates.

The written answer does not end this particular agony because each candidate is faced with a classroom analysis of her approach when she can either defend her solution or amend it after listening to other options suggested by those in her group. Reception of valid suggestions, dismissal of impractical ideas, insistence on sticking to the initial plan of action, and ability to control the ensuing discussion, all reveal vital personality traits. Each candidate is observed constantly, beginning to score plus or minus points which will mean pass or fail. The major in charge of any particular group knows nothing of individual backgrounds, is concerned only with what he or she sees. They must remain absolutely impassive. Not one flicker of approval or disapproval should be evident in either expression or reaction.

The outdoor exercises determine how individuals work together as part of a team and how they react when given command. For some, no leaders are selected, while for others a leader is appointed and briefed on what has to be accomplished. The candidates are confronted by ladders, ropes, toggles, planks and poles. One exercise might involve crossing a pond using two narrow planks which are too short to span it. An added hazard is that the planks appear as if they would crack under the weight of a child, let alone an adult. Or a bucket of water has to be hauled over a high beam – without spilling a drop, and all in the time allocated. The girls are on their own to do as they see fit.

What distinguishes a leader from a follower? It is the ability in these circumstances to sum up what is required, work out the practicalities of certain manoeuvres, make the most economical use of the team as a whole, give clear and unambiguous orders, and pull one's own weight if required. Self-assertion does not necessarily equal ability. A girl may stay in the background while she is studying the situation and only then suggest a well-reasoned solution which works perfectly. But for this kind of temperament will the obstacle course in the gymnasium prove her undoing? It involves crawling through a tunnel, up an assault net, over a high beam, bouncing off a trampette through a window between two wall bars, scaling a narrow plank, sliding down a pole and negotiating a series of tyres suspended on ropes. Three minutes are allowed to complete the circuit and then, if there is time to spare, she can start again. The course requires confidence in one's own ability and a sense of balance, and contains a controlled degree of risk-taking. Fitness is essential and determination to succeed all-important. Back in the classroom candidates may be asked to deliver a 'lecturette' – the official term – on nominated subjects and are then interviewed on an individual basis to determine background, to explore motives for wishing to join the Army as an officer, to examine academic records, to probe friendships at school, university or workplace.

Each member of the Westbury board makes an assessment of each candidate in as many as nineteen categories on a one-to-five rating. Occasionally there is disagreement, and then discussion can continue for hours. If there is any doubt remaining, the decision goes against the candidate on the basis that no chances can be taken with officers who in the future will be called on to command other people.

Successful candidates, about 45 to 50 per cent, are recommended for a cadetship at Sandhurst graded either as plain dogs; Charlies, which are better; Bravos, which are exceptional; or Alphas, which are so rare that few present board members can remember seeing one. Candidates are advised by letter within forty-eight hours whether they have passed or failed and 'foxes' are always given reasons for their not making the grade.

Those who pass Westbury can be assured that they have successfully negotiated one of the most difficult hurdles on the way to earning that revered symbol of leadership – a star on their shoulders, denoting the rank of second-lieutenant. Ahead of them now is Sandhurst where, despite all its male tradition, everyone meets on equal terms. Not all complete the course at Sandhurst even after a successful RCB, but those who do are placed in command of other ranks who have arrived by a different, and rather less demanding, route.

For the majority of girls who are not destined to be officers, the first contact with the WRAC is the recuiting office where she completes a form giving information about her family, her schooling and any former employment. She then sits an army education test, which is in five parts: observation of patterns (dominoes, for example), which require completing; arithmetic problems; simple mechanical posers; word meanings; and instruction questions which determine her ability to interpret orders. This test indicates an intelligence rating as well as highlighting skills that might usefully be employed. After that she will be interviewed by a recruiter who, apart from explaining something about the WRAC and life in the Army, will assess her personality. Among other things, the recruiter must judge whether the girl is the sort of person likely to fit into a communal life or someone who could be susceptible to homesickness. The Army does not want square pegs for the round holes it offers in its variety of jobs.

If the recruit wishes to proceed further, she is required to choose up to three areas of employment in order of preference. She then faces another interview with an army careers officer, during which he or she will discuss her reasons for wishing to join the Army, try to establish any negative characteristics, and confirm or alter the grading which the recruiter has given her. After passing a medical examination the recruit is allocated a number and her details are fed into a computer, which places each candidate in a selection order based first on education scores and then on character assessment. The Army selects only the best and, with recruits applying daily, the list grows longer and longer with some unfortunates dropping further and further down.

If a candidate is called up to report to the WRAC Centre at Guildford, she stays overnight and shares a room with three others, enabling her to sample life at the Centre, meet NCOs and officers, and discuss the WRAC with the regulars. Here she undergoes further written tests and is also required to jog for half-a-mile in a group led by the physical training instructor as a warm-up for the mile run which must be completed in less than ten minutes. Despite being warned about the Army's fitness requirement, which entails a certain amount of application and perhaps training before reporting to Guildford, many girls fail this test and offer as an excuse: 'The mile here is much longer than at home.' It isn't. Those who do pass are invited to enlist for a six-and-a-half week course at Guildford which includes a three-day exercise in the field, drill, first aid and map-reading as well as instruction on nuclear, biological and chemical warfare.

'Join the professionals,' the advertisement proclaims and that is exactly what the men and women in the British Army are. When they enter the ranks at whatever level, each soldier embarks on a journey which will equip him or her for highly specialized jobs – careers for life, if they so choose. The opportunities for women are increasing every year as the barriers fall. Some, in the Army Catering Corps, still wield the traditional pots and pans. Others operate sophisticated computers which control the military destiny of nations in a push-button age.

The story of the WRAC is one of courage, of determination and of glorious achievement after years when the 'Petticoat Army' was often ridiculed, sometimes reviled and only occasionally rewarded. Two world wars were needed before Britain's decision-makers grudgingly conceded that women were a permanent part of what was once considered a strictly man-sized job. Today so essential have women soldiers become that Britain could not go to war again without them.

Yet, ironically, it was not a woman who set them on the warpath but a man – a man of mystery with a vision which never quite worked out the way he intended.

1
A WOMAN'S PLACE

The idea of women playing a role in the British armed forces first occurred to a cavalryman as he lay wounded on the battlefield under a hot African sun in the Sudan, 90 years ago. Sergeant-Major Edward Charles Baker, whether in a moment of delirium or percipience, envisaged a troop of graceful young ladies galloping side-saddle to his rescue, lifting him tenderly on to a stretcher and transporting him back to safety and to regular army nurses and surgeons.

Nurses had been well-established in army hospitals since the Crimea but the notion of exposing women to the battlefield, or even the Lines of Communication, was another matter. Had Baker dared to voice his thoughts to fellow NCOs he would have been greeted with ribald laughter and dismissed as crazy; officers would have spluttered over their whiskies and soda at the temerity of a mere sergeant-major putting forward such a preposterous proposal.

In late Victorian Britain a woman's place was in the home: her circumstances, and the opportunities open to her depended on her status in society. The only changes in attitude demanded of upper-class ladies were the realization that newly acquired wealth was no longer considered vulgar and the acceptance into their ranks of the daughters of recently ennobled magnates and professional men. In fact life went on much as before because new peers adhered to the ethos of landed estates; thus women continued to preside over town and country houses in a world where beauty and breeding were deemed more important than brains.

Upper- and middle-class women met in charitable and voluntary activities; their upbringing was similar in that men wished wives and daughters to do as little housework as possible. The wealthier the family, the more domestic servants were employed in the household and with wages at the turn of the century ranging from about £30 a year for a cook, £25 for a parlourmaid and £14 for a housemaid, even impecunious schoolmasters and curates at the lower end of the middle-class scale could afford such help. One commentator even based his dividing line between middle- and working-class on the possession of servants.

On the fringe of each stratum, 'keeping up appearances' involved perpetual struggle and sacrifice, whether it was a middle-class family seeking to preserve gentility or a working-class family maintaining respectability. Although the wife of a skilled worker carried out her own domestic duties, it was not considered fitting for her to work outside the home. Such a woman took great pride in the neatness of her house, scoured the doorstep, ensured that her children's clothes were spotless, and usually her daughters as well as sons stayed at school until at least the official leaving age of fourteen.

A few girls from better-off families were breaking free from these constraints by taking university degrees, studying to be doctors or making a career in education but, while job opportunities were opening up for girls in other groups, all were very badly paid. Nursing, secretarial or clerical work was a cut above a position as a shop assistant, which in turn was preferred to domestic service. From that level, women in the lower echelons of the working-class were dragged down to the domestic and 'sweated' trades – millinery, dressmaking, sackmaking, boxmaking – and to various regional industries, such as the Lancashire cotton mills. The hours were long, conditions were unpleasant and unhealthy, and wages were derisory. The average wage of women in industrial work was 11*s* 7*d* a week, only one-third of the average pay for men similarly employed; even some waitresses and shop assistants were still forced to supplement their meagre incomes by occasional prostitution. Approximately 30 per cent of the population existed on or below the poverty line and for the women, worn out by hard work and too many pregnancies, life was a constant battle to make ends meet and to avoid descent into total squalor. Members of this group, particularly those living in communities with predominantly male employment patterns, such as mining and agricultural work, were the last to follow the trend towards smaller families. How could these women learn about the latest methods of birth control, let alone afford such devices, when they were trapped within the confines of their homes and immediate neighbourhood and cut off from the circulation of new ideas? The result was too many mouths to feed and children leaving school at an early age or attending lessons part-time while working up to 33 hours a week in factories in order to supplement the family income.

So it was not only military officers who would have scoffed at the idea of women joining the British Army. Unenfranchised, fulfilling their traditional subservient role, the majority struggling to care for their families, women themselves would have been bewildered by the prospect. While women had their dreams, probably it is fair to say that being a soldier was not one of them.

In 1898, at about the time Sergeant-Major Baker was recovering from his wounds, a 26-year-old student, Alexandra Mary Geddes, known to family and friends as Mona, became the first woman to receive the degree of

Doctor of Medicine at Edinburgh University. Commenting on that historic occasion, the *Scots Pictorial* said: 'The men took the innovation gallantly, and when the young lady, modest and charming, but wearing that air of immense capability that distinguishes all her family, appeared to be "capped", she was greeted with the very heartiest applause.'

Mona Geddes had another reason to celebrate that day. She was engaged to an Edinburgh physician but had vowed not to marry until she could write MD after her name. The graduation ceremony was no sooner over than she was hurrying home to exchange her academic gown for a wedding dress in time to drive to the church where Dr Douglas Chalmers Watson waited for his bride. During the next few years Mona established herself as a physician in Edinburgh, but her husband and two sons always took priority over her own ambitions. A Scottish journalist who knew her well described her as the least pushful of people. 'No whirlwind, no electric force, she is a quiet, smiling, tactful and clear-headed woman of the world, seeing the fun of things, getting her way because her way is clearly the right way, never fussing people, never losing her head.' She was a capable housewife and despite her considerable success as a doctor remained thoroughly domestic.

As the *Scots Pictorial* indicated, Mona came from a remarkable family which had already played a leading role in the campaign for women's rights. She was a niece of Elizabeth Garrett Anderson, the first woman MD graduate to practise as a doctor in Britain, and another aunt was Mrs Millicent Garrett Fawcett, president of the National Union of Women Suffrage Societies. During the First World War her elder brother, General Sir Eric Campbell Geddes, was director-general of transportation at General Headquarters and later became First Lord of the Admiralty; later still, after forming the Ministry of Transport, he was appointed chairman of the Dunlop Rubber Company and of Imperial Airways Limited. Her other brother, Brigadier-General Sir Auckland Geddes, a former professor of anatomy, was director of recruiting at the War Office during the First World War and would be responsible for Mona's involvement with the women's service; later he was ambassador to Washington and chairman of the Rio Tinto company. Mona's cousin, Dr Louisa Garrett Anderson, daughter of Elizabeth, was also to play a vital role in Mona's association with the Army. She introduced her to Helen Gwynne-Vaughan.

Like Sergeant-Major Baker, Helen Fraser was in Africa in 1898 but she was in Algiers, about 3,000 miles north-west of the Sudan where her stepfather was British Consul-General. A niece of Lord Saltoun, she was nineteen and facing a crucial moment in her life, determined to rebel against established notions about a woman's place in society: she wanted to read zoology, or at least botany, at university. Three years earlier she had been admonished for daring to discuss geometry with a youth at a dinner table – not at all a suitable topic for a young girl still in her teens. Botany, as it happened, was a most fashionable Victorian pursuit: plants, after all, were a fairly safe subject, just sufficiently aesthetic without any danger of being intellectual and, even more important, properly sexless. Yet despite botany's charms, the family was unsympathetic to Helen's ambition because they felt just as strongly that education spoiled a girl's chances of marriage. The argument raged but as the new century dawned Helen won her fight and was enrolled at King's College, London, reading botany with animal physiology as a subsidiary subject.

In 1904 she passed her B.Sc. examination with second class honours and the same year accepted the post of demonstrator to the professor of botany at the Royal Holloway College. She had matured from being a rather plump schoolgirl, with a thick plait of hair tied back by a bow, into a tall, striking young woman with a fresh, clear complexion and large, almost steely, grey eyes. Her voice, according to her biographer Molly Izzard, was deep-toned and distinctive – cool, patrician, unaffected but daunting. That description matches exactly the memories of others who met her in later life and who served with her in the Second World War. Helen had the voice and bearing of authority, someone who would stand no nonsense from either man or woman. Generally she was uncomfortable in the company of men, only at ease when surrounded by women of equal intellectual ability. Those steely eyes could convey disapproval, anger and outrage just as swiftly as they could suggest sympathy, approval and commendation. There were many who experienced her stern and formidable gaze in the years to come, both women soldiers and servicemen; not even generals were spared the sting of a forthright, and often tactless, tongue.

Helen's independent spirit also showed itself in her open defiance of sartorial convention in academic circles. Those who knew her only in her latter years may be surprised to know that she dressed becomingly in fashionable pale colours and wide-brimmed, elaborate hats, in contrast to the dark suits and unobtrusive headgear worn by other university women. 'I suppose I looked unacademic,' she wrote, commenting on the disdainful glances of her female colleagues. Nevertheless her style brought admiration from male associates who described her as 'a stunner' and 'a peach of a girl'.

Because she enjoyed organizing people and preferred to lead rather than follow, Helen was still secretary of a girls' club in Paddington, a legacy from the time when she and her mother, Lucy, had done social work in London among less privileged families during summer vacations. It must have come as a shock when, in 1906, the thesis she submitted for her doctorate was dismissed. Typically, instead of amending the work as her sponsors suggested, she discarded it altogether and prepared a new thesis which earned her the degree in 1907. That same year she accepted a lectureship in botany at University College, Nottingham; it is likely that the young D. H. Lawrence was one of her students, botany being among the subjects he read for his degree.

Early in 1908 she met the man who melted those large grey eyes, Dr David Gwynne-Vaughan. They met again at the British Association meeting that year but with no thoughts of romance on her side, at least; when she heard he had accepted the chair of botany at Belfast, she promptly applied for his old post as head of the department of botany at Birkbeck College, London, and despite her relative youth and the fact that she was the only woman applicant, she got the job. Later still, in 1908, she attended the British Association meeting in Winnipeg, Canada, and it was then that romance began to blossom. It took three years for David to propose, during another British Association meeting in Portsmouth. They were married on 7 December 1911 but because of career demands only saw each other during vacations and over long weekends for the next two and a half years.

Sergeant-Major Baker left the Army and took a job at Smithfield with the Armour Meat Company. Described by his son Ted as a giant of a man, 6ft 7in tall and immensely strong, he never forgot his vision of women on the battlefield and the idea germinated in his mind until, in 1907, he was ready to put his plan into action. During the autumn of that year Baker advertised in the national press for women to join an organization he called the First Aid Nursing Yeomanry Corps. 'Our mission it is to tend Britain's soldiers on the field,' Baker announced, 'and prove ourselves worthy country-women of the first and greatest of Britain's army nurses' – a reference, of course, to Florence Nightingale.

This was the Edwardian Age when some of the strict conventions of the nineteenth century were being slightly relaxed, and pastimes for women were becoming a trifle more robust. A spirit of adventure was abroad, particularly among women from the better-off middle class and the upper-class rebels. They were inspired partly by the suffragists and partly by the exploits of travellers such as Mary Kingsley in Africa, Lady Hester Stanhope and Gertrude Bell in the Middle East, and Flora Louise Shaw, later Lady Lugard, *The Times* colonial correspondent. Still corsetted, still wearing long petticoats, still cossetted to some extent, they were attempting to break out of the prison of propriety to which society had confined their Victorian mothers, daring to venture out on bicycles and follow their brothers on hikes round the countryside; some even tackled mountaineering and scorned the convention of riding side-saddle. It was to these women that Baker's advertisement appealed and they turned up at his headquarters in the Gamage's building in Holborn to be told that they would have to qualify in 'First Aid and Home Nursing, and in addition go through, and pass, a course of Horsemanship, Veterinary Work, Signalling, and Camp Cookery.' Recruits had to be between 17 and 35 years old, at least 5ft 3in in height, and had to join for at least a year. He expected them to provide their own uniform and first aid outfit and to pay an enrolment fee of ten shillings, plus six shillings a month subscription to the riding school and headquarters.

Baker had judged the mood of the moment correctly. The FANY got off to a good start, although naturally its attraction was limited to those women who could afford the fees. An early recruit was Flora Sandes, the daughter of a clergyman, who worked in London as a secretary and whose chief regret was that she had not been born a boy. Later in her extraordinary life she reflected on this youthful attitude when she wrote in her autobiography: 'I had long realized that if you have the misfortune to be born a woman it is better to make the best of a bad job, and not try to be a bad imitation of a man,' a remark which rings with resignation, but its wisdom still holds good a century later.

Deciding to abide by the limitations imposed by her sex, Flora nevertheless intended to live her life to the full within them. She went abroad to learn French and German, languages which one day would prove more valuable than she could have imagined. She also learned to drive, which was itself a departure for women in those early years of motoring. In her French sports model she roared round the lanes of Thornton Heath in Surrey where she lived with her widowed father, earning disapproving looks from their more staid neighbours who frowned on a respectable young woman, the daughter of a man of the cloth no less, indulging in masculine pursuits. She rode well and had learned to shoot, something else which upset the villagers, who felt she should stay at home to help her father run the house in his retirement. No wonder the FANY appealed to her. Here was an organization which suited her tomboyish nature and offered an opportunity to do something useful and, perhaps more appealing to a woman of her temperament and character, something different. The uniform, too – a scarlet tunic, riding skirt, and high-crowned peaked cap – was elegant, dashing and romantic. Uniform, in the traditional sense, was unknown to all but a tiny handful of ladies: as girls they wore them in the public schools and of course nurses wore them in army hospitals, but the FANY was the first women's organization to adopt military-style dress.

By 1909, when membership was about 100, Baker had promoted himself to the honorary rank of captain, planning to become 'major' when membership reached 250 and 'colonel' when 500 recruits had enrolled. His eldest daughter Katie joined the organization with the honorary rank of sergeant-major and took on responsibility for recruiting, apparently increasing 'the great public interest by recruiting for the Corps at Whitehall, where she stood with the Recruiting Sergeants of His Majesty's Regular Forces' – or so her proud father claimed.

Very little is known about these early years but certainly one of the highlights of the FANY training year was the annual camp. The inaugural camp took place in the grounds of a private estate at Chiddingfold in Surrey, and was the first occasion when a company of women lived under canvas, military fashion. Their activities clearly reflect Baker's dream in the Sudan – there were 'wounded rescue races' in which the 'wounded' feigned agony while the 'rescuers' galloped to scoop them up into the saddles, 'wounds', of course, permitting. There were night route marches and hunts in the open air for casualties. It was all good fun and doubtless the likes of Flora Sandes enjoyed every moment. But the training had a more serious side. One early recruit, Grace Ashley-Smith, a young Scots woman who was initially attracted like many others by the title Yeomanry, with its suggestion of a volunteer cavalry force, summed up the meaning of membership in the Corps thus: 'It is not a corps of shirkers, but of workers . . . Those who look upon the training of the Corps as a pleasant pastime are advised to think twice before offering themselves at headquarters as recruits.'

The Corps was financed by members' subscriptions and private donations, with the occasional charity matinée to raise funds for items such as ambulance wagons. But, although details are sparse, it appears that money became a cause of dissension. Also some members, notably Grace Ashley-Smith and Lilian Franklin, who had joined in 1909, had less romantic notions about the duties and direction of the FANY. A real power struggle developed, breakaway groups were formed, the unpleasantness aggravated by public scepticism and mirth at the sight of women in uniform. By 1911 the Corps was being run by Grace Ashley-Smith and Lilian Franklin and the final break with Baker and his daughter came on 6 January 1912. Under the new régime, a more practical uniform of a khaki tunic and a divided khaki skirt worn over riding breeches was adopted, and riding astride was preferred to side-saddle. Signalling and stretcher drill were now held at a South Kensington flat or at the Yeomanry Riding School. Then Grace arranged for Royal Army Medical Corps sergeants to teach stretcher drill and bandaging, for a signalling officer to give lessons in semaphore and Morse code, and Hounslow Barracks allowed the Corps to ride there, cavalry drill being given by the sergeant-major of the 19th Hussars. Weekend and summer camps were held at Haslemere and Bourne End in 1912, and at Pirbright in 1913 and 1914.

The Pirbright camps were enlivened by the assistance of the Brigade of Guards who generously loaned tents, thus saving the FANY the expense of hiring equipment from the Army and Navy Stores, and also supplied troopers to act as casualties. Of this period, Hugh Popham says in his history of the FANY:

Though they were a voluntary organization, with no official standing, they could reasonably feel that they had at last attained recognition, an identity, a role: all the more so when, at their last camp before the war, they not only took part in manoeuvres, but attended the Guards' Church Parade – an unprecedented honour. [Grace Ashley-Smith wrote] 'It was worth all the labour and slogging, and self-denial and discouragement – all the ups and downs, all the jeers and sneers and laughter – to be there at last – part of the army – yes and with the best of it.' After that, official rejection, when it came, would be all the more galling.

Lilian Franklin and Grace Ashley-Smith, members of the FANY, in 1911.

The campaign for women's suffrage gained in momentum and in bitterness during the years leading up to the First World War. The first suffrage societies had been formed in 1867 and Millicent Fawcett's National Union of Women Suffrage Societies, a federation of sixteen societies, was founded in 1898. Its members were chiefly educated upper- and middle-class women, many of whom had succeeded in breaking down some barriers of male prejudice in professions such as education and medicine.

Approximately 60 per cent of adult men had the vote, the franchise being governed by the qualification of being a male householder, and many suffragists were concerned with obtaining the vote for women on these terms rather than with securing universal adult suffrage. Towards the end of the nineteenth century women householders and the wives of householders were given the vote in local elections, and the right to be elected to positions in local government but little progress had been made towards winning the parliamentary vote. So in 1903 Emmeline and Christabel Pankhurst founded The Women's Social and Political Union, dedicated to 'Deeds not Words', and the campaign entered a new phase. Battling with the police, heckling politicians, smashing windows and chaining themselves to railings, the suffragettes – the term came into popular usage in 1910 – who belonged to the WSPU became more and more militant as the Liberal government failed to respond to their demands. Prison sentences were meted out to protesters and their hunger strikes resulted in the 'Cat and Mouse Act' of 1912, which allowed suffragettes to be released from prison when hunger strikes brought them close to death but to be re-arrested as soon as their health was restored. In 1913 Emily Wilding Davison, an ardent supporter of the Pankhursts, was killed on the Derby racecourse: she ran into the path of the galloping thoroughbreds, caught the bridle of the King's horse and was knocked to the ground, thus becoming a martyr to the cause.

The extreme militancy of the WSPU brought a backlash, not only from the government but from supporters of women's suffrage, including some members of the NUWSS. Helen Gwynne-Vaughan was among those who, while actively concerned with the question of suffrage, disapproved of such tactics, finding the Pankhurst methods immoderate, emotional and extreme. This did not prevent her friendship with Dr Louisa Garrett Anderson and together they started a University of London Suffragist Society, leading the girls on processions through the streets of London. However, while Louisa went to prison for throwing a stone during a demonstration, Helen confined herself to voicing her opinions forcefully from public platforms.

Of course, in the years immediately preceding the hot, momentous summer of 1914 it was not only women's suffrage which dominated the headlines or the Irish Question which was debated. The talk was of war, and the threat of Germany and its militaristic ideals. Since the Treaty of Vienna in 1815 Britain had enjoyed immunity from any serious national danger, safe in an island fortress, the surrounding seas patrolled by the greatest navy in the world. War was regarded by many people as a great adventure, real living with never a dull moment, and there was eager anticipation of the excitement it would bring. Thus the declaration of war on 4 August 1914 was greeted with rejoicing rather than regret. Its coming at long last inspired a spirit of euphoria, even of ecstasy. For many, bored by the dull routine of work, it promised escape, fulfilment and romance. Long queues of men waited outside recruiting offices to join up, enlisting at the rate of 100,000 a month for 18 months – and ironically it was the patriotism of the men which opened doors to women. As the vital industries needed to support the war effort threatened to grind almost to a halt through lack of manpower, Lloyd George, the Minister of Munitions, pointed to the solution: 'Without women victory will tarry and the victory which tarries means a victory whose footprints are footprints of blood.'

Almost overnight the suffragettes became munitionettes, urging their members to work in factories. Most of the women came from the working class, from the textile industry, the metal trades, from Scottish fishing villages, the valleys of Wales, the Irish countryside and from the workrooms and villas of English provincial towns. They took the place of men not only on the factory floor but on trams and buses, in the police and ambulance services and on the land. But not all were working-class girls: a scheme was introduced for training leisured ladies to do weekend work at armaments factories. Though not everyone saw it as such at the time, the war had brought a sudden irreversible advance in the economic and social power of women. It dealt a major blow to the whole domestic service as thousands of working-class girls put away their mops and brooms, their dish-cloths and their dusters and went to work for the well-being of the country.

But the British military remained aloof from these developments, its attitude in the early days of war typified by rejection of the FANY. When Lilian Franklin approached the chief commissioner of the Red Cross, at the War Office, she came away empty-handed: he had nothing to suggest for the Corps. Hugh Popham attributes that rejection to the inability of the military mind to picture women in any wartime role except nursing, and to the fiercely independent nature of the Corps itself. In addition, it must be said that the FANY was a tiny organization – in the *London Budget* 2 November 1913, Grace Ashley-Smith explained that it consisted of 'thirty five gentlewomen, and is really a women's mounted ambulance corps'. On the other hand, they were a strong and resourceful band of young women, eager and enthusiastic, and willing to undertake any job which turned up. The FANY found its wartime role and well-earned recognition. Its drivers and nurses forged links with the more enlightened Belgian Army and also operated under the aegis of the British Red Cross Society but these women did not form part of the British women's service when it was formed. Although not exactly a forerunner of the WAAC, the FANY certainly provided a measure of inspiration for the formation of a women's corps and won Baker – of whom, regrettably, we know nothing more for he disappeared into obscurity – a place in history.

Considering this contribution, it is perhaps churlish to highlight one aspect of Baker's outlook when he founded the FANY; yet the fact remains that the whole emphasis of the organization changed when Grace Ashley-Smith took control. It was the man who saw the women as romantic figures in elegant uniforms, riding side-saddle gracefully as they ministered to a soldier's needs. The women saw themselves quite differently: soberly dressed in practical khaki, riding astride, and doing a serious and useful job of work.

The FANY members must have been angry in 1914 when their offers of help were rejected and undoubtedly Hugh Popham is right when he says that they would have been even angrier had they known of the reception that other women were receiving from the Services. When Vera Laughton Mathews applied to the Admiralty for any job, however humble, she was told: 'We don't want any petticoats here,' and it is gratifying to record that she later became director of the Women's Royal Naval Service. And before one feels too complacent about changes in male attitudes, Popham cites the example of Judith Chisholm, the pilot who set the record for a woman's solo flight to Australia in 1980. Chisholm records how, with 2,000 hours on type, she offered her services in an emergency to Shell, only to be told that their passengers 'would not like it if a little blonde dollybird started to fly the aeroplane'.

In 1914, as the men of Britain marched to war, the women had to battle for the right to make a positive contribution. Perhaps some at least were inspired by the words of Olive Schreiner, a South African writer who had made her mark in 1888 with her book, *The Story of an African Farm*. Since then her literary output had been limited but in 1911 she published *Woman and Labour*. The opening paragraph pleaded: 'Give us labour and the training which fits for labour,' but she went on to make a claim which proved to be prophetic: '. . . the nation which is the first to employ its women . . . may be placed at a vast advantage over its fellows in time of war.'

2
THE STRUGGLE TO SERVE

As men flocked to the recruiting offices in the summer of 1914, a number of women's organizations were established to make a contribution to the national effort, each designed to undertake specific tasks.

Already in existence were the Voluntary Aid Detachments which had been formed in 1909 and were managed by the British Red Cross Society and St John Ambulance as well as having links with the Territorial Force; the FANY; and the Women's Sick and Wounded Convoy Corps which, under the leadership of Mrs Mabel St Clair Stobart, had broken away from the FANY in 1909. Mrs Stobart had taken members of her corps to Bulgaria in 1912 where they ran a complete surgical hospital during the Balkan War with Turkey, the first women doctors and surgeons to serve at a front-line hospital during wartime. In 1914 she organized another women's medical corps, the Women's Imperial Service Hospital. Within a month her new corps was behind the lines in Antwerp and when that city was overrun by the Germans on 10 October 1914, after a heavy bombardment, she narrowly escaped being shot as a spy.

The first of the new organizations was the Women's Emergency Corps, which the Hon Evelina Haverfield helped to launch. The daughter of Lord Abinger, Evelina soon switched her loyalty to the Women's Volunteer Reserve, sponsored by the Marchioness of Londonderry, the Marchioness of Titchfield and the Countess of Pembroke and Montgomery, of which she became the commandant. The WVR was by far the most militaristic of the organizations, designing khaki uniforms and felt hats for its members who saluted their officers army-fashion and were lampooned mercilessly by newspaper cartoonists. The members undertook a variety of jobs, such as scrubbing the floors of military canteens, salvaging waste paper, digging allotments and becoming special messengers for the Post Office.

The early weeks of the war also saw the formation of the Women's Defence Relief Corps, the Women's Auxiliary Force, the Women's Volunteer Motor Drivers and the Home Service Corps. The Imperial War Museum has a letter from Mrs E. M. Garstang which gives some idea of the training women received. When she and her twin brother were sixteen years old, her brother pretended to be nineteen and enlisted in the Army, 'so I enlisted in the "Women's Defence Relief Corps" in Wallasey. We were trained by an elderly Segt in the Cheshire Regt: i.e. Voice drill, military and Swedish drill, semaphore signalling and shooting.'

Dr Louisa Garrett Anderson joined with Dr Flora Murray to form the Women's Hospital Corps, whose members dressed in greenish-grey uniforms with small cloth caps trimmed with veils. Another contributor to the work of 'sustaining the vital forces of the nation', as she termed it, was Millicent Fawcett, who opened a Women's Service Bureau in London in order to direct the efforts of non-professional women. Before the end of 1914 more than 1,300 had been placed, many doing VAD courses or working in auxiliary hospitals.

Rather unkindly perhaps, Professor Arthur Marwick suggests that this proliferation of bodies mushroomed because the founders had 'an urge to boss other people around and a passion to compete with anyone else who had the temerity to set up an organization of their own'. However, although there must have been conflict and rivalry at the top, women in general desperately wanted to be useful and went out of their way to offer their labour to the War Office in almost any capacity. In addition to the rejection of the services of the FANY, another indication of the prevailing attitude can be gauged by the rebuff suffered by Dr Elsie Inglis from a harassed War Office official when she offered to equip a hospital, staffed entirely by women. 'My good lady, go home and sit still,' she was told abruptly. When war broke out the redoubtable Dr Inglis had been secretary of the Federation of Scottish Suffrage Societies. After 4 August she became commandant of the Sixth Edinburgh VAD but swiftly realized that she could make a greater contribution. In no way discouraged by her experience at the War Office, she made the same offer to Belgium, France and Russia, who accepted with alacrity, and founded the Scottish Women's Hospitals for Foreign Service. Dr Inglis is best remembered for her work in Serbia during the great retreat of 1915 where she was joined by Evelina Haverfield and – ironically, in view of her previous service to Bulgaria – by Mabel St Clair Stobart, who took charge of the 3rd Serbian Relief Fund Hospital unit. Dr Inglis became the first woman to be invested with Serbia's highest decoration, the Order of the White Eagle, and the Serbs were lavish in their praise of her efforts. 'In Scotland they made her a doctor, in Serbia we would have made her a saint,' was one tribute paid to her.

One of the organizations which *was* given official recognition in September 1914 was the Almeric Paget Military Massage Corps which supplied 50 fully trained masseuses for work among the wounded in United Kingdom hospitals. Later masseuses were also sent to France and by Armistice Day there were 2,000 serving in hospitals at home and abroad. The enthusiasm of women surmounted all obstacles. Mrs C. S. Reed, writing in *How We Lived Then*, published in 1929, reported a schoolboy's letter to his mother:

'I spend my time being bandaged and unbandaged by the girls who want to be VADs. If some of them ever manage to get into a hospital, Heaven help their patients.' Fortunately many of them improved and did manage to get into hospitals.

When the Army experienced a serious shortage of cooks, Lady Londonderry founded the Women's Legion specifically to recruit women cooks and at the instigation of the quartermaster general, Sir John Cowans, a contingent of women took over a cookhouse in the Convalescent Camp at Dartford as an experiment on 3 August 1915. They found that the new gas ovens had been sabotaged by the men, who resented exchanging a safe billet for the trenches. This attitude was not unusual – on another occasion, as the replaced men marched out, an army corporal remarked to a member of the WAAC: 'You are sending those men to their deaths.' Nevertheless other cookhouses were taken over, first in convalescent camps, then in command depots, officers' and sergeants' messes, the Royal Flying Corps, and the Cadet Battalions where officers were selected for training.

The Women's Legion, officially recognized by an Army Council instruction of February 1916, was a private society run by Lilian Barker from her home. The cooks, who were experienced in domestic employment or teachers with culinary diplomas or merely enthusiastic amateurs, were recruited through the Labour Exchange and paid by the War Office. One of the recruits who arrived at Lilian Barker's flat was Mrs Florence Burleigh Leach, later Dame Florence Simpson, who offered as a qualification that she had kept house for her uncle when he was Governor of Gibraltar. Apparently Lilian was not impressed by this 'vision of radiant beauty' and insisted that the application should be made to the Labour Exchange, in the belief that this curt dismissal would prove discouraging. Within an hour the resolute Florence returned with her card and after a few weeks' training she was posted to a convalescent camp at Eastbourne as head cook. Undoubtedly it was her initial scepticism which took Lilian Barker to Eastbourne a few weeks later to inspect the camp, where she found this 'radiant beauty' on her hands and knees scrubbing the cookhouse floor because half her staff were ill. By December Florence had become commandant of the Women's Legion Cookery Section.

The Women's Legion is a particularly interesting example of these burgeoning groups. By allowing its members into military cookhouses, the Army had stretched its imagination to add cookery to the list of duties which women could perform; nursing headed that list, and some female clerks had been appointed as civilian subordinates at the War Office. The Legion illustrates the initiative taken by women themselves to undertake useful work and the fact that the role of women in such organizations was largely voluntary because, although the cooks and waitresses were paid by the War Office, no official contribution was made towards administrative expenses. Also, the Women's Legion was one of these voluntary groups which did achieve some measure of rationalization, in that its Cookery Section was integrated with the WAAC in 1917.

In previous wars a number of women had performed valiantly in battle and, in a practice which may have begun before the birth of Joan of Arc, some had disguised themselves as men in order to do so. The most notorious example in British medical and military history is 'Dr James Barry', who was born in the 1790s and died in 1865 after reaching the rank of inspector-general of hospitals and serving as a surgeon in the Army for more than 40 years. But no concrete evidence exists as to whether Barry was woman, man or hermaphrodite and Barry's career was confined to the medical field. No such controversy surrounds Christian Davies, who joined a Foot regiment as a private in 1693. Better known today by her nickname, 'Mother Ross', she was wounded at the Battle of Landen, transferred to the Scots Greys and fought in Marlborough's campaigns, but her sex was discovered after being wounded at Ramillies. Discharged from the service, she was granted a pension of one shilling a day for life by Queen Anne and was buried in the Chelsea Hospital cemetery when she died in 1739. Phoebe Hessel, who was born in Stepney in 1713, served for many years as a private soldier in the 5th Regiment of Foot in different parts of Europe and in 1745 fought under the command of the Duke of Cumberland at the Battle of Fontenoy, where she received a bayonet wound in the arm. George IV arranged for her to receive 'comfort and support in her latter years', according to her tombstone at Brighton, where she died on 12 December 1821, aged 108. Mary Anne Talbot (1778-1808) participated in the Napoleonic wars as a drummer-boy and then as a 'powder-monkey' in the British Navy, later receiving a small pension for her services. During the American Revolution Deborah Samson joined the 4th Massachusetts Regiment in 1780 as Robert Shirtliffe and fought in several battles, being wounded at Tappan Bay, Tarrytown and Yorktown, and was only identified as a woman after three years as a soldier.

Making no secret of her sex, during the First World War Flora Sandes won the highest and most coveted award for bravery in action in the army in which she served as soldier, NCO and officer.

During the first week of war in 1914 Flora dashed between Red Cross offices and various volunteer organizations, frantically displaying St John Ambulance proficiency certificates which she had acquired but which did not seem to impress anyone. 'I'll go anywhere and do anything,' she told them, leaving her address and appealing to be notified if anything suitable turned up. When Madame Mabel Grujic, the American wife of the Serbian Secretary of State for Foreign Affairs, arrived in England to seek volunteer doctors and nurses for her beleaguered country, the Red Cross suggested to Flora that she should join a party of eight first aid workers and nurses going to Serbia. She accepted a three-month contract immediately, without even knowing exactly where Serbia was.

Remembering her camping experience, she went well equipped with portable wash basins, sleeping bags, insect powder and hot-water bottles and was glad of her foresight: accommodation was spartan and the group was given only straw palliasses on which to sleep. She also took her violin and at night helped keep up spirits by accompanying sing-songs. The women were assigned to the First Reserve Hospital at Kragujevac to work under Serbian surgeons in appalling conditions with a scarcity of even the most basic medical supplies, such as bandages, and with no anaesthetics. Soon, because of the shortage of doctors, Flora was forced to take up the scalpel and perform some of the more straightforward surgery herself.

Described as a tall, handsome woman with short grey hair and a faultless khaki coat and skirt, the 39-year-old Flora went home after three months and campaigned vigorously on behalf of Serbia, returning with £2,000 and 110 tons of medical supplies. When she went back to Serbia in the summer of 1915 after a second home visit, the Serbian army was in full retreat and the British Consul urged her to leave again as soon as possible. Others did turn back but Flora insisted on staying, so the consul drove her to Prilep where she found a room in the town brothel. With a loaded revolver next to her bed, she shouted at the raucous men who pounded on her door until, discouraged, they left her alone. She went to work in the military hospital and then joined the Second Regiment Ambulance Unit, which provided her with a small bivouac tent in which to sleep. However, at Monastir (today known as Bitola) she was told that the ambulance unit was no longer needed and urged to seek safety, but when she pleaded to continue with the regiment, the commander impulsively enrolled her as a private in the Second Regiment, 1st Serbian Army. He lent her a white half-Arab mare, which she named Diana, and among the soldiers she became *nashi Engleskinja* (our Englishwoman).

As the Bulgarians advanced, the Serbian army engaged in a fast rearguard action in which Flora rode, carrying a thermos flask of hot tea laced with cognac and toting a rifle. At army headquarters her appointment as a private was confirmed and she continued with the regiment on the long, weary retreat in lashing rain, raging blizzards and bitter cold. In her autobiography she wrote of the endless white expanse of snow, lit by the flashes of the guns, and the long column of men trailing away into the dusk, sending up a dirge-like wail. On 28 November 1915 Serbia capitulated and Austria and Bulgaria occupied most of the country. Harried by the Bulgarian forces, the remnants of the Second Regiment continued their flight, subsisting on corn cobs roasted over a fire or beaten into coarse flour for bread. On the march

Flora learned to handle a small mortar and to fire the Serbian rifle, admitting that at first she was uneasy when she had human targets in her sights but that distance helped to make the act of squeezing the trigger impersonal. By Christmas Eve they had reached Albania. Finding some money in her haversack, Flora went to a small hamlet to buy unleavened loaves of coarse bread and a bowl of sour milk which she brought back to the campfire to share with her platoon. Then she picked up her battered violin and played 'God Save the King' and Christmas carols, encouraging the men to join in the singing. Two weeks later in Durazzo, during the orthodox Serbian Christmas celebrations, Flora was promoted to corporal and decorated with the Order of St Sava by Prince Alexander, in recognition of her selfless and heroic services to Serbia. She was fortunate to survive: of the 800,000 who set out on the retreat to the Adriatic, more than half died on the way.

After a welcome rest, Flora, by now a sergeant and with a batman to attend to her needs, rejoined her regiment which was waiting to move out on the start of the Macedonian offensive. The Serbs, skilled mountain fighters and inspired now by the closeness of their native soil, made rapid progress and on 14 September 1916 they took the Gorniceyo Pass, breaking through the Bulgarian front. This was Flora's first experience of a full-scale battle and she found herself in the thick of the action. 'Incessant fighting, weariness indescribable,' she wrote, 'but hand-in-hand with romance, adventure and comradeship.' Days and weeks went by, she recalled, with no chance to remove her boots, as the 'Iron Regiment' contested one mountaintop after another.

At last the Bulgarian army was in retreat and the Serbs drove forward, taking revenge for the long, bitter months of humiliating defeat the year before. On 15 November 1916, during an attack on a strategic hilltop where the enemy was entrenched, a grenade hit Flora in the right side but fortunately the butt of the pistol in her gun belt protected her from the worst of the blast. She collapsed in the snow, exposed to enemy fire and only ten yards from the Bulgarian lines until a lieutenant dragged her to cover. One arm was broken and more than two dozen shrapnel wounds lacerated her back, right leg and right side. A stretcher party bore her to a dressing station and from there she was taken to a Scottish Women's Hospital, where she stayed until she could be sent to Salonika. A week later Crown Prince Alexander's aide-de-camp awarded her the Karadjordj Star for bravery in action, the most coveted decoration in the army.

Four days after Flora was wounded, Monastir fell to the Serbs but the advance was halted for nearly two years. Flora had to undergo a lengthy period of hospital treatment and convalescence but still participated in the bitter fighting of the new offensive, which began on 14 September 1918 and which led to the Serbs' eventual victory over the Bulgarians.

Sergeant-Major Flora Sandes being congratulated by a Serbian officer after she had been awarded the Karadjordj Star, the Serbian equivalent of the Victoria Cross, in 1916.

British troops participated in that final attack and an officer in the South Wales Borderers was awarded the VC for his bravery, but for Flora there was no recognition from the British, no honour or glory. In Serbia she became a legend but, while acknowledging that she could not be given the VC because she was not fighting under British command, the thought lingers that another reason accounted for the averted eyes at the War Office. She was a woman.

Faced with the mounting toll of slaughter in the trenches, the British government had no alternative but to recognize the necessity of employing women in larger numbers not just at home but in France, and to call on them to volunteer for war service.

On 18 December 1916 the War Office instructed Lieutenant-General Sir Henry Lawson to investigate the number and physical categories of men carrying out non-combatant duties in France. His report to the Army Council on 16 January 1917 stated that much of the work on the Lines of Communication, the area behind the battle line where troops were in rest or training and where supplies were accumulated, was done by about 12,000 fit soldiers. As this work chiefly consisted of cooking, cleaning, clerical duties, typing and telegraphy at the base camps, training schools and hospitals, Lawson recommended that the tasks should be undertaken by women but suggested certain safeguards and precautions. 'The women must be carefully selected, suitably housed, well cared for and looked after and must form part of definite units provided with their women officers and NCOs,' he stated.

The adjutant-general, Sir Neville Macready, asked the commander in the field, General Sir Douglas Haig, for his opinion. Haig agreed with Lawson, adding that the women should be properly organized and operate in groups of not fewer than twenty, each under their own officers. However, he sensibly pointed out that some jobs would be inappropriate or impossible for them: 'Clothing storekeepers cannot be women for they cannot assist at the trying on of clothes.' He also said that although the women cooks could be used in hospitals, men 'would be necessary for such tasks as lifting carcasses of beef'.

Clearly a women's corps with a proper command structure was required – in other words a special female unit of the British Army. But still the War Office hesitated and Lord Derby, the War Secretary, cautiously consulted leaders of women's organizations like Millicent Fawcett and Katherine Furse, commandant of the VADs. 'The dilution of the Army by women can only be successfully carried out if the whole mother wit of women can be brought to bear on it,' wrote Miss Furse.

The urgency of the situation demanded swift action, however, and the director of recruiting at the War Office, Brigadier-General Sir Auckland

Geddes, acting on his own initiative, called his sister Mona Chalmers Watson to London in order to attend a meeting of women's leaders on 26 January 1917, convened by Lord Derby, at which the Lawson Report was discussed. Lord Derby opposed the full enlistment of women although he realized that, without total incorporation into the Army, any women who were captured might be considered civilians merely 'dressed up' in uniform. The meeting discussed discipline and the way in which women would be paid for their services, but no firm decisions were taken and for the time being, and despite Haig's approval, it seemed that the idea of forming a women's corps remained pending.

Sir Auckland had already sounded out his sister about her interest in commanding the new Corps and he now urged her to seek a private interview with Sir Neville Macready. Their meeting lasted 90 minutes, during which time Mona was asked to give her opinions of all the women who had attended Lord Derby's meeting. Sir Neville asked her how the scheme would work and Mona gave him some rough notes she had prepared with her cousin Louisa. Sir Neville then set a date for another meeting and Mona returned to Edinburgh to discuss the project with her husband.

She was in a dilemma. She wanted to do all she could to help the war effort but her chief concern, as always, was her home and the welfare of her two sons. The Lawson Report made it clear that the main body of women would be sent to France and her immediate reaction was that she could not accept a foreign assignment. Therefore the obvious solution was to appoint someone as her deputy who would command the women's Corps in France. Mona received all the encouragement she needed from Douglas and when she returned to London for her next meeting with Sir Neville her mind was made up. All the same, she admitted to a friend privately that it 'cost her more than she could well say to leave her home and her children at this call of duty'.

On Friday, 9 February 1917 Sir Neville asked Mona if she would head the corps, saying that although Lord Derby favoured the appointment of 'a lady of title', he preferred a professional woman for the post. Having explained her compromise solution to the problem of the French command, she received his authority to find a suitable candidate. That weekend she consulted Louisa Garrett Anderson, who recommended a meeting with Helen Gwynne-Vaughan.

When war was declared Helen and her husband had been in Belfast, packing his belongings in preparation for a move to Reading in Berkshire. David had accepted the chair of botany at the university there partly in a bid to bring them together more, and waiting for them in Reading was a new home and garden, abutting the university's botany garden. When they arrived Helen joined the local VADs, of which the principal's wife was commandant, and commuted daily to her job at Birkbeck College. Household staff was still plentiful and the Gwynne-Vaughans employed a cook, a parlourmaid and a housemaid to ease the load of domestic duties on Helen, who enjoyed entertaining fellow academics. She was determined to combine matrimony with a career, modelling her life on those of Madame Marie Curie and her husband Pierre. But the happiness of the Gwynne-Vaughans in their first real home was to last for less than a year.

As a young man David had undertaken two scientific expeditions to the rubber forests of the Amazon and to Malaya, and had contracted a disease which caused occasional but intense neuralgic pain. Typically, both he and Helen ignored the warning signs, David in particular regarding the attacks as an irritant rather than as a symptom of anything more serious. In the spring of 1915 he began to show signs of a severe illness but struggled through to the summer while Helen learned first aid in the Reading VAD unit. By the end of June David was confined to bed and his condition became progressively worse, but Helen considered herself sufficiently qualified to nurse him at home. On 3 August he had two successive lung haemorrhages and developed pulmonary tuberculosis, and died on 4 September 1915. Helen accepted his death with stoicism, although inwardly she felt her life was shattered. It was a time of widows and she displayed little emotion, believing her grief to be no greater than that of thousands of other women whose husbands had died in the trenches.

There now being no necessity to stay in Reading, she moved to a flat in London which remained her home for nearly 50 years. During the next eighteen months she filled her spare time by cataloguing David's scientific slides and papers on fern anatomy but also began to think about what personal contribution she could make to the war effort. As a scientist the medical field seemed to offer her the most practical opportunity and, because she was skilled in high-power microscopy, she took a course in bacteriology. Madame Curie was then touring the battle areas of France with a radiological unit and the Nobel Prizewinner's example served to inspire Helen once again. 'I think I had visions of a mobile laboratory on some really dangerous front,' she wrote in her personal reminiscences. But fanciful or not, she confided her ambition to serve abroad to her friend Louisa Garrett Anderson, who recalled the conversation when Mona Chalmers Watson spoke to her about the French command.

Helen returned to her flat after a visit to her sister on Sunday evening, 11 February 1917, to find her telephone ringing. It was Louisa, inviting her to the WHC in Endell Street where she was now senior surgeon. Hurrying round, Helen met Mona for the first time and heard about the projected corps of women for duty in France. To Helen, it was the realization of a dream. Here was a real opportunity to be of service to her country and to pioneer the way for women's advancement. Without hesitation, she immediately asked to be allowed to serve no matter in what capacity. When Louisa whispered that she was actually being considered as a possible head of the Corps in France, Helen could hardly contain her excitement. The new Corps had far more glamour in her eyes than any laboratory, and to be in on the ground floor of a new organization would give her much more scope than if she joined an existing unit.

Mona and Helen established an immediate rapport that evening. They were complete opposites – Mona charming, motherly and good-humoured, and Helen with an hauteur born of her aristocratic background, yet impulsive and at times undiplomatic – but they were both professional women with respect for each other's achievements. In retrospect the combination of Mona's tact and Helen's forceful determination could hardly have been bettered and contributed greatly to the success of the large organization which they were to head.

After agreeing to meet Sir Neville on 13 February, Helen returned to her flat. One can imagine that she hardly slept that night. Within her grasp was the opportunity of obtaining the position of responsibility for which her training had equipped her. She had absolutely no doubt that she possessed the qualities needed in a director at the War Office. Many years later, she reflected: 'The relatively young Mrs Gwynne-Vaughan of those days . . . was a soldier's daughter, which offered hope of the right sort of heredity, she came from the same kind of family as the officers of the pre-1914 Regular Army and presumably spoke the same language . . . she had no family ties, she had held posts which accustomed her to dealing with both men and women, and to exercise a certain amount of authority . . . She was physically strong and healthy . . .'

So convinced was Mona Chalmers Watson that she had found the right person that the next morning she went to Helen's laboratory and the two women lunched together and for the rest of the afternoon discussed plans. On Tuesday Helen arrived at the War Office, excited and somewhat awed at the prospect of the interview: 'I still remember the very excellent little tricorne of black panne which graced the occasion and helped to give me confidence,' she recalled. While waiting in an outer office, she spoke to Lieutenant-Colonel James Whitehead, who told her he was an assistant adjutant-general at General Headquarters in France and that, if appointed, she would work mainly with him.

Other candidates were being considered but none matched Helen's qualifications. Lord Derby had wanted 'a lady' while Sir Neville opted for a professional woman, and Helen was a combination of both – a scientist and a niece of Lord Saltoun. During the course of conversation Helen discovered that Sir Neville had been adjutant of the Gordon Highlanders in 1896 and told

A hurried picture of Helen Gwynne-Vaughan taken early in 1917 for her passport. She was being fitted for her first uniform at the time.

Right A rare photograph of Mona Chalmers Watson, the first director of the WAAC, in uniform in 1917.

him that she had 'come out' at their ball in Aberdeen. She begged to be allowed to go to France in some other capacity if not chosen for the senior post and it was this selfless request that formed one of the reasons for her appointment, which was confirmed by Sir Neville personally in a telephone conversation a week later.

At a subsequent interview with Sir Neville and Lieutenant-Colonel Leigh-Wood, the head of AG11 which was set up to administer the Corps, Mona and Helen were informed that the name of the new organization would be the Women's Army Auxiliary Corps. The two women would share the same rank but Mona would be senior to Helen. They were told that as soon as they acquired uniforms they could put up badges of rank.

Together the two women visited Marshall & Snelgrove where, not knowing quite what sort of uniform would be suitable for officers, they took advice from an assistant. The khaki jackets chosen had side-pockets of the usual officer's type, cloth belts and bronze buttons but no breast-pockets, because it was felt that these would emphasize the bustline. The full skirts were considered daringly short, being twelve inches off the ground and so revealing feet and ankles. At first Mona and Helen opted for tight-fitting khaki caps with khaki *crêpe-de-Chine* veils at the back but in time these were replaced in Britain by round, brown felt hats and in France by khaki peaked caps.

A few days later, accompanied by Leigh-Wood, they crossed the Channel to France in order to inspect the area where the Corps would operate in the offices, cookhouses and stores on the Lines of Communication. After a brief visit to General Headquarters at the Ecole Militaire, Montreuil, they went to the headquarters of Mona's other brother, Sir Eric Geddes. He was responsible for all railway transport in the British Zone and for certain forms of water transport, and had decided to employ a number of women clerks. Brother and sister understood each other well and Mona picked up so many ideas that she decided to return at once to the War Office to set wheels in motion. Helen continued the tour with Leigh-Wood before driving to Le Havre to embark for England. During the journey she tried to make conversation with her rather staid companion and very quickly discovered that he had misinterpreted her relaxed manner. Like many women at that time, Helen smoked and did not abide by all the conventions of society in her relationships with men, although throughout she remained a lady in manner and bearing. When she asked whether Leigh-Wood's wife was interested in the new venture, he replied abruptly: 'My wife, Mrs Gwynne-Vaughan, is a truly feminine woman.'

'It has stuck in my mind,' Helen wrote, 'because it voiced exactly a common point of view that there was something rather bold and "not quite nice" about the auxiliary services. We never had the *réclame* so readily accorded to hospital personnel, yet cooking for hungry men is also a "womanly" activity.'

AG11, which Leigh-Wood headed, was a new branch formed at the War Office under the adjutant-general specifically to administer the Corps and was staffed by military officers. Stationed in London, it was Mona Chalmers Watson who had to liaise with the branch and presumably she was involved in decision making, a conciliatory, diplomatic role for which she was ideally suited but which was fraught with difficulties. Rather caustically, Helen wrote: 'Naturally, in such a time of crisis, the best officers were needed elsewhere, and some of those appointed seemed to have hardly more knowledge of military requirements than Mrs Watson herself, and far less quickness of apprehension.' Reading between the lines, because Mona left no record of her experiences, a picture emerges of a woman trying her utmost to do her duty to the Corps and dealing with the occasional, or not so occasional, stupidity and patronizing of the men while retaining their co-operation; and, at the same time, coping with the more headstrong attitude of Helen, who had to implement decisions in the field and who disagreed with some of the dictates.

Undoubtedly Helen was deeply disappointed at the War Office ruling that the Corps would be civilian. The enlistment of women required an Act of Parliament or at any rate a Defence Regulation, even though the Interpretation Act of 1889 had laid down that, in the construction of every Act of Parliament, masculine words included the feminine. After deciding not to enlist WAAC members, the authorities had to clarify their legal status in the theatre of war. The WAAC was replacing combatant soldiers and therefore was not covered by the Geneva Convention. Even if not enlisted or commissioned, its members would still be under the Army Act on active service since the Act included among those subject to military law as soldiers 'all persons . . . who are followers of or accompany His Majesty's troops or any portion thereof when employed on active service'. This definition, summarized in the term 'camp-follower', was applied to the WAAC serving in France but not to its members in the United Kingdom where civil law was available. Of course, historically the term 'camp-follower' has distinctly derogatory connotations but one would like to think that the WAAC members, with their strong personalities and sense of humour, greeted it with more hilarity than indignation.

However, to Helen, denial of military status was a bitter blow. One imagines that Mona was less disturbed by this state of affairs and that – though this is mere supposition – the WAAC members fell into two categories: those who, like Helen, yearned for full acceptance into the Army and those who, like Mona, cared only about getting the job done. Whatever their feelings, in a decision which went flatly against the Lawson Report and Haig's endorsement of it, the women were informed that there were to be no 'officers' as such or 'ranks' in the WAAC; instead it would be made up of 'officials' and 'members'. Senior women – the 'officials' – received titles based on the term 'controller': chief controller (equivalent to lieutenant-colonel), deputy chief controller, assistant chief controller, controller, and deputy controller. Junior women were unit administrators, deputy administrators and assistant administrators. NCOs were described as 'subordinate officials', and the equivalent of sergeants and corporals received the titles 'forewomen' and 'assistant forewomen' – titles which were most unpopular at first and, Helen suspected, had been given to keep the WAAC in its place. The privates were called workers – mercifully, a suggestion that 'amazon' might be appropriate was rejected.

When the order announcing the appointments of Mona and Helen was published, Helen was shocked to read that they were to be known as chief women controllers of the WAAC. She objected to announcing her sex when writing her title after her signature and lobbied for a change. Because a direct approach appeared to be undiplomatic, with unusual tact she telephoned Sir Neville's secretary and begged her to tell him that a senior's authority would not be enhanced by going to France as the chief WC! Almost immediately an order appeared amending the title to chief controller.

The next disappointment concerned badges of rank. At first the badges for 'officials' were to be the same as those of military officers, the two chief controllers beginning with a crown and star as worn by lieutenant-colonels; but, in a move which emphasized the exclusion of the Corps from the armed forces, these were replaced by properly feminine bronze roses and fleur-de-lis (equivalent to the stars and crowns respectively). Chief controllers started with one fleur-de-lis and one rose but very soon advanced to one fleur-de-lis and two roses, the equivalent of a full colonel. In 1918 a double rose, equivalent to a brigadier-general's crossed sword and baton, was approved for chief controllers and finally the controller-in-chief in London wore a double rose and a rose, in line with the badges of a major-general. But no parity of ranks was ever formally granted or admitted.

The badges of other 'officials' followed the same pattern – a deputy controller wore a fleur-de-lis as a major wore a crown, but in addition insets of coloured cloth on the shoulder-strap distinguished functions: blue for controllers, orange for administrators and green for recruiting controllers. The suggestion of gorget patches was vetoed because it was regarded as too military. Forewomen were distinguished by a laurel wreath encircling a rose on the upper sleeve and assistant forewomen by a laurel wreath. The occupation of members was indicated by coloured insets on shoulder-straps: brown for clerks, red for domestic workers, claret for drivers, and purple for women in other employments. Unfortunately, according to Helen, the Army in general seldom understood the significance of the badges or colours.

Uniforms for members comprised a coatfrock of khaki gaberdine with a washable brown collar, brown shoes, stockings and gaiters and an army greatcoat. Although the greatcoats were excellent in cold weather they proved impractical in summer or in rain, and therefore permission was given for the WAAC to purchase civilian pattern drab waterproofs. The necessity of distinguishing between officials and members on wet days gave rise to an order that members should not wear belts with their waterproofs. This caused some resentment and resulted in an interesting discipline case.

When Helen arrived in Boulogne, the area controller asked her to deal with the base commandant's personal clerk who had refused to go out unbelted. She sent for the clerk and demanded an explanation. Blushing, the young girl replied: 'Oh, ma'am, it would be so bad for the reputation of the Corps' – without a belt, the waterproof bulged suspiciously in front. A compromise was needed. Helen looped the belt across the back only and thus honour was satisfied. Later, the order against belts was withdrawn.

The headquarters of the WAAC was established at Devonshire House in Piccadilly, in offices shared with AG11 and the VADs. The vast mansion, once the scene of sumptuous balls and receptions, is no more but its gates decorate the railings of Green Park opposite the original site. Here Mona and Helen planned details of the new Corps and made preparations for the first detachment to go to France.

Ahead of these girls lay eighteen months of a life beyond their imaginings, doing a man's job in what had been strictly a man's world. When it was all over they would return to a new Britain and some of them would build on the feminist foundations even then being laid. Cicely Hamilton of the *Morning Post* summed it up prophetically after a visit to the Corps in France:

> . . . one speculates as to what Army life will make of the ordinary girl, how affect her in habits and outlook. For the life she is leading is Army life, rubbing elbows with soldiers, domiciled in barracks, hedged round by the barriers of discipline. It leaves its mark on the man who has lived it and will leave its mark on her.

3
WOMEN'S ARMY AUXILIARY CORPS: TRIALS AND TRIUMPHS

On 19 March 1917, exactly a month after confirmation of her appointment, Helen Gwynne-Vaughan crossed the Channel to take up her duties as chief controller, Women's Army Auxiliary Corps, British Armies in France. On a tour which included visits to Abbeville, Rouen, Havre, Dieppe and Etaples, where most of the women would be posted, her first and chief concern was the attitude of the men. The officers were helpful, courteous and kind, co-operating fully during her inspection but back in the mess for lunch or tea she learned their true feelings, finding that there was an almost universal objection to the employment of women.

Of course the Services, of all professions, had the least experience of working with women. Only sheer necessity had forced the Army to form the WAAC and the men in France had no idea whether or not the new arrangements were working at home. The officers were apprehensive about the complications which an influx of women might bring and certainly did not welcome the intrusion of an 'alien' element into offices, workshops and other areas of their professional life. Army circles could be described, at best, as conservative and deeply suspicious of emancipated women, an attitude which was hardened by the militancy of the suffragette movement. But it has to be said that the delicate transition period between antagonism, or polite patronization, and acceptance was not made any easier by the approach of Helen Gwynne-Vaughan.

Doggedly the Army maintained that the status of the WAAC was civilian, while Helen enthusiastically embraced military procedure and protocol. She met with immediate opposition.

When the Corps was formed Mona and Helen had to decide on a feminine equivalent to 'sir' and they settled on 'ma'am'. Right at the outset Helen used it when addressing Mona, causing astonishment among visitors, who assumed that Mona was a member of the Royal Family. But – correctly, as she saw it – she also addressed generals as 'sir', standing up when they spoke to her, and saluting. Having received verbal authority from the adjutant-general at the War Office, she put up her badges of rank and the adjutant-general at GHQ in France approved. However, the War Office objected and Mona wrote to Helen, instructing her to remove the badges.

Stubbornly Helen refused to comply, maintaining that her instructions were to take orders only from GHQ and that, as she had verbal authority to put up the badges, she required a verbal order to take them off. The next time she saw the adjutant-general at GHQ, General Fowke, she asked him for such an order but he flatly refused and instead asked to see Mona's letter. Apparently he was amused by Mona's additional exhortation that Helen should not call generals 'sir' or stand up when they spoke to her, but other senior army officers found it disconcerting to be accorded a courtesy which they did not expect from a lady of her standing. To Helen such behaviour came naturally, as she had always given similar respect to academic superiors. 'I should like to have told the War Office that I was only treating generals as professors,' she said. But also there was method behind Helen's courtesy – she realized it would be easier to disagree with her seniors if she could use a title of respect.

She believed strongly that saluting should be part of WAAC routine because, being 'the basis of discipline, it will place our women in the right attitude of mind towards officers and the latter to them; the best work may be anticipated when our personnel are thought of as clerks, car drivers, typists etc. and not particularly as women . . .'

Helen's determined views and unabated activity earned her another tactful rebuke from Mona, who reminded her that 'there is a great effort being made to establish that the whole of this women's organization is civilian . . .' On 21 April Helen was ordered to report to the adjutant-general at GHQ in Montreuil where she received a 'telling off' from Sir Neville Macready who emphasized, among other things, that the status of the WAAC *was* civilian and that saluting, while not objected to, was not required. However, Helen made no mistakes in her correspondence, quickly learning the distinctions between addressing subordinates, equals or superiors. In her memoirs she admits she was amused and delighted by the solemn courtesies which at the same time allowed veiled sarcasm. Papers were passed to juniors 'for necessary action' and to equals 'for any action that may be necessary', whereas recommendations were submitted to senior officers 'for favour of your consideration'.

Back in Britain Mona Chalmers Watson was organizing the recruitment of women into the camps. The first recruiting pamphlet stated that 10,000 were wanted at once and 40,000 before the end of the year: 'This is the great opportunity for every strong, healthy and active woman not already employed on work of national importance to offer her services to her country.' Therein lay the first difficulty. Many women who might have been eligible were already employed in hospitals, on the land or in munitions factories. The recruiting pamphlet, carefully preserved among

Mona's papers, listed various categories of employment – domestic, cookery, mechanical, clerical and tending war graves, popularly summarized as the three C's: correspondence, cooking and canteening. The rates of pay were not listed in the pamphlet but domestic workers received between £26 and £40 a year depending on their seniority, clerks 25*s* to 32*s* a week, telegraphists, telephonists and postal sorters 26*s* to 34*s* a week, and a category known as 'miscellaneous' a minimum of 20*s* a week. The selection of 'officials' also posed a problem, as few women possessed the sort of experience which qualified them for supervisory posts and most of the recruits, who came mainly from working-class and lower middle-class families, were content with subordinate positions as 'workers' because they were used to taking orders rather than giving them. Mona insisted that only women who had experience of regular employment could be recruited and regulations stipulated that those who were going abroad had to be at least twenty years old. As the Corps did not have official army status, employment exchanges initially acted as recruiting offices. From there candidates were sent to Devonshire House to be vetted by Mona personally; they were required to bring two references and to appear before an all-woman medical board.

Georgina Baxter was 88 years old in 1986 when, at her Edinburgh home, she recalled how meticulous Mona Chalmers Watson was in selecting the girls: 'Being a doctor she told us the facts of life and I can tell you many girls needed that information. We young girls were not as well informed then as the modern generation appears to be. She spared no blushes. It was straightforward talk and we were all given strict instructions . . .'

Although recruiting had begun early in March 1917, the first Army Council instruction about employing women at the base and on the Lines of Communication abroad did not appear until 28 March; and Army Council instruction No. 1069 of 1917, which formally established the WAAC was not published until 7 July. For months the Army kept the WAAC under wraps and reporters were not encouraged to write about the activities of the Corps. For instance, the press was not told about Mona's appointment until the end of August that year, but then a number of profiles about her were published. 'She speaks enthusiastically of the work of the WAAC,' the *Naval and Military Record* stated. 'She rejoices in the patriotism, the pluck, and the *esprit de corps* of the girls who compose it. There is something inspiring in the picture of the vigorous young women marching off for France for all the world as though they were destined to stand side by side with the soldiers in repelling the enemy.' And just to prove that there were no class distinctions in the WAAC compared with, say, the FANY and VAD, both of which comprised girls from what was diplomatically called the 'leisured class', the *Record* continued: 'Another claim made for the WAAC is that it is organized on democratic lines. Efficiency alone paves the way to promotion.'

In August 1917 the *Daily Mail* sent a reporter, H.C., to the Connaught Club, near Marble Arch, where 500 WAAC women of every rank and condition were housed. Clerks, secretaries, shorthand-typists and accountants mixed freely with parlourmaids, cooks and tweenies. All were awakened at 7 a.m. by the sound of a bell carried along the corridors and 50 minutes later they attended roll-call, standing to attention outside their bedroom doors. Breakfast followed at 8 a.m. with the 'draft', as they were called, queueing up for porridge, fish and a couple of slices of 'marged' bread. To their relief they were allowed sugar, which was severely rationed in Britain at the time. Then the girls were divided into two sections, some going off to Hyde Park to drill and others attending lectures by the resident medical officer. While in residence they were re-vaccinated against smallpox, and inoculated against typhoid and paratyphoid, an ordeal for every girl, although some coped better than others. A few even had to go to hospital. Elizabeth S. Johnston, a Scots girl from Anstruther, sent her impressions to a friend in a letter from Folkestone, where the draft was housed in the Hotel Metropole:

> We have 48 hours respite from drill, etc. and if we choose we can remain in bed, but it isn't advisable. There you nurse your pain and are alive to every little twinge – in fact, those who remain in bed become worse. The plan is to get up, and crawl, if you can't walk . . . Some lie about in chairs, not caring if they die right off . . .
>
> I'm enjoying it and finding it intensely interesting, but my advice to others is 'Don't enlist unless you've got a huge lump of humour somewhere.' This experience would kill lots of folk, myself included, if I took it too seriously . . .

Many girls had to be deloused when they arrived and then taught the basic rules of hygiene. Very few bathed regularly, if at all, and had to be compelled to do so once they were in residence. Others found it extremely difficult to adjust to the lack of privacy and even undressing in front of other girls was a trial.

Olivia Moir described her 'First Day in the Women's Army' in an article published by the *Manchester Dispatch* on 10 January 1918. After arriving at the hostel, still wearing the distinctive pink arm tape so that she could be recognized as a recruit on the station platform, she had her tea which consisted of bread, thickly sliced, with the famous 'plum and apple' spread:

> While I was finishing and taking in new impressions, all the girls came in together from a route march. Laughing and chattering, they poured in and settled down at the tables with their rations, which they fell upon with a will. Their flushed and glowing faces and

> happy voices filled me with delight and fired me with tremendous enthusiasm. 'My word,' I mentally remarked, 'this is the life for me!' and I hoped there would be a route march the next day so that I could take part in it. They all looked splendidly healthy and full of life, and amidst the din of their voices and of crockery mingling, we new girls sat dumb and admiring.

She also tells of the embarrassing gaffe she then made. Seeing some girls wearing a cream silk collar, 'I wondered why, if a lighter collar might be worn and so improve the dress, so few took advantage of it to discard the dark brown, which looked far less pretty. So strongly was I struck with this idea that at last I turned to one of the girls nearest me with the remark: "When I have my uniform I shall wear a light collar with it." She stared at me for a moment, surprised. "What, like those?" "Yes", I said, "they look so much nicer!" The girl laughed. "Oh, no," she said, "you won't be allowed to. The light collar is only worn by an NCO." I retired squashed.'

According to the *Daily Mail*'s H.C., the great moment for the girls at every hostel came when they were issued with uniforms and kit. Then they waited for names of the fortunate ones to appear on the board as 'Drafted for France'. This happened almost every day and the selected members lined up for kit inspection in the dining-hall. In that kitbag they were expected to have a second pair of strong shoes or boots, one pair of low-heeled shoes for housewear, two pairs of khaki stockings, two pairs of warm combinations, one dozen khaki handkerchiefs, two pairs of dark coloured knickers, two warm vests, two pairs of pyjamas or two strong nightdresses, and sanitary towels. They had to provide all their own underclothes. At last the order was given to 'quick march' and, to the envious cheers of those left behind, the Great Adventure began.

In what was quick work by any standards, the first draft of WAAC members, consisting of fourteen cooks and waitresses for the officers' club at Abbeville, arrived on 31 March 1917. The unit administrator, M. Finlay, acquired the dubious distinction of becoming the first WAAC casualty when she contracted measles ten days later and Helen visited the club in order to ensure that her quarters were disinfected. She told E. P. Shalders to regard herself as the NCO in charge – a slip of the tongue, perhaps, using terms familiar to all, but it was one of Helen's first indiscretions, in view of the fact that the Army was not prepared to concede military ranks to the women.

The Times special correspondent gave a sentimental account of the arrival of one draft on a drizzling November morning, wintry and wet, 'at a certain port in France' which most probably was Boulogne. The girls' disembarkation was delayed until the men had been despatched to their destinations. 'Then came the little company of WAACs, an officer at their head, neat in their warm khaki coats over their khaki coat-frocks, their stout brown shoes, and their new serviceable pull-on felt hats, each with her soldier-like pack on her neat back.' Willing Tommies manhandled the kitbags on to an army lorry while the girls, in brisk military formation, four deep, marched off to the waterside hostel, an annexe to the Soldiers Institute, where a hot meal awaited them. 'As they passed through the wistful French town, *poilus* [soldiers], with the hoods of their weather capes pulled over their caps, looked at them curiously, and an occasional Frenchwoman, not yet used to the novelty of them, glanced their way with a *"comme elles sont gentilles, ces petites soldates"*. Otherwise France took them as a matter of course.'

That night they slept on the floor on army 'biscuits', as they had learned to call the military mattress. In the morning they received their orders. The correspondent travelled with one party to the Queen Mary's Camp at Rouen. There the WAAC members were posted to the Record Office which, ironically, was housed in the Archbishop's Palace, the very place where Joan of Arc had been tried:

> Little streets of huts stretched before us as we arrived . . . Around the camp was a high barbed-wire fence. A warm and plentiful meal was ready for the new arrivals . . . In the distance they could hear the bugle calls from the men's camp. From the YWCA hut nearby the sounds of a WAAC company going through their twenty minutes' weekly drill, and when it ceased it was followed by the tune of a well-known waltz played by one of the girls . . . Then women who had been drilling joined in and danced until soon after there came the camp call to supper . . .

It is difficult to give an accurate description of a typical WAAC camp because accommodation varied according to the locality, but most camps consisted of Nissen huts housing eight women or large wooden huts holding up to 30 members. When Helen first arrived in Boulogne, her inexperience had been tested by an unexpected telephone call. 'Can women live in Nissen huts?' the inquirer asked. Not knowing what a Nissen hut was, Helen stalled. 'Is it necessary?' When the answer was 'Yes', without hesitation she replied that they could, and later discovered that these tunnel-shaped huts made of corrugated iron with cement floors were in fact ideal for the women.

One pleasant experience which awaited the girls posted abroad was the abundance of food. There was no rationing in France and many girls found themselves faced with larger portions and more nourishing food than they had ever had before: working-class women were used to eating very little, sometimes even going without so that the men in the house could

QMAAC camp No. 4 at Rouen, showing the Nissen huts in which the girls lived.
Below a WAAC dormitory at Rouen in July 1917.

eat. Now, suddenly, they were able to enjoy red meat and vegetables and delicious French loaves and cream cakes. *The Times* reproduced a week's diet sheet, of which Tuesday's fare was typical: tea, bread and butter and rissoles for breakfast; roast beef, carrots, celery, cabbage and bread pudding for dinner; tea, bread and butter, jam and Irish stew for tea; and soup, cheese and savoury biscuits for supper. Had *The Times* been read by the working-class, any recruitment problems would have vanished overnight. However, on 1 September 1917 the *Aberdeen Journal* reported: 'One alteration has had to be made since the women went to France, said Mrs Chalmers Watson. It was found that they did not do their best work on the heavy meals which they were at first allowed. Consequently the meat ration has been reduced.' As *The Times* report was published on 21 November 1917, one wonders what the rations were like before they were reduced.

On the first evening in camp the newcomers unpacked their possessions, turned out their four army blankets, made up their beds, stood their footwear 'at attention' facing the door, produced photographs of family and friends, put away their valuables and then sat on their beds for a talk with their room-mates or an impromptu party on parcels from home. In the administrators' mess the officials were relaxing. Of all the administrators, the letter censor had the most onerous task – the WAAC member wrote two letters to the soldier's one. 'She invited me to come with her to her Nissen hut with its cosy glowing French stove, while she went through her great basket of letters . . .' wrote *The Times* correspondent.

Members of the WAAC, like the soldiers, were instructed not to identify the places where they were stationed but occasionally the censors missed rather obvious clues. Elizabeth Johnston, whose letters to relatives and friends were more like short stories, managed to outwit them: 'To the student of Scottish history, this place should be very interesting, more especially to those versed in the annals of the House of Stuart. Doubtless you can recall the words of Mary Stuart re what would be graven on her heart.' From that there can be no doubt that she was in Calais, the port from which Mary embarked on her voyage to Scotland. In another letter she identifies Rouen by writing about the summit of a hill with 'a splendid building – a church – and also a beautiful monument to the memory of Joan of Arc.' On one occasion she complained to her mother that a letter, ten pages long, had been returned to her because the censor did not approve of the contents. In fact, Miss Johnston must have been the despair of the censors: one of her notebooks contained the names and addresses of 85 people and, according to her biographer, she wrote to most of them.

The camps provided ample recreational facilities and on a typical August evening the girls relaxed in deck chairs, played tennis and hockey or went for a walk. The YWCA hut, which supplied cocoa, a table at which to write letters and several entertainments, was always crowded, particularly in wet weather.

But it was not all fun and games. Cicely Hamilton described the home-sickness of girls fresh from England as they adapted to the lack of privacy and a life lived entirely in common: 'Close quarters, even if comfortable, are not suited to every temperament, and seven in a bedroom may at first be a trial to one used to slumber alone.' Another shock of barrack-room life was the absence of sheets: army issue was only four blankets, which irritated the skin. Helen Gwynne-Vaughan decided to share the same discomforts as the women in the ranks but compromised by folding a towel along the top of the blankets 'where they tickle one's chin'.

'Life in the Army isn't just a "Home from Home" as the popular advertisement has it,' wrote Elizabeth Johnston from Calais. 'The mud is terrible, and since it is so bad here, it helps us to realize how unspeakable are the conditions farther up the line.' That spirit was characteristic of most girls, who realized that, no matter how bad their situation, they lived in luxury compared with the men in the trenches.

The cold was so intense that none of the girls could sleep, Elizabeth relates. At four o'clock one morning she and a colleague had to get up and shake melted snow, which had seeped through two holes in the roof, from their blankets. She managed to patch the hole above her head but the other was more difficult to repair, so the two girls shared a bed, huddled under greatcoats instead of the damp blankets, until reveille. 'Ugh!' her companion shuddered, clinging to her. ' "What's wrong?" I asked. "Oh, I've touched the North Pole with my feet", she said.' The below-zero object turned out to be Elizabeth's hot-water bottle.

Some hardships were incurred voluntarily. The third party to come to France, 22 clerks who arrived on 17 April to be posted to the Directorate of Forestry at Le Touquet in the Etaples district, set a pattern for willing sacrifices by the WAAC members which endeared them to Tommies and officers alike: they discarded the bedsteads they were given. The men they replaced had had to sleep on the floor and they wished to experience the same conditions. The Battle of Arras was in progress and the beds were removed to grateful neighbouring hospitals, but the director of works swiftly replaced them because he was disturbed by the idea of 'long hair trailing on the bare boards'.

The women, in their khaki uniforms, were becoming a familiar sight on the Lines of Communication. Officers were learning the advantages of having women in attendance and some even conceded that they had never known comfort in the office before the arrival of the 'WAACs' – of course, with that nickname, it was inevitable that their places of employment

WAAC on parade in Rouen on 24 July 1917. The French called them 'Les Tommettes'.

should be dubbed the 'waacsworks'. Helen, whose name was far too long and cumbersome, was simply referred to as 'Mrs Waac'. The French were more colourful, preferring the soubriquets 'Les Soldates' or 'Les Tommettes'.

They worked as cooks, waitresses and laundresses; as clerks, shorthand writers and typists; as drivers, storewomen, telegraphists, telephonists and postal sorters; and tended war graves. The group classed as 'miscellaneous' included printers, gardeners, grooms, shoemakers, bakers and tailors. However, some groups undertook more unusual duties – technical workers were attached to the RFC, and in March 1918 an assistant administrator and 44 members took up positions with the Ordnance Survey Department, near St Omer, which was concerned with map-making. A considerable number of women also worked on the quays at Calais, checking and sorting stores as they were unloaded, and consigning them to destinations in the army areas. Perhaps the most specialized group were the assistant administrators who worked in the Intelligence branch of the General Staff at St Omer and who were among the very few WAAC officials employed in direct replacement of army officers. All were experienced linguists and were believed to deal with the translation and preparation of documents. As their activities were highly confidential, they were nicknamed 'Hush-Waacs'.

WAAC technical administrator Miss Nicholls oversees the members of 61st Advanced Motor Transport Section, Abbeville.

Below WAAC girls repair the engine of an officer's car in Abbeville, 15 September 1917.

Friction did arise between WAAC members and the Army but often it was trivial and came from both sides. A staff captain at Wimereux tried to explain to a WAAC administrator local regulations about the disposal of bones and swill, only to be met with the outraged response: 'My dear boy, I was housekeeping long before you were born. You should leave me to manage my own affairs.' Men found the adjustment equally difficult – one sergeant-major, unaccustomed to drilling female soldiers, forgot his usual parade-ground manner and politely requested: 'Will you ladies please fall in.'

In marked contrast to the War Office stance, not only were the members of the WAAC accepted by the Army in France but soon they were positively spoiled. Army engineers tried to provide the best possible quarters with baths, hot and cold water and electric light, and even decorated the camps with window boxes and flower beds. A Machine-Gun School commandant showed his approval by teaching his cooks to handle guns – everyone at his school had to learn and he saw no reason why the women should be left out. 'They probably cooked with added enthusiasm,' Helen remarked and went on to say that when she heard two Army School commandants discussing whose cooks saluted most smartly, she knew the women had made good. At First Army School the WAAC administrators were given the army brassard and made honorary members of the officers' mess.

Final acceptance from the men on active service came when the women were subjected to air-raids. In an account written for the Imperial War Museum in 1976, Mrs Elsie Cooper described bombing raids on the base at Etaples. The women had been detailed to dig trenches outside each hut and were ordered to take shelter in them as soon as the alarm – the firing of a nearby gun – sounded. The trenches were not big enough to accommodate all the girls and some of the less nervous remained in bed but were usually chased out by officers. Later, another trench leading to chalk caves on the banks of the River Canche was dug at the back of the field where they were camped. As the girls ran for cover, shrapnel clattered on the sheets of corrugated iron covering sections of the trench.

'Occasionally there would be fights between planes within a short distance of the camp,' Mrs Cooper wrote. 'The girls did not appreciate the danger and invariably went outside to watch, much to the consternation of the officers who insisted on us taking cover.' One night the camp received a direct hit and among the huts demolished was one which housed the YWCA. Scraps of furniture were scattered over the parade-ground. Helen tells of a direct hit on Camp II at Abbeville, on the Montreuil road. While the girls in her HQ cellar played games, sang songs or sewed, huts outside were blown to pieces, uniforms scattered far and wide and some garments left suspended on the branches of trees. But by the time work was due to start, the women, in a variety of clothes salvaged from the wreckage, were back on duty.

Members of the QMAAC sit on the edge of a crater caused by a bomb at Abbeville on 22 May 1918. Helen Gwynne-Vaughan says that while the girls in her headquarters cellar played games, sang songs or sewed, huts outside were blown to pieces. Eight days later nine members of the QMAAC died in another air raid.

Another member of the WAAC, A. B. Baker, wrote an account of an air raid on Etaples in 1918. Near the bridge there, on a sunny spring day, she saw 'half a company of men blown to pieces by bombs' which also hit the graveyard close by. 'Coffins and dead men were blown from their graves. Into those graves limbs of living men and fragments of shattered dead men were flung.' The scene was too much for her; she became hysterical and nauseous and wished she were home. In the shelter she prayed that the war would stop.

On 30 May 1918, eight women were killed outright in a raid on Camp 1 at Abbeville. Seven others were wounded, one of whom died later. The bravery of the survivors earned commendations from all and three military medals were awarded to the women who helped in the rescue. One forewoman, whose shoes were blown off, helped rescue her comrades; another worker, who was seen to be limping when she scurried backwards and forwards, had been too busy to realize that a nail was embedded in her foot. At the women's funeral next day there were wreaths from the local troops, a fly-past, and a large number of soldiers and officers joined the cortège behind the gun-carriages bearing the coffins.

Up to this time the only 'army' women killed had been hospital personnel. Journalists were intent on berating the enemy for killing women but Helen typically reminded them that because the women were replacing combatants, the enemy could be excused for killing them if he could. The reporters conceded the point and toned down their outrage. All the casualties had been new arrivals and paradoxically this caused a little envy among those who had been in France for some while. They felt it 'inappropriate' that the 'honour' of suffering war casualties had gone to newcomers.

Helen was always striving for official recognition of the Corps but never quite achieved her ambition in the First World War. However, after one air raid at Boulogne, the devotion to duty of signalwomen in the telephone exchange caused the signal officer to recommend to his HQ that the WAAC girls should be mentioned in Orders. Back came the laconic reply: 'We do not thank soldiers for devotion to duty; we do not propose to treat these women differently.' Staunchly, Helen turned the rebuff to advantage: 'We could have had no greater praise than this assumption that devotion to duty was to be expected from us as from the troops. We were admitted to a great fellowship.'

Disquieting reports about Helen's militaristic attitude had been filtering across the Channel ever since her arrival and Mona therefore decided to visit France in order to assess the situation. Her permit, signed by Lieutenant-General G. H. Fowke, adjutant-general of the British Armies in France, is still in existence; it allowed her to travel to Montreuil and Hesdin via Boulogne. The visit took place between 6 and 16 June 1917 and Mona was accompanied by Florence Burleigh Leach who, when she succeeded to the directorship of the Women's Legion, had organized a merger between 7,000 women of the Legion's Cookery Section and the WAAC. She was now controller of inspection with the WAAC.

It is clear that the talks were frank. Helen's response was to suggest that the War Office should ask her to resign if they were dissatisfied but the more Mona and Florence saw, the more they were impressed. Quick to give credit where credit was due, Mona wrote to Helen stating that she was 'awfully pleased with the way things have started'.

Perceptively she realized that Helen, who had not formed any close relationships with subordinates, needed someone who could speak freely to her so she persuaded Helen's sister, Marjorie Pratt Barlow, to join Helen in France. Helen foresaw difficulties in having her sister so close at hand but in fact no such problem arose and she conceded that Marjorie's presence was the greatest help – she was able to explain frankly when any of Helen's orders caused difficulty or was misunderstood. Helen always took the precaution of posting Marjorie to a unit directly under Corps HQ and for a long time no one guessed that they were sisters. 'We were carefully formal in our official behaviour, and it was only in private that her "Yes, ma'am" and "No, ma'am" changed suddenly to "Helen, you idiot . . . .",' Helen wrote. But on one occasion in her sister's mess when Helen asked abruptly for more tea, Marjorie reminded her sharply: 'We say "please" in this unit, ma'am!'

The amalgamation of the Cookery Section personnel had been an important step in the expansion of the WAAC at home – an expansion which gathered momentum after that visit to France in June 1917. The headquarters staff was increased, a training camp and a cadet wing were formed, and a depot was established at Folkestone for the despatch of drafts overseas. The Folkestone depot also prepared 22,000 meals a day for soldiers en route to the Army in France – an activity which Helen describes as 'one of the most striking' of the Corps at home but which also indicates that many WAAC members were employed in traditional, 'womanly' occupations.

In London Mona began a campaign to have two women doctors appointed to an auxiliary corps of the RAMC so that they could be responsible for WAAC members. Helen backed this initiative, chiefly because the male doctors occasionally erred on the side of too much concern for supposed female frailty. 'I have known a medical officer order medical comforts for perfectly fit women, as though to be female was to be permanently invalid,' she commented acidly. Such treatment was obviously not good for morale and might have prompted some women to take advantage of sympathetic medical staff.

When the War Office agreed to the appointments of a woman president of the Medical Boards in England and a woman medical controller in France, the incumbents were given rank equivalent to a lieutenant-colonel in the RAMC. The Finance Department, however, refused to pay them the £700 per annum plus allowances which men of similar rank and qualification received. Instead they offered an insulting £420. Dr Laura Sandeman, who was appointed to take up the post in France, refused to accept and Mona complained to the Permanent Financial Secretary of the War Office, Sir Charles Harris, who promptly told her that patriotic ladies could always be found to work for less than men. Sir Charles might well have had a twinkle in his eye, for he was facing one such woman – Mona had accepted a salary of £500 per annum – but this was an issue on which she refused to budge: after all, her family had pioneered the way for women to qualify as doctors. Accompanied by her brother Auckland, Mona held a meeting with Lord Derby after which it was laid down that the pay for men and women doctors would be the same, but still the War Office Finance Department would not sanction the salaries. Dr Sandeman again refused to leave for France. Lord

Left Recruiting members of the Women's Army Auxiliary Corps in Trafalgar Square in 1917.

Below WAAC cooks at Abbeville, 15 September 1917.

Derby found himself 'between the devil and the deep blue sea' but he was 'obliged to agree to this salary'.

Dr Sandeman arrived in France on 14 October 1917 and Army Council instruction No. 1676, founding an auxiliary corps of the RAMC, appeared on 12 November. Laura wore the badges and dull cherry shoulder-straps of the RAMC but the badges of rank of the WAAC – a fleur-de-lis and two roses. The battle had been won and had ended in 'a victory for women', Mona said in an interview.

Discipline was another vexatious problem which required clarification. Absentees from WAAC service and those accused of thefts and other misdemeanours at home were prosecuted in the civil courts. Newspapers occasionally reported these cases and a typical example was published in *The Times* on 8 February 1918. Headed 'Women Army Cooks Fined', it told how seventeen members of the WAAC, employed as cooks to an officers' training corps at Pirbright, were charged at Aldershot with wilfully disobeying orders.

> It appeared that on February 2 the girls refused to do their work in the kitchen under the forewoman cook, who, they alleged, bullied them. Some of the strikers also stated that they resented being refused permission to go out in the evening, after they had done work. The magistrate fined each defendant £3, to be stopped at the rate of 5*s* a week out of their pay.

When the first WAAC drafts arrived in France, no disciplinary code had been laid down. WAAC members on duty in France were, like civilians, employed under military law 'as soldiers' and could be tried by court martial for serious offences. However, a commanding officer could not award summary or minor punishments for less serious offences. When this subject was discussed at GHQ in France, an officer, to Helen's astonishment, recommended field punishment, one form of which entailed tying the spreadeagled defaulter by the ankles and wrists to a limber, or carriage wheel, for specified periods. When Helen expressed her alarm, the proposer hastily explained that he did not advise the physical punishment, only the accompanying forfeiture of pay.

By October a new form of enrolment had been introduced requiring WAAC members to accept liability to fines 'for any act or neglect in breach of this contract or of any of the rules, regulations or instructions laid down from time to time for this corps'. First offenders were fined 2*s* 6*d*, 5*s* on the second occasion and 7*s* 6*d* thereafter. Helen rightly points out that it was not a satisfactory arrangement, since the amount of the fine took no account of the seriousness of the offence or the pay of the offender.

One of the reasons why the fines imposed on defaulters were considered inadequate was that girls were more than prepared to forfeit these small sums for the pleasure of a night out: it was no more than they might have paid for an evening's entertainment back home. It was certainly cheap at the price for one group among the WAAC since it was soon discovered that, despite precautions designed to identify those joining up expressly to practise prostitution, some had evaded the net and found the Lines of Communication a lucrative hunting ground. One regularly used to slip out of camp after roll-call but although her activity was suspected officials found it difficult to prove. According to regulations only on the fourth occasion she was caught and after a total fine of 15s, could she be sent home.

Certain places, such as the more notorious *estaminets*, were out of bounds to WAACs but this did not deter the adventurous. A favourite pastime for many girls was 'lorry-hopping' but as they often did not know their lift's destination they generally found themselves farther from base than expected and were late for roll-call. Most of these cases, Helen was quick to emphasize, indicated a failure of adjustment rather than depravity.

Another ever-present problem was irregularity of dress. The women were expected to pay for shoe repairs and to replace stockings and other items out of a renewal grant of £1 but, apart from cost, uniformity was difficult to enforce when there was a shortage of supply. Although adornments such as jewellery were forbidden, some of the WAAC members were tempted to disobey regulations in the interest of making themselves look more attractive. Just as Olivia Moir was taken with the lighter collars worn by NCOs, others tucked in the collar of the coatfrock and fastened it in place with a brooch, thus ensuring a longer, more alluring V-shaped opening at the neck.

Naturally, relationships between the men and women in the Army were of great concern and were subject to considerable discipline. During an early conference at GHQ, it was agreed that men and women should be permitted to make friends and walk out together openly with the full approval of the authorities. Nevertheless, one general told Helen: 'If these women are coming, we shall have to wire all the woods on the Lines of Communication,' whereupon Helen snapped back: 'If you do so, sir, you will have a number of enterprising couples climbing over.' Needless to say, no wire was raised round the woods.

Rule No. 14 of GHQ instructions on the employment of the WAAC in France stated that, when off-duty, members of the WAAC 'will not normally associate with officers or other ranks of the British Army in France, except with those holding ranks comparable to their own grade.' It was a regulation more honoured in the breach than the observance. During a tour of Wimereux Helen saw two 'workers' walking out with two young subalterns and, stopping her car, ordered the 'officials' who accompanied her to take the names and numbers of the women while Helen remonstrated with the subalterns, chiding them for encouraging other ranks to break army regulations. 'We never thought these nice girls could be anything but officers,' one subaltern replied innocently. He certainly gained the best of the encounter, Helen conceded afterwards and hoped that his subsequent career was as successful as his resourcefulness promised. She also told of a sergeant who called regularly on a clerk at her headquarters. Only after the war did she realize that the sergeant had really been an officer who had borrowed an NCO's uniform in order to court the young WAAC girl. The couple were married after the Armistice.

Reflecting many years later on the wisdom of allowing association between the women of the Corps and the troops, Helen said that it was natural they should make friends, walk, talk and play together. From that good comradeship sprang many marriages. Soldiers had to seek permission to marry WAAC members and at first, because of the rule that wives might not serve in the same theatre of war as their husbands, the unfortunate couple were parted almost at the church door. On 29 April 1918 a more thoughtful approach by Brigadier-General J. B. Wroughton, deputy adjutant-general, resulted in newly married couples being able to rent a villa or a cottage for a week's honeymoon in France. In turn, Helen's staff ensured that the correspondence about the woman's return to England was suitably delayed.

Hilda M. Love had written in the *Daily Mail* on 21 December 1917 about 'Waacs and Weddings':

> Of all the romantic unions of the war, surely none pleases the eye and the heart of the onlooker more than the wedding of a khaki man and a khaki-clad girl? It is the apotheosis of romance . . .
>
> Many a girl who might have bloomed and faded in some retreat of the Homeland, or taken unto herself an indifferent male through sheer lack of selection, has found the man in all the world for her somewhere in the war zone.
>
> I saw a Waac wedding today; the bride and bridegroom first met in France. One forgot to notice the singularly stiff arm that hung by the man's side in watching his proud face. What a love story they will have to relate in the years to come, and how young ears will revel in the tale of the days when he was a soldier and his bride a member of the Women's Army.

For the most part the picture which emerges *is* one of companionship between the men and women of the Army. The WAAC members invited the men to tea, held dances and concert-parties in the YWCA huts and the soldiers reciprocated their hospitality. The girls visited the wounded in hospitals, entertained convalescents to tea and bought oranges and cigarettes for their guests. Yet they provided more than just female company because they, too, were part of the Army: they could talk about the same things, understand the men's feelings and see the point of a story.

The WAAC officials did not rely only on discipline to keep order but took a genuine interest in the welfare of their members. Betty Vetch, who became a chief commander in the ATS, recalled how Helen lectured her officers on the need both for vigilance and for keeping a kindly eye on the women who served under them. 'Remember that war makes a man more ardent, a woman more vulnerable,' Helen told them. 'You don't have to bother about the attractive young girls – they've been looking after themselves since they were fifteen. The woman at risk is the slightly older, plain-looking cook who has never had a boyfriend in her life and now finds two handsome sergeants competing for her favours.'

The naïveté of some girls did lead to unfortunate incidents. A. B. Baker, who wrote about her wartime experiences in the book *Everyman at War*, was a farmer's daughter and only eighteen when she enrolled in the WAAC but because she was fluent in colloquial French, the authorities overlooked her misrepresentation of her age as 21. Before she was posted to France her father

Convalescent soldiers playing cricket with the QMAAC in France, 1 May 1918.

took her down to the pigsties where he attempted to tell her the facts of life. Tommies might be heroes, he warned, but they were also men. However, if she respected herself they would in turn respect her. He must have spoken in very general terms because when she arrived in France some while elapsed before matters became clear to her.

One day she and a friend set out to go to the cinema in Etaples and joined a queue of Tommies, only to be puzzled by the amusement which their presence caused. At last one soldier, taking pity on the unsuspecting WAACs, blushingly informed them that the performance was for men only. They left, still bewildered, and only much later did they realize that they had probably joined the queue for a brothel. Miss Baker also tells of translating letters, many of which were from French girls complaining that they were expecting the babies of British soldiers. Often the expectant mothers arrived at camp with relatives, distraught and in threatening mood. She recalled one particular grandmother: 'She cursed me; she cursed the Colonel; she cursed the British Army; she cursed England and all the English. She went away cursing. I sat shivering and ashamed.' At first she was shocked but later became more blasé about her experiences, especially after she herself had a brief romance.

Her young man was a sergeant named John who had been in France for more than three years. He had been wounded several times and when she met him was fit only for work at the base, but in time he was recalled for active service and on the day he was due to depart he and Miss Baker went for a stroll in the woods. 'He asked me if he could kiss me. I said "Yes." He kissed me many times, and held me very tight. He held me so tight that he hurt me and frightened me. His whole body was shaking. I felt for him as I had never felt for any man before.' Later she heard that he had been killed.

It is evident that one of the reasons why the British Army was from the beginning reluctant to form a women's corps was fear of exposing young women to the 'animal instincts', as one commentator expressed it, of soldiers abroad. In the highly charged atmosphere of death and destruction, soldiers were expected to indulge in affairs. On the orders of Lord Kitchener, every soldier went to war with an exhortation pasted in his paybook: 'Keep on your guard against excesses. In this new experience you may find temptation both in wine and women. You must resist both, and while treating all women with perfect courtesy, you should avoid any intimacy.' Realistically, since no soldier could be expected to heed such an admonition, the Army issued prophylactics in an attempt to reduce the incidence of venereal disease.

'Of course, Mrs Gwynne-Vaughan, you will have some pregnancies,' the medical authorities declared when the first WAAC drafts arrived in France.

'Of course,' Helen replied.

'Would you like us to send them home "not yet diagnosed"?' she was asked. Making a spur-of-the-moment decision, she insisted that she would report all pregnancies to the adjutant-general. Later she was thankful for this impulsive reaction because it provided proof that pregnancy was not the cause of every sick WAAC's return home. But in Rouen on 13 October 1917 a pretty redhead was sent to Helen in the orderly room. 'They tell me you are going to have a baby,' Helen said. At first the girl denied it but eventually dropped to her knees and buried her face in Helen's lap. 'Oh, ma'am, I am so glad you know about it.' The girl was sent home immediately but no disciplinary action was taken against her because none could be taken against the father.

The first 'WAAC baby' was born in France in May 1918. Apparently the young woman did not know she was pregnant and neither did her companions suspect her condition. She had been on duty all morning but did not return after breaking for 'elevenses'. She was discovered in bed with her baby. Helen says this surprise event caused a stir in the adjutant-general's office and he wrote a postscript to a letter to the War Office demanding reinforcements: 'If you don't hurry up, we shall provide our own, we already have one fine boy.' Another young woman had her baby three weeks after competing in the camp races.

Doubtless some pregnancies did result from relationships between soldiers and members of the WAAC. While nurses looked after the wounded, WAAC members were in contact with 'fit' men whose physical and mental resources were stretched to the limit and who shortly had to face again the deafening roar of artillery, the stench from unburied bodies, the screams and groans of the wounded, the blood, the mud and the rats, and the constant presence of the enemy across no-man's-land. Some soldiers cracked under the strain. Others were eager to have one more fling in case it was their last and the women, trapped by the heated emotions of time and place, could not be blamed for providing a form of comfort. Nevertheless, the number of pregnancy cases and the instances of liaisons between army men and women provided no foundation for rumours which mysteriously began to circulate, alleging that members of the WAAC were guilty of loose conduct and immoral behaviour. The rumours soon became a major scandal.

One source of such rumours was entirely innocent – the wicked humour of Tommies, whose jokes were accepted as fact by an earnest audience. For instance, one clergyman visiting France met a group of civilian women with babies and asked a passing Tommy who they were. Not realizing the mischief he would cause, the soldier replied: 'WAACs, of course.' Back home the padre repeated the tale to a shocked congregation. On another occasion a sentry on duty outside a base joked that he was guarding a maternity home for WAACs. His story was also swallowed by a gullible visitor who related the incident when he returned home. At one time, according to Helen, the WAACS were reported to have produced more babies than there were WAAC members in France. More than ever was she glad of her decision to report pregnancies:

> It is submitted for favour of your consideration that No. 1234 Worker Smith, M. N., being pregnant, is unfit for active service. It is recommended that she be returned to home establishment. This condition appears to have supervened about 1st May, 1917; the woman *reported for duty in France on 9th August, 1917* . . . (Author's italics)

Some rumours may have been started simply by the tendency of men in the barrack-room to talk about their conquests, to fantasize and to exaggerate, but some stories were malicious fabrications, spread by soldiers who were frustrated, jealous of comrades enjoying WAAC company or just resentful of the women who had taken their safe jobs and freed them for the trenches. Many soldiers immediately blamed WAACs for their venereal disease – it was a penal offence to communicate a venereal disease to a soldier – but in one company seven accusations were found to be untrue and three of them malicious. As a result WAAC officials were asked to warn women of this risk and to 'impress upon them the danger of going into lonely places, or in any way compromising themselves with unknown men'.

The scandal about the alleged licentiousness of the girls in France reached its height early in 1918; it was even affirmed that the WAACs were being recruited for army brothels. Serious credence was given to the theory that the rumours were started by enemy agents. In January 1918 there were 22,479 serving members of the WAAC, nearly 5,000 of whom were stationed in France. Many more were needed to take the place of the men required to repulse the anticipated spring offensive by the Germans but suddenly, as a result of the stories, the flood of WAAC applications slowed to a trickle.

Visiting London in January 1918, Helen was appalled by the blatant distortions of the truth and decided to attend several recruitment rallies. At one rally the Lady Mayoress demanded an interview and repeated some of the allegations she had heard, but was placated by Helen's reassurance that the women led a disciplined and carefully safeguarded life in France. As Helen later wrote: 'With however little justification, immorality is an excellent stick with which to beat a Corps of women . . .'

The Minister of Labour, G. H. Roberts of the Labour Party, defended the honour of the WAAC when he spoke at an exhibition at the Bradford Technical College on 31 January 1918. 'Unfortunately some allegations that these women were guilty of improper conduct in France have been spread,' he said. The WAAC was trying to trace the origin of these allegations and,

Members of the QMAAC relax at Paris Plage, 29 May 1918.

although there was not the slightest truth in the suggestions, he was requesting certain independent ladies to go out to France to conduct an exhaustive inquiry. Generally the newspapers played down the 'wild and varying stories about the relations between the rank and file of the Waacs and the Regular Army', as the *Daily Sketch* described them. Apart from a few sensational accounts, the bulk of public complaints were in the form of letters to the War Office, though rumours were still repeated as fact from public platforms.

Another eminent person to spring to the defence of the WAAC was the Archbishop of Canterbury, Randall Davidson, who had visited bases in France in July 1917. Speaking at the Convocation of Canterbury at Church House, he refuted the slanders about women's work at the front and said he wished to dissipate absolutely the untrue statements which had been made as to the alleged immoral results arising from the employment of women in khaki. The *Daily Telegraph* reported his speech on 6 February 1918 and quoted him as saying: 'One would think from [these statements] that whole boatloads of women connected with the WAAC and other organizations were coming home, the women having fallen grievously into evil ways.' Any such assertion was a gross libel. He said he had undertaken the fullest possible inquiry and was convinced that although there might have been some evil results and some wrong-doing, the percentage of such cases had been of the very smallest dimensions.

It was unfortunate that at this juncture Mona Chalmers Watson resigned as chief controller of the WAAC. Inevitably her departure was linked to the rumours. Interviewed at Devonshire House, she said: 'The real reason I am leaving is that I am needed at home. My husband and my children need me. I was called on at a few days' notice to start the scheme of a women's auxiliary army and now it has taken shape and is working smoothly. I am extremely sorry to go, but I feel I am leaving a workable machine, and someone else, probably one of our own officers, will move up and carry on the work, as well as I can. One of my children has been seriously ill. He has just been operated on for appendicitis, and the anxiety has not been good for my work here, so I have decided I must go back to my family and my profession.' The persistence of 'these evil stories' made her believe there *was* an organized attempt, deliberately planned by enemy agents, to stop useful girls from joining the women's army.

> The Germans at the beginning did not take our organization seriously, but now that they know we have made good and are releasing thousands of young men for the fighting line, they may well want to put a stop to our recruiting, and no other means would serve so well to discourage women of good character as the stories of immoral conduct in France.

The Globe, commenting on 9 February on Mona's resignation, said that it was satisfactory to learn it was not due to the malicious rumours concerning the morals of the WAAC, adding: 'No more disgusting form of treason can be imagined than these quite outrageous slanders on a body of patriotic women.' Mona had been among the first recipients of the newly-instituted CBE on 25 August 1917 and now there were many tributes to her work. The *Ladies' Pictorial* on 20 February 1918 said she had 'nobly done her bit' and the *Daily Sketch* that she 'had organized and set going that most useful corps with conspicuous success'. After returning to Edinburgh, Mona and her husband bought a farm, Fenton Barns, in North Berwick, East Lothian, where they retired from medicine to breed a herd of tuberculin tested cattle. Mona died there on 7 August 1936.

The War Office announced the new appointments at the head of the WAAC on 19 February. Florence Burleigh Leach was to succeed Mona as chief controller, and Mrs V. A. Long, who was Florence's sister and had been controller of administration, became her deputy. These moves did not affect Helen, who continued to be chief controller in France. Miss E. M. Thompson and Miss E. M. Trotter, both 'forewomen', were promoted to controller of inspection and controller of personnel respectively. These last two appointments were in line with Florence's preference for officers who had come up through the ranks.

When Florence took over command, she was asked to swear an affidavit declaring that she was well aware of the purpose for which every woman was enrolled and that no member of the Corps had ever been 'requisitioned or sent to France for any immoral purpose whatever'. This curious request no doubt revealed familiar double standards but it also emphasized how serious the situation had become, and demonstrated the strength of feeling about the issue in certain quarters.

The Labour Minister moved swiftly to authorize the appointment of a Commission of Inquiry. Mrs Deane Streatfeild was chairman and Miss Violet Markham secretary. The other members were Miss Carlin (Dock and General Workers' Union), Miss Varley (Workers' Union) and Miss Ritson (Women's Friendly Society of Scotland), a panel which demonstrated the progress women had made since the war began: there were no men on the panel and two of the women were trade union officials.

Accompanied by Florence, the Commission arrived in Boulogne on 5 March 1918 to be met by an indignant Helen, who resented the inquiry. She believed it was a bitter humiliation and an affront to the Corps, and as usual she made her feelings known. She had been asked to give the Commission every courtesy and to co-operate fully in drawing up a programme, but on the first day she learned that the Commission members had their own ideas, so she had to adjust the itinerary. She spent some time attending to the alterations and, after the Commissioners had gone to their rooms sent a WAAC conducting official to inform them of the new arrangements. Within a few minutes the embarrassed official raced back to Helen.

'Ma'am,' she burst out breathlessly, 'I knocked at the door and Miss — said "Come in", and I went in, and there was a staff officer there – and Miss — was wearing her camisole!'

Helen laughed and explained that Miss — used her maiden name for official purposes but was in fact the wife of an army major at GHQ. Next morning all this was relayed to Miss —, who quite saw the joke about her suitability to adjudicate on the morals of the Corps.

The Commission was confronted with a 'joke' of a different kind when they attended a meeting with General Fowke, the adjutant-general at GHQ in France. He produced a copy of the *Sporting Times* and read out the caption to a cartoon: 'Would you rather have a slap in the eye or a Waac on the knee?' He looked up gravely from the paper and added: 'This, ladies, is the sort of thing which we rely on you to prevent.'

The Commission's report was published on 20 March 1918 and was described by the *Daily Telegraph* as a complete vindication of the honour of the WAAC. According to the Commissioners, 'The general impression left upon us by the corps is that of a healthy, cheerful, self-respecting body of young women.' The medical reports of the Corps in England and France had been examined and the Commission found that there had been 21 (or 0.3 per cent) pregnancy cases and 12 (0.2 per cent) cases of venereal disease. Of the pregnant women, 2 were married and the majority of the others had been pregnant before going to France. Several of the cases of venereal disease were of old standing. In addition, 19 women had been returned home on disciplinary grounds and 10 for inefficiency, 59 had been discharged on medical grounds – including the 12 venereal disease cases – and 21 on compassionate grounds. They found that 17 women had been fined, 41 confined to camp, 23 had privileges restricted and 7 received admonitions – a total of 88 cases of various kinds and degrees.

'Compare this,' Miss Tennyson Jesse demanded in her book *Eve in Khaki*, 'with the morality of a village in England – or anywhere else in the world – and then (if you dare to be so obviously dishonest) say that there is any reason why the Women's Army should be aspersed.' She maintained that girls were shielded far more effectively from sexual temptation in the WAAC than they had been in civilian life. Although Miss Jesse does not say so, it would also be interesting to compare the statistics with those for an equivalent number of male soldiers.

What must have particularly pleased Helen was the statement that the Commission was impressed by the good discipline and tone of the Corps, both as regards administrators and the rank and file. One other interesting point emerged about the success the Corps had achieved in France: the Commission was told that a distinguished French senator had inspected the WAAC in one area with a view to the possible establishment of a French corps of women organized on similar lines. In fact, a women's corps was established in France only after the Second World War.

It had been an unhappy episode but the WAAC recovered from the scandal, helped, no doubt, by the appointment of Florence Burleigh Leach and Helen Gwynne-Vaughan as Commanders of the British Empire in the New Year Honours List. Both Florence and Mona received their awards for civilian work, but Helen gained the distinction of being the first woman to receive the military CBE.

She wore the decoration with great pride.

4
QUEEN MARY'S ARMY AUXILIARY CORPS

On 21 March 1918 a thick morning mist shrouded the 50-mile front line from Nieuwpoort, Belgium, in the north to Rheims, France, in the south. At 5.10 a.m. the largest concentration of artillery ever assembled began its bombardment of the Franco-British positions. It lasted for five hours and as the crack German stormtroops advanced, the battered Third Army under General Julian Byng and the Fifth Army under General Herbert Gough fell back. Three days later the Germans poured across the Somme and in another two days they captured Bapaume and Albert.

At first there was little alarm along the Lines of Communication because news took some time to filter through, but by 25 March the château at Gezaincourt, near Doullens, was certainly within sound and almost within sight of the big guns, and the WAAC cooks and waitresses there were withdrawn. Other women were moved back to Abbeville, the corps headquarters, from forward positions, travelling for many hours in cattle trucks to escape the German spearhead which threatened to bisect the British forces. At every station the cooks and waitresses worked, sometimes for 24 hours at a stretch, to make thousands of sandwiches and urns of tea for the tired and hungry troops cut off from their units.

Towards the end of the month it was clear that Amiens was in danger of falling and as Abbeville was a mere 25 miles north along the Somme, the safety of the women stationed there caused concern. Helen realized that if it became necessary to evacuate large areas, new accommodation and redeployment of her workers would be necessary, so she prepared a detailed plan. On 31 March she was ordered to report to GHQ where, with the Germans now within ten miles of Amiens, Field Marshal Sir Douglas Haig admitted that the British had their 'backs to the wall'. When Colonel James Whitehead asked Helen what she proposed to do about the women, she produced her recommendations. Relieved, the colonel raced off to see the deputy adjutant-general: 'Look, sir, Mrs Gwynne-Vaughan has it all worked out.' As Brigadier Shelford Bidwell says, she had anticipated the question as a good staff officer should, but for the time being it was agreed that the removal of 10,000 cooks, clerks and signallers, at a time when troop reinforcements were urgently needed, would be disastrous.

King George V and Queen Mary inspect a parade of QMAAC. Iris Feneghan is with Her Majesty while Miss Stevens accompanies the King. At the rear General Sir Archibald Murray accompanies the young Princess Mary who was in later years to become controller commandant of the ATS.

This was the real testing time for the Corps as it faced the possibility of actually coming under fire. Not only were the women within range of the guns, which were blasting away relentlessly at the Allied lines, but they were subjected to the constant threat of air raids. At Aire, on 11 April, Deputy Administrator G. Penrose, commanding a group of women employed on camouflage work in the Northern Special Works Park, was commended by her commanding officer for her coolness and the way she steadied the spirits of the workers as bombs fell and shells exploded in the vicinity. At St Omer two days later, the signals officer stressed the importance of the corps telephonists and telegraphists who had stayed at their posts during air raids, but still GHQ had doubts and that very night Helen received a message from the assistant quartermaster-general to withdraw the women from St Omer. Perplexed, she queried the order with GHQ who remained firm until the Directorate of Signals intervened, arguing that all 142 women were indispensable and must remain. The order was rescinded, the first and last attempt to withdraw members of the Corps from duty because of fears for their safety.

During this crisis period the spirits of the Corps received a tremendous boost by a mark of Royal approval. On 9 April 1918 the Secretary of State for War published an announcement:

> As a mark of Her Majesty's appreciation of the good services rendered by the Women's Army Auxiliary Corps, both at home and abroad since its inauguration, and especially of the distinction which it has earned in France by its work for the Army during the recent fighting on the Western Front, Her Majesty has been graciously pleased to assume the position and title of Commander-in-Chief of the Corps, which in future will bear the name of Queen Mary's Army Auxiliary Corps.

On 19 April Florence Burleigh Leach was commanded by Queen Mary to convey to her members that 'The Queen was very much interested in the work and welfare of the Corps [and] is pleased to be the Commandant-in-Chief and wished it every success.' The Queen had inspected WAAC quarters at Wimereux on 4 July 1917 and she and the King had lunched at the officers' club in Abbeville on 10 July when they were served by WAAC waitresses, so they both knew the contribution being made by the women in France.

With the first offensive, 'Operation Michael', weakening, the Germans launched a second thrust, 'Operation George', further north in France along the River Lys. In a do-or-die attempt to break through the defences the attack lasted from 9 April until 30 April, but this time the British and French lines did not buckle and gradually the flap on the Lines of Communication subsided. For the time being, the emergency was over.

Now the Americans were arriving in force. Their commander, General John Pershing, recognized the need for clerks in the Record Office at Bourges but the War Department in Washington was adamantly opposed to the idea of American women serving on army posts. When General James G. Harbord, commander of US Services of Supply in Europe, requested 5,000 military women as clerical workers, he was sent 5,000 limited-duty unskilled enlisted men. In October 1917 General Pershing had cabled Washington for 100 female uniformed telephone operators but instead he received contract women civilians. In addition, Pershing had about 5,000 American women volunteers to contend with, recruited by welfare organizations for service in Europe and over whom he had no control. Major-General Jeanne Holm, USAF (Ret), says that the lack of co-ordinated supervision of the diverse independent groups running loose in Europe added to the general confusion, as there was no ultimate authority who could direct their efforts.

The reaction of the US Army was curious, not least because the US Navy was far more progressive in its attitude to employing women. This was due in no small measure to the foresight of Navy Secretary Josephus Daniels who, as early as March 1917, before the US had even entered the war, authorized the enlistment of women. They were ranked as Yeoman (F) but popularly known as 'Yeomanettes'. They not only performed clerical duties but also became draughtsmen, translators, camouflage designers and recruitment personnel. What is more, the navy top brass had found an ingenious way round their own rather rigid rules which decreed both that all yeomen were to be assigned to ships and that all women were forbidden to go to sea. Some bright fellow thought of assigning the yeomanettes to sunken tugs on the bottom of the Potomac.

Pershing looked enviously at the well-organized and disciplined QMAAC, the British Army nurses and the US Army's own nursing corps and, according to General Holm, yearned to bring some order out of the chaos which surrounded him. The only solution was to appeal to the War Office in London for assistance. Accordingly, in the spring of 1918, 1,000 QMAAC clerks under Chief Controller Hilda Horniblow were posted to Bourges. Miss Horniblow's title posed a problem for the QMAAC, since effectively it now had three chief controllers. To differentiate between them, Florence was promoted to controller-in-chief, the equivalent of a major-general.

Brigadier-General J. J. H. Nation instructed Helen to detail 100 clerks for the Americans and at first, uncharitably, she seized the opportunity to dispose of some of her less useful members, only to be promptly told: 'We always send our best troops to the Allies.' So her best troops had to go. A far more relaxed attitude pertained at the US Army base and, strangely, the girls preferred the stricter régime of the British. By July the Americans needed more clerks to help them organize the files of the Central Record Office at Tours and another QMAAC team was chosen for the task. The unit administrator was Olive Bartels. In 1914 she had become chief organizer of the WSPU and had been placed on the police 'wanted' list, evading their search by adopting the pseudonym Margaret Cunningham and wearing the disguise of a widow in mourning, a thick black veil concealing her face as she darted from hiding place to hiding place. After the campaign against the suffragettes was called off, she joined Christabel Pankhurst on a tour of the United States but she had managed to keep this secret and the War Office was not aware of her former role. By 1917 Olive was in the uniform of the WAAC and worked in the coding and parliamentary branches of the War Office, where she was commended for her ability and initiative. She also earned many compliments from the US Army, who mentioned her in despatches.

Later that summer Mrs Long, Florence's sister and her deputy in London, crossed over to France to inspect the QMAAC detachment at the American camp in Bourges. On 2 August she re-embarked aboard the hospital ship, *Warilda*, carrying 600 wounded as well as QMAAC members back to England. In mid-Channel a torpedo struck amidships. One hundred and twenty-two men were lost and one woman – Mrs Long – was crushed to death against the ship's side while transferring to a lifeboat. It was a tragedy felt throughout the Corps.

By now Helen had gathered round her a group of loyal assistants who between them, she says, kept her in good order. Her head clerk throughout her eighteen months in France was Forewoman N. Campbell, described as a benevolent despot. Helen often used her as a sounding board: when they had been together for a year Campbell was asked whether she noticed any difference in the attitude of the soldiers. 'Oh, yes, ma'am, the men talk shop to us now,' she replied. Helen's driver was the untiring Jolly, a great character and an outspoken critic if she spotted anything out of order. During their trips Helen often chose to sit in front and held long discussions with Jolly, who she describes as having a distinctly masculine appearance and a deep-rooted scorn of all men, to such an extent that she would not allow them anywhere near her vehicle.

On 13 June 1918 the corps headquarters was moved from Abbeville to St Valéry-sur-Somme. Calling on the town major, who had been a general officer in the South African War, Helen asked about the procedure in air raids and was assured that there was absolutely no compulsion to take to the shelters if it was not considered necessary. She dutifully pointed out that at Abbeville part of the general orders was that all personnel should be under shelter when an attack was launched.

'Ah yes,' the major replied, 'but that was on the Lines of Communication where they have an inquiry if anyone is killed. Here we expect it.'

The corps office was set up in a villa with the sleeping quarters in an annexe at the bottom of the garden. The washing arrangements soon proved inadequate so additional facilities were installed in the garden, entailing a run through the fresh air to a cold bath every morning. Drill was possible in the spacious grounds and for the first time headquarters staff were expected to turn out for parade every morning. Helen not only joined in herself but instructed visiting officials to do the same, much to their consternation.

Helen also initiated a Corps School at which administrators and forewomen attended refresher courses. At first instruction took place at various camps which had space available, but in the summer of 1918 a site close to the sea at Mesnil-Val, three miles south-west of Le Treport, was chosen for a rest camp and the school moved there. As well as offering the opportunity for women from different areas to come together and exchange experiences, members could enjoy the sea air and have a break from camp routine.

In August Helen's portrait was painted by war artist William Orpen and, when completed, looked so lifelike that an orderly, entering the room where it was placed, came smartly to attention. But that August was to be Helen's last full month in France: on 1 September she was ordered to London where she was informed that she was to succeed the Hon. Violet Douglas-Pennant as head of the Women's Royal Air Force. Her immediate reaction was to say 'no, thank you' but she was told that it was an order.

When the adjutant-general interviewed her later, he asked: 'Well, Mrs Gwynne-Vaughan, have you heard about the Air Force?'

'Yes, sir,' she replied.

'Are you pleased?'

'No, sir.'

'You surely don't think yourself indispensable to the Corps in France?'

'It hadn't occurred to me to think myself indispensable to the Air Force, sir,' she retorted.

Sadly Helen returned to St Valéry to say her farewells and to be consulted about her successor. Miss Lila Davy, deputy controller at Rouen, was selected. She then travelled to Etaples, Dieppe, Abbeville, Havre and Rouen, warning the women that it would be her duty to ensure that the WRAF was more efficient than they were. 'Don't let me succeed in that,' she pleaded. On the way to Calais her career was almost ended precipitately – her car collided with a train at a level crossing but Jolly, in a brilliant feat of driving, managed to keep the car upright after the bonnet was struck. Helen sailed for England on 11 September and when she returned to France on 22 March 1919 she was wearing the badges of an air commodore.

Within four days of Helen's departure her sister Marjorie Pratt Barlow, by now deputy controller at Etaples, wrote a letter to her 'darling CC', telling her of the effect on Jolly. She recounts a doleful drive with the chauffeuse who cried nearly the whole way, although 'she tried all the time to appear to have a cold and continuously blew her nose'. Campbell joined Helen in the WRAF where she became an officer and remained as personal assistant to the director.

On 28 September the Fourth Army broke through the Hindenburg Line, capturing 35,000 prisoners and 380 guns, and soon the German High Command sued for peace. The war diaries of the Corps recorded the event in a variety of ways. QMAAC headquarters: 'Office routine, news of armistice arrived.' Le Havre hinted at some form of celebration: 'Owing to the announcement that the armistice had been signed very little work was done' but Etaples ignored the event completely, saying merely: '1 worker transferred to Boulogne; 1 to and 5 from Base depot; 1 admitted to and 2 discharged from hospital.'

Left Portrait of Helen Gwynne-Vaughan painted by William Orpen in France, August 1918. *Right* Florence Burleigh Leach, who succeeded Mona Chalmers Watson as director of the WAAC in February 1918.

A far fuller picture of Armistice Day in Rouen was provided by Elizabeth Johnston, in an article published by the *East of Fife Observer* on 5 and 12 December.

> The dawn was alive with promise; large issues were at stake, and a nation's fate hanging by a thread. Throughout the night we had heard of peace, and rumours of peace, and now we entertained 'great expectations'. Being Night Signallers, the day was ours to do with what we chose. After an hour's journey we reached the city, where all was excitement and suppressed emotion. In pitiful little groups, refugees thronged the streets . . . In the Place de la Cathedrale, the Daughters of Mary were hurrying to High Mass . . . newsvendors were making small fortunes; Yankees and Tommies, English residents and Jocks, were eagerly paying francs and half francs for the Continental edition of the *Daily Mail*. The crowd was dense – 'the world too much with

> us', so we decided to leave the town, and await the news, on the hill-top. We knew what the signal was to be, and how the signing of the Armistice was to be proclaimed. When we reached the summit of the hill we came on a party of German prisoners burying a dead comrade. How significant it seemed! In the shadow of the Eglise de Bon-Secours, we sat on the grass and listened to the convent children singing. Listening, we
>
> Heard a carol, mournful, holy,
> Chanted loudly, chanted lowly.
>
> Suddenly the hillside echoed and re-echoed, as volley after volley was fired from the big gun on the ramparts. In the distance, the cathedral bells pealed and clanged out the glad news. Flags were run up to the masthead on every boat and steamer in the river, and the Allies' colours were unfurled everywhere.
>
> After sundown the city was transformed. Was it the same place through which we had passed in the morning? Or was it a dream city? One connected the sights with scenes described in Aladdin, only here there were *hundreds* of wonderful lamps. Spanning the river the bridges seemed like magic constructions – fairy arches. The myriad coloured lights suspended from the arches of the Pont Corneille were reflected in the river. Along the Quai de Paris a band was making its way. Crowds followed and clambered up beside the bandsmen.
>
> Upon the wharfs, they came.
> Knight and burgher, lord and dame
>
> grown-up children gone wild with delight. A young French girl threw both arms round a Black Watch Kiltie, and ere he had time to know what was happening, she kissed him, first on one cheek, then the other, after French fashion . . .

An Australian band played the Allies' national anthems and a Scottish piper led a procession – of French soldiers in their picturesque blue uniforms, wounded Belgians, Australians in their hospital suits, Americans, Portuguese, Chinese, South African Scottish, Canadian Highlanders and Indians. Early in the evening she made her way back to Camp 4, walking for miles between avenues of poplar trees along a road made by Napoleon. Then she turned into a by-path towards the British cemetery where, side by side, lay fallen Highlanders and Tommies, Australians and Canadians, Americans and New Zealanders, and nurses and members of the WAAC.

Before the month was out Elizabeth Johnston became a victim of the influenza epidemic which swept the world and she wrote letters home telling of her convalescence. On Christmas Eve 1918 she went on night duty at 11.15. Leaving the signal office at 8 a.m. on Christmas Day, she went to Rouen and the fourteenth-century church of St Ouen. There she told the verger she wished to go up to the central tower, to see the glorious views of the city below. He was the last person to whom she spoke. At 2.30 that afternoon two American soldiers saw her, lying unconscious on the roof of a chapel, after plunging 80 feet from the top of the tower. She was carried through the church and taken to No. 8 General Hospital, where she died with a friend at her side.

Miss Christian Lorimer, the QMAAC camp administrator, wrote: 'She was carrying books, and was often known to get into quiet corners to read. What happened after that is a mystery. My own theory is this: she must have perched herself up in some corner, and possibly fallen asleep, reading, and in awakening, must have been taken by dizziness and fallen . . .'

Elizabeth Johnston was given a military funeral in St Severs cemetery on Monday, 30 December 1918. A South African Scottish firing party fired a volley as her coffin was lowered into the grave, surrounded by girls from the Signal Corps and QMAAC officials.

With the commencement of demobilization in 1919, the disbanding of QMAAC units in France began, although new detachments were still being sent out. In Perth, Georgina Baxter, then 21 years old, joined two of her fellow workers in an appeal to their colonel to be sent abroad. She arrived in France in July 1919 and was posted to an RAF engine repair shop near Rouen. In September the corps headquarters moved to Boulogne and soon afterwards to Wimereux. By December 1920 nearly everyone had gone home, except for a small unit remaining with the Graves Registrations Commission at St Pol. They were demobilized in London on 27 September 1921, and with their departure the QMAAC was no more.

About 57,000 women had served in the WAAC and QMAAC over four and a half years. The Army was the only service which had forbidden the use of the word 'officer' for women and which did not allow them to wear the same badges of rank as the men.

This had been 'the war to end all wars' and therefore little need was seen for the retention of women's services, despite the recommendation of a committee to the Army Council that a Queen's Reserve be formed within the Territorial Force.

Yet by 1918 women had proved, beyond all doubt, to be capable substitutes for men in industry, in organization, in transport and, indeed, on the battlefield itself. Nurse Edith Cavell, who had been shot by the Germans on 12 October 1915 for helping wounded Allied soldiers to escape, had even drawn from the then Prime Minister, Herbert Asquith, the belated admission: 'There are thousands of such women, but a year ago we did not know it.'

In addition, women partially won their fight for the vote when the Representation of the People Act 1918 gave the franchise to married women, to women householders and to women university graduates of 30 and over. This Act gave the suffrage movement a world-wide impetus and two years later the United States followed suit. Though one cannot attribute this governmental *volte-face* directly to women's war work – enfranchisement would have come eventually, anyway – it certainly played a part and probably saved the face of Lloyd George's administration. The old arguments about women not being able to help defend the realm were now no longer valid. A year later, on 28 November 1919, Nancy, Viscountess Astor, took the place of her husband as Conservative MP for Plymouth, becoming the first woman to take her seat in the House of Commons. That same year the Sex Disqualification Removal Act paved the way for women to enter the Civil Service and the professions.

And so the women returning to civilian life discovered a whole new world of opportunity open to them – a world where the Pankhursts and the suffragettes were out of date; where offices, once a male domain, were now prepared to allow, even to encourage, women to work side by side with men; where the number of parlourmaids and domestic workers had dwindled by more than a quarter. Thousands of women did grasp the new challenge. Within three years of the war's end, there were 94,381 nurses – 20,000 more than in 1914; the numbers of women doctors and surgeons had tripled to 1,253 during the same period; there were 296 women dentists compared with 250 in 1914; and 43 chartered accountants, a rise of 27. And in a notable move, 20 women had become barristers and 17 solicitors, while 1,663 chose social welfare for a career. There were even 41 women civil engineers and 42 additional women architects. The number of women employed in commerce had nearly doubled to 934,500. In all, more than seven million women were now in full employment throughout Britain.

'When I got into Parliament,' Nancy Astor proclaimed, 'I felt like a bullet out of a cannon. The Women's Movement was the cannon. I have been exploding ever since.'

The suffragists had lit the fuse, the women war workers had touched off the powder and fired the first salvo. Now it was up to the next generation to set the sights and aim for new targets in their bid for total equality. The feminist movement, although still in its infancy, was clearly on the march. The next few years would decide whether it really could achieve what seemed so easily within reach as the bells began pealing joyously at the eleventh hour on the eleventh day of the eleventh month in 1918.

5
BETWEEN THE WARS

Perhaps the most obvious evidence of the new world which emerged after the First World War was the radical change in the dress and appearance of women, for more than anything else the fashions epitomized the newfound freedom which women were enjoying. The elaborate clothes and ample curves of the appropriately named 'S-bend' style, worn by ladies of the Edwardian Era, were replaced by the flapper or *garçonne* look. Slimness was the vogue and the well-dressed girl of the 'twenties looked flat-chested, waistless, wearing a slip of a dress ending just below the knee. Hairstyles also demonstrated the boyishness of the 'twenties woman, with the emphasis on short hair cut into a 'bob', a 'shingle' or an 'Eton crop'. To some extent the new generation was influenced by the tendency of women who had worked in factories or on the farms to cut their hair short because of the hazards posed by machinery, but chiefly girls were expressing the independence brought by a career, a pay packet and better prospects of employment.

They had exchanged the sombre war years for a mood of gaiety and frivolity, laced with determination. Instead of trailing a fan the young girl of the 'twenties wielded a tennis racquet; instead of taking dignified drives in the country she sat behind the wheel of a sports car; and instead of cultivating a pale complexion she turned her face to the sun and positively encouraged a healthier-looking tanned skin. The use of cosmetics became respectable and lipstick was freely and liberally applied. Lingerie was advertised openly and for the first time women went to the seaside in order to bathe in daring costumes. At Wimbledon the 1919 women's champion, Suzanne Lenglen, set the sporting trend with a loose-fitting, flowing white frock. She still wore white stockings but there was a hint of even less inhibiting styles and shorter hemlines to come, until by the mid-'thirties some Women of Wimbledon, led by Alice Marble, were donning shorts. In the home, too, a revolution was taking place. Having once escaped the drudgery of domestic service, the girls who had done war work sought jobs which paid better wages and demanded fewer hours of labour, and they found them in abundance in commerce and industry.

'There must be time to think, to read, to enjoy life, to be young with the growing generation, to have time for their pleasures, to have leisure for one's own – to hold one's youth as long as possible, to have beauty around us – line and colour in dress, form and colour in our surroundings,' the spanking new *Good Housekeeping* magazine advised its readers in its first issue of 23 February 1922. It promised the house-proud woman, 'in these days of servant shortage', features on every new invention which was practical and economical to use; household equipment, such as vacuum cleaners, was advertised. Gas and electricity were becoming standard in the homes of the better-off, as was the telephone. Expanding wage packets provided money to spend on houses, cars and entertainments such as the cinema and on crystal sets to tune into radio stations. The 1920s saw the dawn of Hollywood with stars such as Greta Garbo, Clara Bow – the 'It' girl – and Mary Pickford, drawing longing sighs from the men and envy from the women. For those who preferred reading, a new French novel, *Chéri* by Colette and a volume of short stories, *The Garden Party* by Katherine Mansfield, set the tone.

But there was something artificial about the world which the younger generation inherited in 1920 – as artificial as the new synthetic fabrics such as rayon, which were rapidly becoming more fashionable than wool, cotton or silk. W. L. George sounded a note of caution in *Good Housekeeping*:

> Great movements of mankind, like a European war, which tend to remake the face of the world, can affect women more than they do men, because they leave men where they are, while they make for women a new world with which they must cope . . . Such change as has come over the world is merely the change which would have come without any war, but it has come quicker . . . We are a little ahead of ourselves, and therefore we come everywhere upon difficult readjustments . . .

Those prophetic words were given more force by the warning:

> Woman knows that if anything deprives her of her work, public opinion quietly but obstinately propels her back towards the shelter of the home, and that if she is driven in she may never get out again . . .

It is worth looking more closely at the various categories of women who emerged into the new decade after the war ended. The flighty 'flappers' were dancing the fox-trot and the Charleston, smoking in public, venturing out unchaperoned in twos and threes to restaurants and cinemas and becoming more and more captivated by jazz music and the swing bands which were to follow. They were bright young people who came from middle-class homes and their aim was to enjoy themselves to the full, to indulge in the spirit of hedonism which was abroad and eventually to catch the eye of a beau and settle down in one of the thousands of new semi-detached houses being built in the freshly created suburbs. Although many were employed in offices and shops, they were in truth merely 'birds of passage', on their way to housebound domesticity when they married and had children – and they had every prospect of marriage because they and their male contemporaries had been too young for war service.

The slightly older, more mature woman had less optimistic prospects. In this category were many war widows whose chances of remarriage were diminished by the enormous death toll of the war. They could not go out to work because they had school-going children to bring up and had to scrape by on a paltry pension. Many others, whose husbands were permanently maimed (about 40 per cent of all soldiers who had served) had to find means of supplementing the meagre pension while coping with the demands of a growing family and caring for a disabled husband. Also in this category were the surplus women – those who would never marry because there were not enough men to go round: the ratio of females over 14 rose from 595 per 1,000 of population in 1911 to 638 per 1,000 in 1921. Thus a vast number of women were forced to fend for themselves, though some did make a conscious decision to become career women because they found work more interesting than marriage. The more fortunate, whose husbands had escaped death or serious injury, could combine the wartime careers they had carved out for themselves with housework, their salaries providing the difference between pinch and plenty.

Most of the older women, however, lacked the required education for a career: they had been born in an age when women were deemed not to need learning and had inherited a legacy of staid Victorian and Edwardian conventions. Trapped in a world neatly poised between the prudishness of their mothers and the flamboyance of their daughters, they shook their heads disapprovingly at the antics of the younger generation, perhaps concealing an element of envy behind the disparaging expressions. This generation of women had won the vote at the cost of a husband or a son lost. They were a disillusioned and, in some respects, a bitter generation, who believed fervently that the world in which they now lived was a worse place because of the war.

The men who were killed in that war are often referred to as 'the lost generation' but, in retrospect, perhaps it was the women they left behind who were lost in the new world for which they had laid down their lives. And the tragedy was that as the decade advanced so the plight of the women who had been loved and left became even more difficult, because the economic boom which marked the end of the war was soon to turn into a devastating Depression.

Into this booming new world was born, on 19 June 1920, Eileen Joan Nolan. Eileen was scarcely six months old when the post-war bubble burst and the economy started a slide towards the 1929 catastrophe, signalled initially by an increase in government borrowing rates, a fall in prices and the beginning of a rise in unemployment. As the last of the demobbed soldiers returned to reclaim their jobs, the 'caretaker' women were pushed aside and by June 1921 almost two million people were out of work. The road to ruin for millions in America and Europe was, even at this early stage, well-signposted. But in many ways the girl who was brought up in the 'chocolate village' of Bournville, near Birmingham, was protected against the vicissitudes which were to overtake the children of the 'twenties. The firm of Cadbury Brothers, founded by John Cadbury in 1824, had grown into an important enterprise under the management of his sons, Richard and George. They had moved from the original premises in Bull Street to Bridge Street and then, in 1878, they found an ideal 14½-acre site about four miles south of Birmingham in open country crossed by a tiny stream, the Bournbrook, from which the factory took its new name of Bournville.

George Cadbury, a Quaker, became renowned for improvements in the working conditions of his employees, who were treated almost like members of the family. Football and cricket fields were provided for the staff – among the products of the Bournville works cricket team was England wicket-keeper Arthur Lilley – and a separate garden and playground adjoining the factory was set aside for girls. But the development which most demonstrated the concern the Cadbury brothers felt about staff welfare was the creation of a brand new housing scheme for Bournville employees. When the firm first moved to its new site the brothers had built for key workers 24 semi-detached houses with large gardens and rooms much bigger than was usual at the time. These houses set the pattern for what was to folllow. In 1895 George bought 120 acres of land adjacent to the factory and began the Bournville experiment, the formation of a garden village. The scheme began with 143 houses which were sold to staff at a cost price of about £150 on a 999-year lease and low interest loans. Eventually George created the Bournville Village Trust to administer the 330-acre estate and 370 houses, together valued at £172,724. The residents were secure not only in their jobs but also in their homes and, with the Quaker influence of the brothers, all staff at the factory were required to join in prayers before work every morning.

'It was really like having a royal family in the village,' Eileen recalls. 'Dame Elizabeth Cadbury, George's widow, was a very regal lady, not unlike Queen Mary, and everybody loved her.' Eileen was barely two years old when George died but the Cadbury family traditions were maintained. The Nolans were very much part of this close-knit community: Eileen's father, James John Nolan, who had served in the First World War with the Royal

Horse Artillery and was decorated for gallantry in 1915, was employed by Cadbury's as a technical adviser. Eileen's mother, Ethel Mary, had trained as a singer but the war had cut short her ambitions to become a concert soprano. For all its advantages, Bournville was a closed community which welcomed only Cadbury employees and as such it was virtually sealed off from the rest of England.

Some other young girls also escaped the full effect of the declining standards of living and the gathering unease of the business community. Mary Tyrwhitt, approaching her coming-of-age, had seen her father end the war as a naval hero who had commanded the Harwich flotilla aboard his flagship *Arethusa* during the battles of Jutland, Heligoland Bight and Dogger Bank. After the Armistice Rear Admiral Reginald Tyrwhitt met the surrendering German submarines on 20 November 1918 and escorted 129 of them into Harwich. Thereafter Mary accompanied her father to Gibraltar. 'I never did any work after school in the local convent during the mornings and so I hunted, rowed, swam and played tennis and had a jolly good time,' she reminisces. From Gibraltar the Tyrwhitts had moved to Malta, then to Scotland and after that to Hong Kong before eventually returning to London and Admiralty House. Mary's father became admiral of the fleet and his last posting before retirement was commander-in-chief of the north. It was all good experience for young Mary, by now busying herself as a Girl Guide leader.

Not quite so fortunate but nevertheless just as secure in her home life during those war-weary years was Irene Ludlow. She lived in the Wiltshire village of Marten where her father was the local police constable, patrolling the byways on his bicycle. Uniforms had been part of the Ludlow tradition for three generations; Irene's great-grandfather, grandfather and now her father and uncle were all members of the police force. Irene was one of seven children, five girls and two boys, and the Ludlows, although poor, were an exceptionally happy family. By the 1930s domestic service had made a comeback, as more and more girls from the less privileged classes discovered that this was the only type of work available to them. And so, in the late 1930s, the teenaged Irene took a job as a maid at a local farmhouse.

These three young women, so typical of the class structure of Britain during the inter-war years, were to meet during the conflict which even then was looming as the National Socialist Party began its spectacular rise in Germany, propelling Adolf Hitler into power in 1933. Memories of the 1914-18 war were far too fresh in the minds of the British people for anyone to wish for another conflict in Europe. Besides, the country was just beginning to regain momentum after the Wall Street crash and its dislocating effect on the world economic structure and Europe's political stability. If the people of 1920 could be described as optimistic about the future, eager to make up for the lost years of their lives spent in the trenches and hoping for a swift reversal of the privations they had endured, then those who greeted the decade of the 'thirties could be summed up as disillusioned, wary of what lay ahead, afraid, perhaps, that the good times would never return. The mood of the day to a large extent persuaded Western governments to pursue a policy of disarmament rather than maintaining military preparedness. While in retrospect it is easy to see the flaws in this strategy, few politicians in those unsettling years would have risked the popularity of the electorate by imposing extra tax burdens to finance re-armament.

By 1933 unemployment had begun to fall and this promising sign of an economic recovery coincided with a staggering upsurge in consumerism. This was the dawn of a new era – the age of convenience. In the shops housewives could buy tinned fruit, meat, fish and every variety of vegetable. If fresh produce was preferred, it could be stored in refrigerators. Cereals were available for breakfast, the legacy of John Harvey Kellogg, and in 1932 Nestlé had introduced instant coffee. Growing affluence went hand-in-hand with increasing thrift – Building Society deposits rose from a mere £82 million in 1920 to £717 million by 1938. Cars came down in price and the famous Austin 7 and Ford 8 could be purchased for as little as £100. Houses – semi-detached with bathroom and garage, now the vogue – were selling for £450, with interest on mortgages of 4½ per cent. In entertainment, the new Hollywood phenomenon of the 'talkies' had swept the world after Al Jolson's pioneering role in the 1927 production of *The Jazz Singer*. Gary Cooper and Clark Gable were the screen idols of millions of women and the child star, Shirley Temple, enthralled mothers with her first film, *Redhaired Alibi*. Technology had advanced to the point where in 1931 the world's tallest building, the Empire State, had reached a height of 1,250 feet (381 metres). There was also hope of a breathtaking new form of entertainment after J. Logie Baird's demonstration of television in 1926.

In this era of opportunity women continued to demonstrate their versatility, particularly in aviation, the Cinderella of transport. While Americans hailed the triumph of Amelia Earhart in becoming the first woman to make a solo flight across the Atlantic, Britons found a heroine in Amy Johnson, who established several long-distance records with her solo flights to Australia in 1930, to Tokyo in 1932 and to Cape Town and back in 1936. Women were also prominent in the best-seller literary lists – Mazo de la Roche with her Jalna saga, the first volume of which was published in 1927, and Pearl S. Buck who wrote the classic *The Good Earth*, which won the Pulitzer Prize in 1932. Still busy scribbling in those early years of the decade was Margaret Mitchell, destined to publish the international best-seller *Gone With the Wind* in 1936, the year in which Britons were shocked by a constitutional crisis when Edward VIII abdicated to marry Wallis Simpson.

But the post-war plan for women to play a role, albeit a limited one, in the three Services continued to gather dust in the archives at army headquarters. Although women had made inroads in almost every other profession, the barriers remained lowered against them there and there was little hope in the early 'thirties that the male exclusivity of these Services would be breached again.

Through all these years Helen Gwynne-Vaughan had continued her work at Birkbeck College. On 4 December 1919, when her First World War service ended, she had been made a Dame of the British Empire. Two years later she received another title, becoming the first academic at Birkbeck to assume the status of Professor of the University of London. Her wartime contribution had not been forgotten by the authorities and she sat on three Home Office committees while devoting leisure time to the Girl Guides, the VAD Council, the National Union of Scientific Workers, the Service Women's Association, the RAF Benevolent Fund and the National Union of Conservative and Unionist Associations. In the three general elections of 1922, 1923 and 1924 Helen stood unsuccessfully as a Conservative candidate in the North Camberwell constituency, and then decided to withdraw from the political arena and concentrate on her work. Her reputation as a scientist grew and in 1929 she was created a Dame Grand Cross of the Order of the British Empire 'for public and scientific services'.

As she grew older her choice of clothes became more in line with the image of her later years so well remembered by her Second World War colleagues. The light, colourful fabrics of her youth were discarded in favour of darker costumes and cardigan suits, with plain blouses of silk or chiffon. Pictures of her in evening dress reveal a preference for velvet and brocade gowns adorned by lace scarves. She concentrated heavily on her scientific work and, in collaboration with a graduate student, wrote a textbook on fungi which was well received, and several notable papers on the same subject. But Helen was a disillusioned lady, restless, missing the furious activity of her years in France, yearning to re-enter public life by channelling her energy into a worthwhile project. Opportunities to relive the memories of 1917 and 1918 came about through the QMAAC Old Comrades Association, founded in December 1919 and the forerunner of today's WRAC Association, of which she was a vice-president. From July 1920 the association published a gazette which is now titled *Lioness*. Helen also became president of the WRAF Association which was constituted in 1920.

The chance to help in organizing women to take a more active role in emergency duty arrived in June 1934 when Helen received a telephone call from Lady Londonderry, who had a scheme to combine all the women's voluntary organizations – the Women's Legion, which she had founded twenty years earlier; the VAD; and the Women's Transport Service, more familiarly known by its original name, FANY. Helen became Chairman of the proposed body and developed an idea for an Officers' Training Section to function within the Legion. However, the new body was disbanded in 1936 when the Home Office withheld recognition and its individual components continued as separate entities. Helen's Officers' Training Section became the Emergency Service which, with the backing of the authorities, was to select and train officers 'for any women's corps that may be employed on duties other than nursing, in a national emergency', as it was termed by the Army Council. Camps were held at Hemel Hempstead and at Abbotts Hill. About 400 potential officers were trained and the cadets were given an idea of the duties which might be performed during wartime service, taking it in turns to give and to receive orders. They were subjected to tough tests, during which they had to give spontaneous answers to questions such as: 'You are a junior officer attending a cinema performance at which there are about twenty women of your unit. The cinema has caught fire. What action are you taking and what orders are you giving?' Faced with a problem of this nature, most people would require a moment to stop and think. The rapidity with which the girls reacted revealed the difference between the leaders and those who were content to wait for orders.

One of the cadets was Belinda Boyle, the daughter of Lady Trenchard. Drilling a squad for the first time, she marched them until the leading file became entangled with a partly built aircraft and then improvised the curious order: 'Backwards march', which the squad executed smartly enough. 'I even managed to halt them on the right foot,' she claimed. Once again army drill instructors found themselves confused: throughout one session the sergeant referred to Belinda as the 'right-hand man' until in the middle of an order he hesitated and offered an apology. 'I beg your pardon, I should 'ave said the right-' and lady.' Cooking also had its brighter moments. On one occasion a Royal Signals brassard was dropped accidentally into the rice pudding, turning it blue, and everybody complimented the chefs on their gastronomic variation. The cooks also had to tackle an intruding rat with a rolling-pin and despatched it with several well-aimed blows.

Tensions were rising again in Europe by 1936. On 16 March 1935 Hitler, denouncing the terms of the Treaty of Versailles that mandated German disarmament, had reinstated conscription and upgraded the army to 36 divisions. A year later Germany reoccupied the Rhineland, the first in a series of expansionist moves. July 1936 saw the start of the Spanish Civil War in which the Luftwaffe grasped the opportunity, while helping Franco's forces, to test German air strategy. With Hitler now firmly in control in Germany, Benito Mussolini ruling Italy and Joseph Stalin consolidating his position in Russia, totalitarianism was on the march in Europe.

The British Army, alert to the possible dangers ahead, dusted off the files of almost forgotten memoranda prepared after the First World War and reconsidered the question of employing women. However, the Committee of Imperial Defence submitted a report to the Cabinet which, in a manner more typical of the times, decided that a reserve of women during peacetime was not necessary. Fortunately, when Lieutenant-General Sir Clive Liddell replaced General Sir Harry Knox as adjutant-general in December 1937, the idea was revived and three women's organizations were recognized by the Army Council – Helen's Emergency Service; the FANY; and the Women's Legion which now had a Motor Transport Section. Representatives of all three were in constant touch with Sir Clive and after one interview Helen reported optimistically to her council that plans were being drawn up for a women's service, a Government *volte-face* that underlined the anxiety existing in the minds of the authorities in those uncertain months.

After Hitler occupied Austria on 13 March 1938 and proclaimed the Anschluss, it was clear that he had also set his sights on Czechoslovakia. Two bodies of opinion prevailed in Britain – those who were in favour of appeasement and those who recognized the inevitability of another war. While Neville Chamberlain's government relied on protest to combat Hitler's provocative acts, the army generals were forced to take contingency action. This time there was no question of ignoring womanpower: senior officers were old enough to remember the enormous contribution women had made in the First World War and were sufficiently percipient to realize that in another emergency they should be ready to tackle the same tasks.

At a meeting held on 6 May 1938 representatives of the three women's societies were informed of the intention to create a women's unit. This was followed by a letter outlining details of the scheme and announcing a further meeting on 23 June. The proposal was to incorporate all three recognized societies into the 'Women's Auxiliary Defence Service' within the framework of the Territorial Army: the FANY would provide a core of trained women and potential officers; the Emergency Service would become a training school; and the Women's Legion would recruit the trades – 600 drivers, 1,800 clerks and 3,600 domestics. Except for the name – which Helen and others foresaw could be abbreviated to WADS, the meanings of which were not particularly appropriate or appealing – the scheme was generally welcomed, although there were points of disagreement. Quite apart from these, however, the FANY, which all along had been proud of its independence and in many ways considered itself a cut above the other two organizations, agreed to participate only if it could retain a separate identity. There being no time for argument, they were given short shrift and told to comply or be excluded. All the same, the deputy director-general of the TA, Major-General Sir John Brown, promised that their request would be borne in mind.

The 23 June meeting was chaired by Sir John and, having been given time to examine the implications of the scheme, the women came prepared to argue several points. The name of the unit was probably the major consideration and it is not difficult to imagine the differing opinions voiced round the table. The Emergency Service had suggested Territorial Army Auxiliary Service or Auxiliary Defence Service, ruled out because ADS stood for Army Dental Service; another favourite was Auxiliary Defence Corps, but ADC was the accepted abbreviation for aide-de-camp. Eventually a compromise was reached and the name Auxiliary Territorial Service was chosen, even though the initials ATS were already in use for the Army Technical Service. (Later official documents referring to 'the boys of the ATS' caused much consternation among the women who read them.) It was at this meeting that the foundations of the ATS and its successor, the present-day WRAC, were laid and for this reason it has an important historical significance. The ATS was officially born by Royal Warrant on 9 September 1938:

> George R.I.
> WHEREAS WE deem it expedient to provide an organization whereby certain non-combatant duties in connection with Our Military and Air Forces may from time to time be performed by women:
>
> OUR WILL AND PLEASURE is that there shall be formed an organization to be designated the Auxiliary Territorial Service.
>
> OUR FURTHER WILL AND PLEASURE is that women shall be enrolled in this Service under such conditions and subject to such qualifications as may be laid down by Our Army Council from time to time.
>
> Given at Our Court of St. James's this 9th day of September, 1938, in the 2nd year of Our Reign.
>
> By His Majesty's Command
> Leslie Hore-Belisha.

On 21 September 1938 representatives of the three societies signed the statement defining their relationship to the ATS. The Women's Transport Service (FANY) undertook to 'assist the TA Association in raising' ten motor driver companies of 150 personnel each, for service with the Army. The Mechanical Transport Section of the Women's Legion agreed to 'assist the TA and RAF Associations' in raising 23 driver companies of about 50 personnel each for the Royal Air Force; the Legion itself was to assist in raising clerical and administrative staff. The Emergency Service was to be 'responsible for undertaking such duties in connection with the training of officers as may be decided by the Army Council'.

The signatories were as follows: Lady Hailsham and Miss Baxter-Ellis for the FANY; Lady Londonderry, Agatha Lady Hindlip, and Mrs Munro Ferguson for the Women's Legion; and Lady Trenchard, Mrs E. Harnett and Dame Helen Gwynne-Vaughan for the Emergency Service. On 27 September 1938 the BBC broadcast the first official release on the foundation of the ATS in a special announcement after the 9 p.m. news bulletin.

Two days later Neville Chamberlain flew to Munich to meet Hitler, Mussolini and Edouard Deladier, the French Prime Minister. After agreeing to Nazi demands to cede the Czechoslovakian territory of Sudetenland to Germany, Chamberlain returned home to cheers as he stepped off the aircraft proclaiming: 'I believe it is peace for our time.' By 10 October Germany had annexed Sudetenland, thus acquiring 10,000 square miles (29 per cent) of Czechoslovakian territory inhabited by 2.8 million Germans and 700,000 Czechs. The hungry German jaws were now ready to crunch down on Czechoslovakia itself, the head of which, on the maps of Europe in that year, lay ominously inside the lion's mouth. Six months after Munich the jaws clamped shut and overnight Czechoslovakia was made a vassal state of Germany. The illusion of 'peace for our time' was shattered.

Obviously Germany's next target was Poland, but this time Britain made its position abundantly clear in advance – if Hitler attacked Poland it would mean war. The stage had been set, the players were in their places and the world waited for the curtain to go up.

6
THE AUXILIARY TERRITORIAL SERVICE

Unfortunately the ATS got off to a terrible start – even Helen Gwynne-Vaughan admitted that. Others politely called it a 'lack of co-ordination' or less politely 'a monumental muddle'. In fact, it was absolute chaos as thousands of women, responding to the public announcement, besieged TA units in every county seeking information about the service. Bewildered adjutants, many of whom had not even heard the news bulletin on the wireless, complained that they had received no orders – although details of the scheme had been sent to TA Associations ten days earlier, no information had filtered down to unit level.

Those details, addressed to the presidents of the TA Associations, recommended the appointment of a county commandant who would be responsible for selecting suitable officers: to say the very least, a rather haphazard method of choosing the women who were to be the future officers of the new women's army. The ATS scheme allowed for the enrolment for four years of 20,000 women between the ages of 18 and 43, with an extension to the age of 50 for ex-servicewomen. They could volunteer for general service or for local service in their own neighbourhood and they would be affiliated to military units. But, once again, the Army, wishing to retain some of its traditions, ruled out commissions and insisted that the volunteers, rather than being 'enlisted', would be 'enrolled' on a civilian basis and would be subject to military law only as 'camp followers'. Although recognizing that women were essential if efficiency was to be maximized, the Army was still not prepared to concede the women any military status. The term 'official' still rankled and this time the women pleaded successfully for the adoption of the term 'officer'.

Obviously, in its search for officers, the TA Association presidents approached leading local ladies who, in turn, looked for women in the community who had enough time on their hands to take up the posts, thus effectively ruling out women who were busy running their homes, bringing up families, or in full-time employment. In many areas totally unsuitable people were selected; in others those with titles were preferred, resulting in severe criticism of the ATS in its early months. The ATS inherited a number of officers who were not only incapable of performing tasks properly but were also grossly inefficient and who, eventually, had to be asked to resign.

However, the adjutants of the TA units did have the foresight to write down the names and addresses of volunteers and, when some order was restored, these women were formally enrolled. With few exceptions, there were two types of company – the higher establishment company which had 2 officers, 1 senior leader (equivalent to a warrant officer, Class 11), 5 section leaders (sergeants), 8 assistant section leaders (corporals), and 40 volunteers (privates); and a lower establishment company with 1 officer and 23 members which included 7 sub-officers (NCOs). Some of these companies were intended solely for clerical employments while others were designed for general duties and included clerks, cooks, storewomen and orderlies. In addition motor driver companies were formed and just before the outbreak of war a few women were enrolled for signal duties. Some companies were raised for duties with the RAF but these were transferred to the Women's Auxiliary Air Force when it was formed in the summer of 1939.

Mary Tyrwhitt was living with her parents at Hawkhurst, Kent, when she was asked by a friend whose father was chairman of the Tunbridge Wells council whether she would be interested in raising an ATS platoon.

'Thank you, I'd love to,' she replied and formally enrolled on 11 November 1938. She then set about the difficult task of finding 23 young women who were prepared to give up some of their leisure time for the service.

'We had a meeting with the army recruiting staff,' she recalls, 'and mothers who were interested came to me and pleaded: "If my daughter joins you won't let her leave home, will you?" I told them that if war broke out we could be called up to go anywhere.'

Mary's platoon was soon affiliated to its local military unit and fortunately a sergeant instructor took them under his wing. However, the male officers had not yet adjusted to the idea of women soldiers. 'We had only one visit from the commanding officer and the adjutant, and you could see from their attitude they were terrified by us. In turn, we were frightened of them. They took very little interest in us, which was rather disheartening.'

The platoon joined other ATS units for a week at a military camp on the north coast of Kent, but although they were taught drill and disciplinary regulations, the girls were not told about army procedures.

Another early recruit was Lucy Anwyl-Passingham (later Davies), whose father was secretary of the Middlesex Territorial Association. Like Mary, she became an officer immediately.

'I was fairly young and knew nothing about the women's service because nobody did at that time. I found myself in command of about a hundred women in a drill hall at Willesden, helped by the Territorials, but they didn't know, any more than I did, what to do with us.'

She quickly became disenchanted and in March 1939 resigned. Lucy's experience was typical – the women were part of an army yet not accepted by the men of that army, and so the ATS lost many of its more capable recruits who were not content merely to play at being soldiers. Many girls had made sacrifices in order to join up and they never envisaged spending precious leisure hours marching up and down a drill hall being barked at by despairing sergeant-majors. While they accepted the necessity for drill, they wanted to learn their wartime roles and to feel that their contribution was vital.

Many highly qualified would-be recruits were handled with great insensitivity, including the wife of one of Helen's University of London colleagues. During her interview with the local commandant, she listed her qualifications as a good Cambridge honours degree and considerable experience of newspaper work, both in the editorial department and in the administrative section. The commandant informed her: 'I think the best place for you would be in the clerical staff. We have classes where you can learn to write letters and fill in forms. Or perhaps you can do a little cooking?'

Dorothy Humphery lived at Bembridge on the Isle of Wight with her father, the local vicar, and joined in 1938 as an orderly.

'I had visions of dashing behind the lines delivering top-secret papers saying attack or withdraw. In fact, I spent my time scrubbing the orderly room floors.' Hers was a common misapprehension but Dorothy, whose father and two brothers had military backgrounds, was more fortunate than some recruits. She attended a camp with the 2nd battalion of the Lincolnshire Regiment whose men accepted the girls totally and taught them accounts, finance and the basics of administration. An exchange was organized of cooks and clerks, the men coming over to show beginners how things should be done, the women going to learn from experienced soldiers.

'The men took us seriously – they didn't give the impression that they thought it quite fun having girls around. I know this was the impression a lot of other ATS recruits gained.'

To some extent the disorganized scramble had been anticipated by Helen and while the formation of the ATS was under discussion she had stressed the importance of selecting and training officers before recruitment began. It is astonishing that the Army, with its disciplined approach to such matters, should have adopted the attitude that women would not need much training and that provided the recruits were well-intentioned they would be able to manage. One senior officer even expressed surprise that the ATS should need sub-officers, or non-commissioned or warrant ranks, and many women with experience of organization were turned away. Evidently the lessons of the First World War had not been learned.

While the embryo ATS was struggling to find its feet, the FANY held itself aloof. Within weeks it had recruited 1,000 driver-mechanics, launched a recruiting drive for 500 more, and begun an officer and NCO training course at Camberley. Though officially an integral part of the ATS, from the outset it virtually ignored the service and went its own way. The result was almost open warfare between Mary Baxter-Ellis, the tall Northumbrian veteran of the First World War who had become commandant of the FANY in 1932, and Helen Gwynne-Vaughan. In particular, Helen could not countenance the FANY tradition of informality between officers and so-called other ranks. While on duty they observed the distinctions of rank and obeyed orders in a disciplined manner, but off-duty they were all equal, and officers, NCOs and privates messed together. They had the curious custom, too, of calling each other by their surnames in correspondence and in conversation, to such an extent that it is often impossible to discover Christian names or even initials of some members in official records.

Probably the heart of the problem lay in the alleged arrogance and snobbishness of the FANYs. They considered themselves the élite of the women's services and there was a general assumption among members that each was automatically 'officer material'. An anonymous writer to the FANY *Gazette* summed it up thus: 'We have the privilege of belonging to the educated classes with all the tradition of ruling behind us, and therefore rank as officers in everyday life.' Most of the FANYs did belong to the privileged class, being what could be called the 'mink and manure set' or perhaps, in today's terms, Sloane Rangers. All of them could drive and a good proportion owned cars which they willingly placed at the disposal of their companies. Many senior male army officers were driven in these private cars and because the chauffeuses were often the daughters of family friends, FANY drivers of any rank were invited into the officers' mess when the destination was reached.

By contrast ATS rules enforced a clearcut distinction between the ranks and, in accordance with army tradition, officers remained aloof. Some ATS officers went out of their way to confront FANY drivers who flouted these regulations without apparently appreciating that they were in the peculiar position of being privates in the full army sense of the term and so were committing a punishable offence if seen in uniform in public with male relatives who happened to be military officers. Antagonism built up on both sides.

Helen disliked the FANY drivers intensely. On one occasion, while on an official visit to one of their motor companies, she was entertained by the general officer commanding the 7th Ack-Ack Division, General Heywood, and his wife. Next day, to her consternation, she found that her driver was Mrs Heywood, and later she was invited into an ante-room to have a drink with the drivers. On Helen's insistence, Mrs Heywood was posted to another unit.

No wonder the FANYs considered the ATS officers interfering busybodies and for a long time they thought it far smarter to be a driver than 'counting Ats knickers and making sure they hadn't got nits in their hair', which was the way they saw the life of a junior ATS officer. They much preferred driving staff cars, ambulances, ration trucks and convoy vehicles and, most of all, being billeted in units of two or three rather than the ten under a sergeant that ATS regulations laid down. The more the ATS officers tried to bring the FANYs into line, the greater the degree of resentment. Had they not been promised their independence in the original agreement? A debatable point.

Helen's differences with the FANYs dated back to 1923 when she had attended a meeting with Baxter-Ellis's predecessor, Lilian Franklin, at which Helen suggested that the FANY should become an officers' training corps for a future women's service. Had the scheme been acceptable much of the confusion in the early years of the ATS could have been avoided. This sort of practical solution was typical of the well-ordered and scientific mind Helen possessed, but, as always, her manner in putting forward such proposals hardly inspired a spirit of confidence and co-operation. She had seen herself as the doyenne of women's services and, quite naturally, wanted to be head of any combined operation. Franklin had rejected the scheme outright and so the FANY, who had a proud war record as drivers in France and Belgium, maintained its independence.

There were two other reasons for Helen's antagonism, the first of which concerned the training of officers for the new ATS. Immediately after the announcement of its formation, Helen and her sister Marjorie had been enrolled by the secretary of the County of London TA Association, although both were over the official age limit for ex-servicewomen. Suffering the indignity of accepting lower ranks as majors, they organized five-and-a-half day courses of instruction at the Duke of York's Headquarters in Chelsea to train officer cadets. Conditions in the draughty drill hall were distinctly uncomfortable and hardly befitted women, one of whom had once held the equivalent rank of brigadier-general – for instance, Helen had to interview cadets in the ladies' cloakroom. From the outset Helen lobbied for support from the Army to make it compulsory for all ATS officers to attend her courses but Sir John Brown did not agree. Accordingly, attendance was made voluntary and, to Helen's chagrin, FANY MT officers were specifically excluded. It was undoubtedly a major victory for Mary Baxter-Ellis.

The second reason, which played a far more important part in Helen's vendetta against the FANYs, concerned the overall leadership of the ATS. When Helen enrolled she was delighted to be 'back in the Army again' almost exactly twenty years after being transferred from the QMAAC to the WRAF, and although she was still a professor at the University of London she found time to lecture at the officers' school in history, discipline and the problems of command. However, her eyes were fixed firmly on higher office.

In December 1938 the question of 'a head woman' for the ATS was raised but nothing was done until May 1939. In the interim, although Helen appeared to remain in the background, she was firing off memoranda to TA headquarters on the need for a proper organization and at the same time working frantically behind the scenes to obtain the appointment.

During the First World War Helen had met Lord Trenchard, then chief of air staff; in 1927 he became the first marshal of the RAF. In 1920 she met his future wife, Kitty Boyle, the widow of a son of the Earl of Glasgow, while on a visit to her cousins in Kilkerran. The two women forged an enduring friendship and later, when Kitty married Trenchard, Helen dined frequently at their home. By 1938 Lord Trenchard had retired as Commissioner of the Metropolitan Police, a position he accepted when he left the RAF, and was chairman of the United Africa Company, but he still had enormous influence in military circles and was a close friend of the Secretary for War, Leslie Hore-Belisha. It was natural that Helen should use the Trenchards as a conduit for her ideas on how the ATS should be run, and the receptive Hore-Belisha was bombarded continuously with complaints about shortcomings which could be rectified if only a woman head was appointed rather than the ATS 'being mismanaged by whatever junior male officers could be spared from other duties'. The very existence of the ATS was due in no small measure to Lady Trenchard, a fact Helen frankly admitted: 'The service owes more to Kitty and her husband than it has ever realized.'

In response to Hore-Belisha's representations the War Office typically proposed the appointment of a junior woman staff officer, with the rank of captain, to TA5, the department which was created to deal with women's affairs. However, the Advisory Council on the ATS – which consisted of the Parliamentary Under-Secretary of State for War, the deputy director-general of the TA (Major-General Sir John Brown), the TA Associations through their permanent, professional secretaries, and the representatives of the women's voluntary societies – was invited to consider instead the advisability of either appointing a woman head within the War Office or, preferably, appointing an inspector outside the War Office. Helen swung into the attack and immediately canvassed ATS county commandants to support her contention that a woman head be appointed. Not everyone agreed with her, notably Miss Justina Collins. But by far the most hurtful response came from Mary Baxter-Ellis, who said she saw no need for such a position and in her opinion there was no lady in the country with the necessary knowledge of military matters, or the capacity, to take over the work of TA5. This was a slap in the face for Helen, who saw herself as the only woman with the experience and qualifications for the job. Perhaps Helen had also heard that Mary Baxter-Ellis had herself been sounded out for just such a position in 1938 but had declined because she did not wish to leave the FANYs.

Helen now hedged her bets and began urging the Air Ministry to form a women's auxiliary service for the RAF. It was logical that the ATS units earmarked for service with the RAF should evolve into a separate corps and Helen told Sir Charles Portal, the Air Member for Personnel, that if she was not offered the army appointment at the War Office she would consider accepting a similar position at the Air Ministry. One of the main arguments against Helen's appointment anywhere was her age, for she had turned 60 in January 1939, but this was overlooked diplomatically when the army candidates were being considered. It seems highly probable that once again the Trenchards used their influence to secure the appointment for Helen but another factor which possibly played a part was that the Earl of Munster, Parliamentary Under-Secretary of State for War, was her cousin. On 27 June she was called to a meeting with Hore-Belisha and the new director-general of the TA, Sir Douglas Brownrigg, and offered the position of director of the ATS with the rank of chief controller, equivalent to a major-general in the Army with a total salary of £1,338 a year, roughly two-thirds of a major-general's pay. She was to head a directorate, assisted by an ATS deputy director and two other ATS officers, under the TA director-general and took up the appointment on Monday, 3 July 1939.

The FANYs maintain that Helen did all she could to destroy their organization and there is some truth in that allegation. Helen was not the sort of woman who could tolerate criticism of her methods or any form of insubordination, no matter the quarter from which it came. In strictly military terms she was absolutely within her rights, but from the point of view of human relationships she would have received far more co-operation if she had employed a little more tact in dealing with subordinates. Her first target was Mary Baxter-Ellis herself, who ran the motor companies from the FANY head office in Ranelagh House in London. In December 1939 Helen persuaded the War Office to instruct Mary to set up a Driver Training Centre at Camberley and to take the FANY headquarters with her. She expected this to be the end of FANY autonomy but she overlooked the fact that the Ranelagh House operation fell outside the ATS, being run privately from donations and members' subscriptions. Mary Baxter-Ellis had to comply with the War Office request but she sent an urgent message to Marian Gamwell to return from Northern Rhodesia to take over in London. Mary made one last attempt to remind Helen of the 'agreement' that the FANYs could be a corps within the service but the redoubtable Helen remained adamant: all previous arrangements had lapsed and there was no room for 'special arrangements' or two command structures within the ATS.

Throughout the war those who had been FANYs before 1 September 1941 were permitted to wear a FANY flash on the shoulders of their ATS uniforms, but because of Helen's obduracy many FANYs felt they had been betrayed and harboured a permanent grudge against her. Mary Baxter-Ellis wrote to the FANY president, Princess Alice: 'It is extremely difficult to keep conversation with Dame Helen consecutively on any one subject, or even to finish a subject. One cannot pin her down to definite statements.' Marian Gamwell became head of the Free FANYs: they did undercover work in France and other countries and counted among them Odette Churchill. Marian was outspoken in her condemnation of Helen: 'She was the most tactless person I think I have ever had the misfortune to know.' This intractable nature counted against Helen in her dealings not only with the FANYs but also with senior army officers.

On 4 July 1939, the War Office, in announcing Helen's appointment, stated that the ATS had 912 officers and 16,547 members, a ratio of almost 1 in 16 which demonstrated clearly that the ATS was top heavy. The press reports brought cables and telegrams from ex-servicewomen throughout the empire expressing a general feeling of relief and hope: 'Now we shall get something done' and 'Now the muddle will end.' However, it would take Helen several months to achieve that end because in the Army the wheels moved very slowly

She chose as her chief assistant Christian Fraser-Tytler, a cousin of Jane Forbes who had become head of the WAAF on Helen's recommendation and also of Marjorie's former husband. Christian had been running an ATS company in Inverness-shire and was prepared to move permanently to London. So that they could learn the work of TA5, the ATS women shared a small room in the War Office with Major A. N. S. Corbett, deputy assistant adjutant-general of TA5, and his two assistants. To Helen's intense annoyance all three men smoked pipes. Her discomfort was increased by the fact that shelters were being constructed in the basement and the noise was so distracting that they were forced to work with the windows shut. Also, meticulous in everything she did, especially her correspondence, Helen soon became dissatisfied with the male clerks. Matters improved when Christian persuaded the authorities to allocate another room, on the ground floor, to Helen and herself and later additional accommodation became available. Soon Helen and Christian took over the work of TA5 which concerned the ATS, and Major Corbett was moved to other duties. Women clerks replaced the men but, to Helen's disappointment, they were civil servants – the deputy under-secretary over-ruled her pleas for ATS clerks, and this wish was not granted for nearly two years.

On the question of uniform, Helen's practical suggestion that buttons be on the right instead of the customary left side for women had been agreed because it meant that the left lapel, on which ribbons were worn, would be uppermost. For the ranks the driver-organizations had won the day with shirts and ties instead of a coatfrock such as the WAAC/QMAAC members had worn.

One of her first tasks now was delineating badges of rank. ATS officers had been given titles as follows:

ATS 1938–41	*ATS July 1941*	*Military equivalent*
Chief Controller	Chief Controller	Major-General
Senior Controller	Senior Controller	Brigadier
Controller	Controller	Colonel
Chief Commandant	Chief Commander	Lieutenant-Colonel
Senior Commandant	Senior Commander	Major
Company Commander	Junior Commander	Captain
Deputy Company Commander (later Junior Commander)	Subaltern	Lieutenant
Company Assistant	2nd Subaltern	2nd Lieutenant

Sergeants' and corporals' chevrons were used by the NCOs but special stars were designed for junior officers. Instead of a major's crown, senior commandants wore a laurel wreath and this, with one star above, was also worn by chief commandants. Later, a specially patterned crown replaced the wreath. Ranks above controller had no badges and, unlike the First World War, Dame Helen received no authority to put up any badge of office but by February 1940 crossed laurel branches had been designed for a chief controller.

Her chief concern was organizing the mobilization of the ATS in the event of war. This involved solving the problems of transport, accommodation and pay, and her requests for decisions contained a note of urgency unfortunately not matched by the War Office. (The atmosphere of non-co-operation would be aggravated by the hostility between the new chief of the general staff, Lord Gort, and the Secretary for War, Leslie Hore-Belisha, who was forced to resign in January 1940.) On the vexed subject of pay Helen had to concede that men and women in the Army were not of equal value, although in many respects women proved to be better clerks or cooks than their male counterparts: in the last resort, the Army Council argued, a soldier clerk or cook was also a potential fighting man whereas women were enrolled as non-combatants. Consequently the women were paid, like herself, two-thirds of the salary of the corresponding officer or soldier.

During the summer of 1939 Helen spent much of her time visiting camps to discover how ATS members were coping with the rigours of sleeping in tents, cooking out-of-doors, running across dew-wet grass to ablution huts, and mounting guard at night. Most of the officers and other ranks were see-

Left Dame Helen Gwynne-Vaughan before her enforced retirement in 1941. Somehow the ATS uniform never seemed to fit smartly on her. The fact that she wore braces to hold up her skirt did not help her appearance. Here (*right*) she watches a march-past at Hounslow.

ing their director for the first time and her visits inspired that feeling of awe experienced by virtually every member of the ATS in her presence. Tall and with a stern expression, the khaki uniform made Helen an imposing, formidable figure and, as she was accustomed to lecturing students, the pitch of her voice demanded attention and implied authority. Yet at the same time she was somewhat ungainly because she never wore her uniform well. The belted jacket, with capacious breast-pockets (no longer considered risqué) was unbecoming and since she supported her skirt with braces it billowed voluminously round her calves. Her soft-crowned peaked cap, which photographs suggest was much too large and which was described by her biographer as 'bulky', shaded her eyes and she also insisted on wearing gaiters which creaked embarrassingly when she curtsied to the Queen. 'I'm quite sure Her Majesty won't mind,' Helen assured her junior officers. Her staff tried to smarten her up, suggesting that she go to a tailor, a shirt-maker and a hairdresser, but Helen refused to see the necessity for any change.

Immaculate she was not but Helen was every inch a woman general and there was no mistaking the military bearing she had acquired during the First World War and re-adopted so swiftly in 1939. Her 'troops' felt they were in the presence of a living legend when she appeared, and so they were, for Dame Helen's name is uttered in hushed tones still.

War was now seen as inevitable. In April Mussolini had seized Albania and the following month concluded a military alliance with Hitler. By August the USSR had announced a ten-year treaty of non-aggression and neutrality with Nazi Germany. With his frontiers safely sealed, Hitler struck at Poland on 1 September 1939 and Britain and France issued an ultimatum. On 3 September Chamberlain spoke to the nation, gravely announcing that Britain was at war with Germany. While he was broadcasting, a young ATS telegraphist was transmitting the formal declaration of war to the German Foreign Ministry in Berlin.

On that momentous Sunday Mary Tyrwhitt was at the foot of Ben Nevis, enjoying a walking holiday in Scotland with a friend. She stayed one more day, then hurried back to London where she arrived during the first evacuation of children into the country.

'Try as I might I could not make contact with my army unit in the first few days,' she said. 'When I eventually got in touch, they told me: "Oh, we've lost the file!" ' Almost a week went by before she received her orders to report with her platoon to Chatham.

Dorothy Humphery was at the Bembridge Vicarage on that fateful morning. She telephoned her nanny who said: 'I suppose you're off to do your bit?'

'I thought it was an awful cliché but nevertheless that was what I was doing. I suppose there was an air of excitement about, that we were going off on an adventure in a way.'

Lucy Anwyl-Passingham heard the news at Juan-les-Pins in the south of France where she was on holiday.

'I had my Studebaker car with me and I drove across France, through convoys, to Dieppe where it was practically impossible to get a boat to take my car, because so many people were dashing back to England. Fortunately the AA man knew me from previous trips abroad and he managed to get my car on to a ship. When I landed at Dover I rang my father and his first question was: "Where is the car?" I felt thoroughly deflated at not being congratulated on at least managing to get home.'

Eileen Nolan was in church at the critical hour and, unaware of the dramatic news, hurried to see her maternal grandmother after the service: there was to be a family gathering later to celebrate her cousin Janet's birthday. After informing Eileen about the declaration of war her grandmother lamented: 'And on Janet's birthday, too. How terrible to spoil a child's birthday.'

The following day Eileen reported as usual to Cadbury's where she was on a special training course for a career in sales and advertising. War would bring that to an abrupt halt – advertising would no longer be needed when chocolate production was governed by strict confectionary rationing.

In the little village of Marten, Irene Ludlow was at the farmhouse carrying out her domestic duties and did not listen to Chamberlain's announcement. She heard the news later in the day but for her, at that stage, the war meant little change in routine. She had never been out of the village where she was born and had no reason to suppose that the war, which to her seemed so remote, would make any difference to her life.

A week earlier all members of the ATS had received orders to report to their Territorial regiments and 20,000 women, many of whom had regarded their service as a novel, part-time activity, now faced the real prospect of life in the Army. Some were completely unprepared for the emergency, having no uniforms and possessing only unsuitable civilian clothes. Others discovered that because of family commitments they were unable to leave home and had to resign. A few stipulated that they could serve only in locations close to their home, but only a very small minority had anticipated the emergency and were ready for service.

The confusion which had reigned a year before returned tenfold. One company was instructed to proceed to a town 150 miles away while another company, raised in that very town, was posted to the town the other company had left. In the gigantic muddle ordnance depots, which expected clerks and storewomen, received cooks and orderlies, and kitchens were staffed by secretaries and typists who knew little or nothing about cooking and catering. Other companies stood idly by awaiting instructions which never came from the regiment to which they were attached. The commanding officers could not be blamed: at the outbreak of war thousands of men were flooding into training units and officers were trying desperately to cope with the mobilization of troops. In some circles the ATS was regarded as a private army, the position of which had yet to be clearly defined, so the women were not provided with accommodation, had no designated work to do, and felt like outcasts.

Later there were notable exceptions. J. M. Cowper, author of the official history of the ATS, wrote of one company which found that every detail had been foreseen by their army regiment and everything possible had been done for their comfort. The morning after the company had settled into its quarters, the officer, Junior Commander A. Bell, shy, inexperienced and overawed at being in the Army, was confronted in her office by a major who announced that he was escorting her to attend 'orders'. She had absolutely no idea what 'orders' meant but was far too frightened to refuse. At the commanding officer's office she was ushered into a room full of male officers whom she recognized as the company commanders of the battalion. Then it dawned on her that she was attending the CO's orderly room at which he dealt with offenders.

Bell's recollections of the next hour were hazy. Her first realization was that she had forgotten to salute the colonel when she entered the room. Her next impression was of the inordinate amount of noise: the regimental sergeant-major shouted orders as if on a barrack square, heavy army boots stamped on thin wooden floorboards, charges were bellowed in incomprehensible military language, evidence was given in stentorian tones and, after an agonizing, nerve-racking silence, sentence was delivered and the unfortunate offender removed at the double. The process was repeated several times before the nightmare was over.

Only later did she realize that her attendance was a mark of respect and that it had been designed to impress on officers and men that henceforth she and her company were to be accepted as part of the unit. The colonel ensured that she was handed over to the company sergeant-major for instruction on administration, to the pay sergeant who told her how to keep company accounts, and to the regimental quartermaster sergeant who showed her how to run a clothing store. She was made an honorary member of the officers' mess but, not wishing to intrude on male privacy, remained in her room until one evening she plucked up enough courage to send a message to the colonel inquiring whether she might arrive for dinner. To her horror the colonel himself came to chide her for asking permission to enter a mess to which she belonged.

7
FALLING IN . . .

Widespread publicity in the national press ensured a steady flow of eager recruits for the ATS in the first months of the war but generally the ATS at this point of its history was, as Bidwell aptly described it, a shambles. Its officers were untrained and floundering in a welter of unfamiliar military terminology and regulations; its disciplinary code was inadequate and often misinterpreted or ignored; its uniform was unavailable for issue; its accommodation was primitive and wholly unsuitable for women; and its duties were undefined or so vague that no one knew exactly what was required. The ATS desperately needed direction and there was no one better suited than Helen to fight the red tape and the top brass at the War Office who still, apparently, had little time for 'women's affairs' now that war was declared. Her first aim was to remove the impression that she was running a 'Petticoat Army' and to build the image of an efficient, well-drilled organization ready to fit into the military machine.

Unlike many of her contemporaries, Elizabeth (Betty) Macfie *was* prepared for war and was also the sort of person who could see the funny side of any experience. She participated in two sports which few women in the 1930s attempted – yachting and skiing. In 1936 she had represented Great Britain at the Winter Olympic Games at Garmisch-Partenkirchen in Germany, and while on the ski slopes had been persuaded by a fellow competitor to join the FANY. Her family had a military background – her father, uncle and brother were officers in Highland regiments – and Betty felt that the FANY, which was the nearest equivalent at that time to a women's army, provided a way for her to follow the Macfie tradition.

'The staff at the school where I was a physical training teacher were very Left-wing. They were very nice to me but I could see they disapproved of me going off on a Monday to the Duke of York's training evening for FANYs. I used to change into uniform at the school and they considered me a little warmonger. With the blessing of the headmistress I was allowed to join up when war broke out. I drove loads of blankets to various places in London.'

Betty was ordered by FANY headquarters to instal her motor company in a hotel in Kensington Church Street which had been commandeered for military use. As section commander, Betty was in charge of about 60 girls, 'most of them débutantes and people of that class', who were required as chauffeuses for War Office staff cars and drivers for laundry vans which had been converted into ambulances. The vehicles had no self-starters so the girls had to crank the engines to get them going. With a sergeant and a corporal Betty reported to the hotel, which had been vacant for two years.

> We had our sleeping bags and nothing else. There was no furniture, no running water, nothing, so we dossed down on the dining-room floor. A candelabra was hanging from the ceiling and we decided to sleep near it. In the middle of the night the corporal switched on her torch and immediately let out an eldritch scream when she saw what looked like a man standing in the middle of the room. We discovered that it was the sergeant's pair of dungarees which she had hung on the candelabra, and burst into laughter.
>
> By the third day we had arranged to have the water turned on and the rest of the company arrived to take up residence in these hastily contrived barracks. A fortnight later Esmé Worthy, the senior subaltern, contacted the medical officer urgently. 'It's just awful,' she complained. 'The war has only just begun and I think the whole lot of us have measles.' There were spots all over our bodies. When the medical officer arrived and began examining the girls, she quickly discovered the cause. 'This isn't measles, it's bug bites!' We found out then that the hotel had been condemned because it was bug-ridden and was taken over by a quartermaster desperately searching for buildings as billets. None of us had ever seen a bug or heard of one. We had been used to mixing and living in camps but not to meeting real bugs. Within 24 hours we were out of that place and into a domestic science college in Kensington.

Betty still has an irrepressible sense of humour. At her cottage in Nether Wallop in Hampshire, she told – with a wicked smile – how years later she came across a plastic bug in a joke shop and sent it off to the ATS museum 'as a relic of the bughouse'. For a long time the 'bug' was on display in a glass case until, when she retired as a colonel in the WRAC, she revealed the truth.

Mary Tyrwhitt also had to tackle the accommodation problem when she was ordered to take her company to Chatham, where she was assured billets had been arranged.

> I suppose I really ought to have inspected the quarters first but I didn't. I collected all my girls and we took the train to Chatham, only to find that we were billeted on local residents in a street which was considered of rather ill-repute, to put it mildly. There

was nothing else we could do but occupy the billets for that night and the girls complained about the very uncomfortable and dirty beds. I went to the police and demanded more suitable accommodation so they found a house which had been used as a day-school. It had two or three classrooms and a sitting-room, dining-room, kitchen and bathroom but no furniture of any kind. All we had were desks – no cooking-pots or any utensils and not a bed in sight. While my sergeant dashed off home to collect spare pots and pans, I managed to obtain some palliasse covers and some straw from which we made our own mattresses. I also managed to scrounge some blankets. Luckily that September was warm and we settled down quite happily.

Next day Mary reported for duty to the Ordnance Corps at Gun Wharf in Chatham but no one had bothered to inform the retired major temporarily in charge to expect the ATS, and no jobs had been specified for them.

When a commanding officer eventually arrived, his first question was: 'What do the girls do?' I told him that they were cooks and orderlies whereupon he said that orderlies were no good to an Ordnance depot. 'In that case,' I said, 'they will have to learn to do something else.' So they all became clerks. A lot of retired soldiers were working in the depot, doing the accounting and indenting, and they were reluctant to co-operate with us. I said that this was impossible and the girls were terribly disappointed so the commanding officer undertook to have the girls properly trained. The second month saw them installed in two houses and at least they were able to sleep in proper beds but, because no orders had been received, we could not draw stores from the Army. We didn't even know what pay we were to receive but I ascertained that the girls got 1*s* 9d a day and I took 9*s* 4*d* a week for myself. On pay day I used to take a certain amount from each girl for messing, which was an unheard of thing to do but no one knew any better.

Then came the first bombing of London. We saw the aircraft going up the river and then the flashes as bombs exploded. Later my sergeant reported that the entire platoon had vanished – they had all flitted after panicking and went home to find out what had happened to their families. The next day they came back and I explained that they could find out all they needed to know from the police.

We were still having trouble being accepted by the Army. None of the senior officers really understood what we were supposed to do. They all wanted clerks and used to say: 'I want a nice girl who can sit on my knee when she takes down dictation.' They got a fairly short, sharp answer from me for that.

Lucy Anwyl-Passingham had now joined the FANY and drove Chief Commandant Dame Regina Evans – formerly Chairman of the Women's Advisory Committee, Chairman of the Central Council, and of the Conservative and Unionist Party – in her Studebaker for three months. Driving at night was particularly hazardous because the only lights on the car were about the size of an old penny, in accordance with blackout regulations. When she was ordered to drive Dame Regina off her usual beat to a training centre at Durham and not knowing the route, Lucy made several wrong turnings – all road signs had of course been removed.

The lack of suitable accommodation was a recurring complaint and, in part, was due to Helen's guiding principle that women should receive the same treatment as men: she believed fervently that if women were to claim equality with men in the Army they should endure the same conditions without any compromise on feminine needs. To some extent her judgment might have been clouded by her own spartan standard of living which made little allowance for personal pleasure or convenience. Furniture in her flat was functional rather than aesthetic or comfortable and she scorned housekeeping, preferring to live a frugal life. Her stand on uniforms, too, necessarily affected the ATS. During the first winter of the war the weather was particularly cold and because proper uniforms were not yet available the girls' only protection was a light gaberdine raincoat. Helen insisted that they should take their turn with the men on the waiting-list for full kit or they would lose all long-term advantages in their battle to be fully accepted and integrated into army life.

'I can't help it, m'dear,' she told the staff officer who brought complaints to her attention. 'It's the only way I can prove that women can do *anything* they are asked to do,' and went on to argue that of course one armchair for ten women in a recreation hut was ample and an eight-hour day for a cook in the steaming atmosphere of an army kitchen quite satisfactory.

'The same as the men,' she informed male officers anxious to formulate proper standards for the women. Helen, with memories of conditions in the First World War still influencing her judgment, was too often wont to argue: 'We managed then and we'll manage now.' But a barrack-room with no cupboards, no curtains and only the crudest form of heating was a demoralizing environment for women thrust suddenly into a depot straight from the comforts of a late 1930s family hearth and they found it difficult to adjust to conditions which were not only foreign to their way of life but, quite often, positively sordid. Many army barracks dated back to the Crimean War and the bleak huts had only bunks with army 'biscuits' as mattresses, and nowhere to even display a few family photographs. No one had heard of kit lay-out, either, and equipment was piled on every bunk like clothes for a jumble sale before the pricing, according to J. M. Cowper. Ablution blocks and latrines could be some distance away – just acceptable, perhaps, in day-time but at night, although the less timorous girls would venture out, others improvised chamber pots out of tin helmets for use outside the hut door.

Helen's staff remonstrated with her constantly but details of welfare administration bored her and she dismissed suggestions that a minimum standard of comfort would greatly increase efficiency and restore morale. Day after day complaints poured into the two branches of her directorate – TA5 had been divided into AG15 which dealt with officers' questions, discipline and training, and AG16 which handled all other-rank matters. At last an exasperated assistant exploded: 'It's all very well, Ma'am, to keep on saying the girls must have the same as the men, but men's urinals aren't much use to a camp full of women!'

This obstinacy upset many of the men who genuinely wished to put matters right, among them General Sir Robert Gordon-Finlayson who in the autumn of 1939 had replaced General Brownrigg at the War Office. With her seniority and experience of a previous war, Helen was the obvious person to consult but her attitude forced the men to seek information from her junior officers, who were less able to foresee what might be required. Had Helen felt able to relax her fight for equality, she might have anticipated many of the problems which arose in the initial stages of the war, problems which were compounded when, by June 1941, the establishment of the ATS had doubled to 40,000.

Dorothy Humphery, who was posted to the control ordnance depot at Chilwell, near Nottingham, had to rush out and buy a greatcoat at the last moment before leaving home:

> Things were very spartan in those days and hundreds of women drivers, whose job was to take vehicles from depots to ports, had no proper kit. They drove in more or less anything they possessed – a pair of slacks if they had it. Only the convoy leaders knew where they were bound and no stops were allowed, even for obvious reasons – everyone had to stay in the convoy. The girls were billeted all over Nottingham and I remember going round to pay the landladies out of an old biscuit tin filled with pound notes.

Irene Holdsworth, who wrote about her experiences in a training depot, describes the conditions endured by the initial intakes. She was more fortunate than most in that her barracks consisted of two large red-brick houses, which were a converted county school for boys and girls, and several green army huts.

> Reveille was at 6.30. We leaped out of bed and rushed down the passage to the washroom. This contains four wash basins, four

> bathrooms and two lavatories, and is used by 75 girls who sleep on this floor. It is lit by one very faint blue light – a fact which irritated me that first morning, but which I now think is possibly all to the good. 'What the eye doesn't see . . .' From a purely personal point of view there is nothing more nauseating than having to face a crowded and far from fragrant lavatory at the crack of dawn on a cold winter's day . . .

Many of the girls cracked under the strain. 'Military discipline or no,' Irene wrote, 'they can't stop entirely feminine hearts beating behind these khaki shirts of ours, and every person I have talked to in my intake (about 50 of them) has had their crack-up. In some cases it is homesickness, in others loneliness. In mine it was the constant atmosphere of every element in life which I loathe. Noise, hurry, smells and lack of privacy.' For others it was the endless queues – for meals, for ablutions, for medicals, for lectures, for just about everything.

Generally the girls were of two distinct types: the upper-class and the upper middle-class who, because of their experience of Girl Guides or boarding schools, were used to communal living, either in open-air camps or in dormitories; and the lower-middle-class and lower-class who had never been away from home before. Irene Ludlow, when she joined up, went to a training camp at Honiton in Devon.

> When we arrived the first event was a medical and then we had to queue up for our kit. Mine didn't fit because I am six feet tall. Then we went to the cookhouse and by this time I was thinking that I had made a mistake. Goodness, there were an awful lot of girls in that room. Never having been with crowds before, we all found it a very embarrassing experience. I can remember that about five girls ran home that evening but they were caught and brought back again. Being strangers, we did not wish to undress in front of each other and tried to get into a wardrobe for the purpose. Of course, I was too big so I undressed under my greatcoat. We had 'biscuits' on our bunks, some sheets and, to me, tatty army blankets. And I thought, well, this isn't me. The corporals came round and told us: 'You have got to make the best of it – you can't go home, can't go back to mother and father, you're in the Army now and you've got to do as you're told. Don't complain.' After PT, we had to take showers in a great, big, long hut, with no curtains but just little cubicles and cold water. Again this was terribly embarrassing but the NCOs put everyone at ease by saying: 'You're no different, you're all the same, all equal, never mind who you are or where you come from.' To me this was lovely because

some people were higher up the social scale than me, who was just a country girl, but the Army is a great leveller.

In December 1939 Helen was able to escape the administrative details she detested so much: she was ordered to GHQ, British Expeditionary Force in France, where the possibility of using ATS members on the Lines of Communication was being discussed. The moment she crossed the Channel with her personal assistant, Junior Commander Gill Dearmer, she felt on familiar ground. It was a marked contrast to her initial visit in 1917 when she was a stranger to army procedure and also to the officers she met. Now she found herself among friends – General Brownrigg, adjutant-general at GHQ France, who welcomed her to Arras, and Brigadier Whitehead, with whom she had worked in the First World War, were among the recognizable faces.

Helen was in her element discussing the trades and employments needed, the places where the ATS could be posted and the disciplinary arrangements. She dined with the commander-in-chief, Lord Gort, at his

An ATS recruit is kitted out with her new khaki uniform.

château and met a 'very kind and friendly major-general' who turned out to be the Duke of Gloucester. The Duke's sister, the Princess Royal, had joined the ATS in October 1938 and had accepted the honorary appointment of controller of the West Riding of Yorkshire, thus beginning an association with the ATS and later the WRAC which was to last until her death. Soon after the outbreak of war the Queen accepted the office of commandant-in-chief, becoming in fact commander-in-chief of all the women's services, and in February 1940 she appointed the Princess Royal honorary chief controller of the ATS. The Princess was formally enrolled, signing the same undertaking as all other officers, and then in August 1941 she was gazetted controller commandant.

The first members of the ATS arrived in France in the spring of 1940, to be followed by a platoon of bilingual telephonists and then by groups consisting mainly of drivers who were posted to Dieppe, Le Havre, Nantes, Le Mans and other towns. They were accommodated in requisitioned houses or in Nissen huts and everything possible was done for their comfort and well-being – in fact, it is fair to say that the ATS abroad were looked after far better than their colleagues at home. The ambulance drivers at Dieppe, with their administrative staff of clerks, cooks and orderlies, were the first ATS to come under attack when German aircraft bombed the base, and they helped evacuate sick and wounded. On 19 May 22 members were sent from Dieppe to Nantes, mostly travelling under cover of darkness and ducking into trenches when necessary by day, on a journey which lasted five days. After one night's rest they took on duties on the Nantes switchboard and at the Reforce Station. On 25 May Calais fell and three days later Belgium surrendered. On 29 May, 25 ambulances and 70 drivers moved south from Dieppe to Nantes where they immediately began work, driving wounded men from trains to hospital ships.

During the evacuation of the British Army at Dunkirk between 27 May and 4 June, ATS telephonists were still in Paris and remained there until 14 June when they were among the last Allied troops to leave the French capital, actually driving their truck out of Paris as the Germans marched in on the other side of the city. After a rough ride along roads jammed with evacuees and troops, the contingent was held up at St Malo and a despatch rider was sent to escort them. Abandoning their heavy luggage, they sailed from France at 0500 hours on Sunday 16 June, the last of the ATS to return to England.

Throughout May and June the ATS in cookhouses, in offices and communications centres all over Britain, worked day and night not only catering for the returning troops, but helping to supply the Army with new equipment to replace the enormous quantities that had been left behind on the beaches of Dunkirk and in Norway: Royal Navy destroyers had evacuated troops from Bodö after the abortive Norwegian campaign and had landed them at

Thurso in Caithness on the north coast of Scotland. Everyone was expecting an invasion and the Army was put on emergency alert. Senior Commandant Belinda Boyle, with memories of her embarrassing drill session at Regent's Park barracks fast fading, went to visit her two ATS clerks attached to the garrison at Thurso and was confronted with a massive catering crisis. The newly disembarked troops were starving and needed to be fed before being sent south, but the commander of the small garrison had nothing like enough stores to go round. At first Belinda was in despair, wondering how to cope with a situation which certainly had not been anticipated by those who wrote the ATS information books. But her own resourcefulness came to her rescue and, grabbing a sheaf of billeting forms, she began amending the wording which requisitioned accommodation to read: '. . . a flock of sheep', '. . . a field of cabbages', or '. . . groceries'. She fetched a troop of Boy Scouts from the local school and set them to work rounding up sheep, she located butchers to slaughter and joint the animals, and she persuaded eleven housewives to join her two ATS clerks in making a gigantic stew in a variety of commandeered pots, buckets and a bath. She saved the day but presented a major problem to the financial staff at the War Office when they were faced with her adjusted forms.

Coping with crises was a daily routine for the ATS girls who were all encountering situations which they had never expected and for which they had certainly never been trained. Air raids were becoming more frequent and all ranks had to learn how to deal with incendiary bombs. One group of four pay clerks were bombed out twice in one night and yet appeared on duty the next day, grimy and clad only in pyjamas and greatcoats, after being buried in débris and losing all their clothes. These 'daughters' of First World War veterans displayed the same indomitable spirit but now, as well as the increased frequency of bombing raids, armaments were far more sophisticated. Great courage was shown by civilians and by servicemen and women in dealing with unexploded bombs after the night-time raids: scorning danger, ATS drivers worked fearlessly with bomb disposal units. Extracts from letters written to three ATS (FANY) auxiliaries tell of their remarkable bravery:

> . . . thank you . . . for your pluck in carrying one (unexploded) bomb in the back of your car . . . that risk had to be taken by someone . . .
>
> thanking you . . . for travelling with a live load of gun cotton, primers and detonators . . . for 107 miles.
>
> . . . thanks for helping me get rid of unexploded bombs . . . regard yourself as being the first and only woman to have carted three at once in a lorry . . .

The officers might have been inexperienced but they used their common sense and the harassed military authorities, faced with the task of equipping a new army to defend Britain from invasion and of raising another expeditionary force, realized once again the usefulness of women in filling the places of men in offices and in other non-combatant duties. At this point the attitude of the Army Council towards the ATS took a dramatic turn: from the autumn of 1940 the total manpower resources of the country were assessed by counting men and women together.

From the outset Helen had argued that women should be totally incorporated into the Army and so be subject to military law, something she regarded as a privilege rather than a restriction on the behaviour of the ATS. The military authorities had refused to extend military law to the ATS generally, maintaining that women were gentle creatures who did not need coercion. Nurses and VADs were not governed by military law, so why should the ATS be treated any differently – as in the First World War, military law applied only to members on active service. Helen foresaw that inevitably some of the volunteers would become bored or dissatisfied with service life and would take their discharge. Her fear was that this attitude could prove infectious and lead to massive desertions. Although the women were required to sign a contract which stipulated that they agreed to accept certain obligations and undertakings, such as fulfilling rules and regulations and instructions laid down for the service, obeying orders and doing work required of them, no specific mention was made on this form defining penalties for insubordination or misbehaviour. However, the War Office did lay down guidelines for a scale of punishments, of which the maximum was fourteen days' confinement to barracks, but it was clear that the only effective method of dealing with a volunteer who refused to accept disciplinary action was to discharge her. In practice, the carrying out of punishment depended entirely on the goodwill of the offender – no legal power existed to enforce the penalty. Therefore ATS members were at liberty to walk out when they chose and could not be compelled to return to duty. And walk out they did. The discharge rate rose from 26 per cent in August 1940 to 29.9 per cent in December 1940, while desertion in the same period rose from 0.19 per cent to 0.47 per cent.

This situation could no longer be tolerated and the Army realized that drastic action was required to remedy the glaring omission in the status of the ATS. On 10 April 1941 the Secretary of State for War, Captain H. D. R. Margesson, announced the change in the House of Commons:

> The Auxiliary Territorial Service has proved so valuable to the Army in replacement of men that the Government have decided to increase its numbers greatly and to enlarge the range of duties which it performs.

Dame Helen Gwynne-Vaughan inspecting a searchlight at Sheerness during the Second World War, *c.* 1941. The ATS girls attached to the artillery units wore blue blazers and white skirts.

Members of the Service are already discharging important functions connected with the air defence of Great Britain as well as with the rest of the Forces at home, and these are of a character which renders it desirable that the volunteers performing them should be definitely declared members of the Armed Forces of the Crown. The whole Service will accordingly be given full military status. Women will, of course, be employed only on work for which they have a special aptitude, but the House should know that such work includes duties at searchlight and gun stations. We have a particular need for women with good educational qualifications. The Service will remain a Women's Service under the general direction of women, and the disciplinary Code of the Army will be applied to it only in so far as the wider responsibilities now envisaged necessitate. I should explain that existing members of the Auxiliary Territorial Service enrolled on the specific understanding that they would be subject on active service to military law and to such penalties as might then be prescribed. They are therefore not being made subject to conditions inconsistent with the terms on which they were enrolled, and I have every reason to believe that they will welcome their new status.

An ATS pay parade.

Fifteen days later a Defence Regulation laid down that medical women, nurses and members of the ATS were members of the Armed Forces of the Crown and that the Army Act applied to them 'in such manner, to such extent and subject to such adaptations and modifications' as the Army Council might determine. On 20 June instructions were circulated that officers, warrant officers and NCOs of the ATS could be tried by Field General Court Martial for absence without leave or for conduct to the prejudice of good order and discipline. The scale of punishments for other ranks was restricted and allowed an officer to award summary penalties at an orderly room of fourteen days' confinement to barracks and fourteen days' forfeiture of pay in addition to extra duties and admonition, except in the case of damage to or neglect of government property, when the stoppage of pay was on a scale up to a maximum of £4. An NCO was liable to admonition, reprimand, severe reprimand and forfeiture of pay. Women could now accept the punishment of the commanding officer or elect to be tried by court martial, which could impose a maximum of 28 days' forfeiture of pay and reduction in rank in the case of an NCO. Officers and warrant officers were liable to dismissal and NCOs to discharge from the service by sentence of court martial.

By far the most satisfying result of the change in status was that officers would now receive commissions. The wording of the commissions was in the time-honoured phrasing of such documents:

> GEORGE, by the Grace of God of Great Britain, Ireland and the British Dominions beyond the Seas King, Defender of the Faith, Emperor of India, etc.
>
> To our Trusty and well beloved
>
> Greeting!
>
> We, reposing especial Trust and Confidence in your Loyalty, Courage and good Conduct, do by these Presents Constitute and Appoint you to be an officer in our Auxiliary Territorial Service from the . . . . . . day of 19
>
> You are therefore carefully and diligently to discharge your Duty as such in the Rank of 2nd Subaltern or in such other Rank as We may from time to time hereafter be pleased to promote or appoint you to, of which a notification will be made in the *London Gazette*, or in such other manner as may for the time being be prescribed by Our Army Council, and you are in such manner and on such occasions as may be prescribed by us to exercise and well discipline in their duties women serving under your orders, and such officers and soldiers as may be placed under your orders from time to time, and to use your best endeavour to keep them in good Order and Discipline. And we do hereby Command them to Obey you as their superior Officer, and you to observe and follow such Orders and Directions as from time to time you shall receive from Us, or any of your superior Officers, according to the Rules and Discipline of War, in pursuance of the Trust hereby reposed in you.
>
> Given in Our Court at . . . . . the . . . . day of . . . . 19 in the . . . . . Year of Our Reign.
>
> BY HIS MAJESTY'S COMMAND

In July 1941 the term 'member' was replaced by 'auxiliary'. Warrant Officers Class 1 were authorized as well as Class II, as were lance sergeants and staff sergeants as well as sergeants. But the Army still baulked at approving military titles for women officers. Slight adjustments were made in the rank titles (see table on page 104) – company assistants, who until then had to endure the embarrassing abbreviation of 'Coy Ass', must have been particularly pleased.

However, army officers' badges were authorized, so the women's 'Christmas cracker' decorations, as Helen described them, could be discarded in favour of the appropriate form of stars and crowns. Helen's own tailor could not supply general officers' buttons but the director of personal services, Major-General C. J. Wallace, discovered this and dropped a complete set in her lap. She wore them for less than a month. On 26 June she learned that the Army had decided she must retire on 21 July. It was a moment of sadness but nevertheless she could draw some consolation that at last she had held the King's commission.

'I had spent a month in my promised land,' she recorded.

8
THE HOME FRONT

There was, of course, much more behind the precipitate retirement of Dame Helen as director of the ATS than the official version suggests. Her biographer Molly Izzard states that a legend grew up among some of the ATS that Helen had been martyred, and displaced as the result of a personal intrigue, but she dismisses this theory and claims that there does not seem to be much evidence for it. On the contrary there seems to be no doubt that personal intrigue did take place, although 47 years later the facts are difficult to confirm. Perhaps in the end Helen was defeated by a combination of intrigue, her own obstinacy which increased as she grew older, and the mood of the country, which was facing the most critical phase of the war.

1941 was a bad year for Britain and the first five months were the hardest of the war. From 7 September 1940 to the end of May 1941 the battle raged in the skies as the Luftwaffe pounded the cities and ports, dropping 54,420 tons of bombs. During those tense months, when Britain stood alone against the might of Germany, more than 40,000 civilians died, 86,000 were seriously injured and 150,000 others were slightly injured. Two million houses had been destroyed or damaged, 60 per cent of them in London. At sea the Royal Navy was valiantly fighting the Battle of the Atlantic, trying to contain the crippling losses of merchant shipping falling prey to Admiral Karl Dönitz's U-boat pack. Elsewhere British forces had been ejected from Greece and Crete, and Lieutenant-General Erwin Rommel, as commander of the Afrika Korps, had begun the German offensive in North Africa. With the whole of the Balkans occupied by the Germans, it seemed inevitable that Hitler's next target must be Britain itself and the summer of 1941 was considered the key period for an invasion.

Obviously it was necessary to make more use of women in the defence of the country so that men could be diverted to offensive operations abroad. However, recruiting for the ATS was lagging behind the target which had been set – in June 1940 there had been 1,060 officers and 30,443 other ranks and a year later the full complement had risen by little more than 10,000. The problem was threefold: first, the Army, which

ATS recruits arrive at an army camp for training. *Below* Square-bashing.

had suffered reverse after reverse abroad, was not considered glamorous next to the RAF and the Royal Navy. Certainly the women in blue were far smarter and looked far more attractive than the women in khaki, who presented a dowdy, almost shabby appearance. 'Khaki is a colour detested by every woman and makes a well-developed girl look vulgar,' wrote a correspondent to *The Times* on 21 November 1941. Even army underwear was khaki, referred to by the girls themselves as 'passion killers'. British soldiers adapted the wartime refrain, 'She'll be coming round the mountain' to the ribald 'She'll be wearing khaki issue when she comes' and the reputation of the ATS sank to an all-time low. Second, the same rumours which had circulated in the First World War were now becoming current about the ATS – the girls were accused of immorality, drunkenness and disorderly behaviour. Mothers read the adverse publicity in the press and prevented their daughters joining up. One girl confided: 'Oh, I couldn't join the ATS. All my friends would think I was one of "those".'

In addition, a government monitoring survey found that the ATS was considered by the public to be a legion of Cinderellas, comprising domestic workers of low degree among whom one expected, and got, a low degree of morality. While the WAAF and the Women's Royal Naval Service were depicted doing interesting and important jobs, the image projected by the ATS was one of constant drilling on parade grounds, cooking in army messes or clerking in military offices.

Gradually the empire Helen had built since 1939 began to disintegrate, leaving her with fewer staff and reduced responsibilities. Air raids on London had resulted in the dispersal of War Office branches. Helen moved to Hobart House while Christian Fraser-Tytler transferred her personnel staff to Cheltenham, where they came under the control of the Directorate of Organization. The Army transferred the training of the girls to the director of military training, thus removing it from Helen's direct control. Thus the planning and control of the ATS now came under the same authority as the manpower. Helen's reluctant acquiescence to this reduction of the director's powers was one of her last actions in the service. With men taking over part of the responsibility for drilling and inspection of quarters, the training was more regimented and far tougher than it had been. Word spread that the discipline was almost degrading for women, who were enduring long hours on the parade ground and almost ceaseless intimidation by army officers who had little sympathy with their charges and treated them no differently from the rookie men conscripted into the forces.

Mrs Joan Savage Cowey summed it up when she described basic training as hell. 'Everything had to be done the right way, the correct way, and it didn't matter how nice your bed looked, they'd come in for inspection, kick it and the officer would say "Now do it again" . . . The sergeants were terrible. They had trained in India and all these places. They were all sergeant-majors, and the roar of them! We almost needed earplugs . . .' One sergeant arrived at 6.30 a.m., ordered the girls to dress and despatched them on a route march, with packs on their backs, until their feet were blistered. An ATS driver told of 'punch-ups' between the girls. Some girls, who really detested the Army, used to go across the barrack square to the men's quarters and yell 'Para 11', a reference to an appendix in the Regulations for the Auxiliary Territorial Service, 1941, of which paragraph 11 stipulated that a ground for discharge was 'For Family Reasons', in other words pregnancy.

Through all this growing dissatisfaction Helen had remained virtually aloof. As her authority declined, so her bouts of temper grew more frequent. The meetings of the ATS council were stormy and often deteriorated into vitriolic arguments in which Mary Baxter-Ellis, who had been appointed to the Directorate of Military Training, was the chief target. Military officers approached Helen's office with trepidation and used to inquire about the state of her temper before daring to enter. Wherever possible people preferred to bypass her, seeking advice from junior officers rather than from 'the old battleaxe' herself. Leslie Whateley, one of those junior officers on Helen's staff in Hobart House, admits that she was terrified of Dame Helen.

> We were all terrified. She didn't think I would be much good when we first met – I enjoy remembering that! Later, of course, she asked me to work for her and I was the lowest of the low among her assistants, who were Daphne Mulholland, the late Lord Cavan's step-daughter, Jacqueline Vereker, the daughter of Lord Gort who became Lady de L'Isle and Dudley, and Christian Fraser-Tytler. Dame Helen was a snob and she gathered all kinds of titled people around her.

Leslie Whateley's own family connections were impeccable: she was the granddaughter of one of the Army's legendary nineteenth-century field marshals, Sir Evelyn Wood VC, and her father was a colonel in the City of London Regiment. She had joined the ATS at its inception in 1938 after working for her grandfather at his home near Winchester, where she received a thorough grounding in army administration and methods. Her first husband, William Balfour, by whom she had a son, had died as a result of being gassed in the First World War; she had married H. Raymond Whateley early in 1939. Of all Helen's assistants, Leslie was perhaps the most capable and efficient. In her book, *As Thoughts Survive*, she says:

> Our director was so imbued with the military spirit that she was quite unable to see that women could not be treated as men, and I am quite certain that it was this factor which was responsible for her not remaining longer in office. I suggest that her age had little to do with her retirement . . .

Another staff officer, who went on a tour of Western Command with Helen, wrote in a letter to a friend:

> She was very rude to some people . . . from some of the comments I heard I don't think she's very popular up there. You know – from all sides you hear people complaining about her. There are intrigues going on all over the place particularly around this region . . . The senior officers are the worst offenders in egging the trouble on. I know there's lots to be said against her, but no one seems to be backing her up. I've heard from several different and outside sources that the men in the W.O. think she's impossible and that when she's not being rude to them she's fawning on them. They hate it . . . I think she probably ought to go . . .

As Molly Izzard states: 'A cynical conviction had grown up that an officer needed to know the right people to get anywhere with the ATS directorate.' Clearly a new image was needed for the ATS, far removed from the caricature which Helen had become and which inspired newspaper cartoonists to depict ATS officers as elderly, tyrannical, titled ladies with a propensity to order younger girls around like subservient orderlies. Lord Beaverbrook's newspapers were probably the worst offenders. Beaverbrook, who was Minister of Aircraft Production from 1940-41, believed women should be employed only in industry, and this view led the *Daily Express* and its sister newspapers to maintain a constant barrage of criticism against the women's services. They printed exposures of maladministration and incidents of irregular conduct which undermined the authority of Helen.

And so Helen had to go, but the problem remained of who should replace her as director. Izzard admits that the greatest and most baffling of the controversial issues surrounding Dame Helen was undoubtedly her supersession by 33-year-old, stunningly attractive Senior Commander (Major) Jean Knox:

> This event excited feelings of the most partisan nature among her associates, and has made it difficult, even at this distance of time, to obtain an objective account of what occurred. It is possible that only with the release of the relevant State papers, at the end of the fifty-year period, will the full story be known.

As it happens the true story is known to most senior officers who served during that period but all evade the question when asked to explain the mystery – all, that is, but the one person who was there and who knew better than anyone else, including Dame Helen, some of the reasons why Jean Knox was chosen over the heads of other candidates. That person was Leslie Whateley who, in August 1941, was appointed Jean Knox's deputy with the rank of senior controller, thus becoming the first ATS officer to attain the equivalent rank of brigadier.

Izzard suggests that Helen put forward Jean Knox's candidature in the belief that this younger, newer type of officer would be seen as inappropriate next to the older, First World War veterans like Justina Collins and Mary Baxter-Ellis, and that all three would be shown up by her own choice, Christian Fraser-Tytler, who, as it were, held the middle ground. In March 1941 Helen had been told that she must retire. No reason was given. Deciding to fight for her survival as director, Helen attempted to lobby the support of influential friends and even tried to send Jean Knox to Canada to get her out of the way. But Captain Margesson had been the Government Chief Whip before his appointment to the War Office and was far too experienced a campaigner to allow himself to be outmanoeuvred. On 26 June, barely three months after the decision was taken, Helen was summoned to his office again and told to name the date for retirement. She chose 21 July. It is said that she took a train to Scotland that night, and lay in the sleeping berth and wept.

Dame Helen's age was given as the official reason for her retirement. This excuse presented the War Office with an excellent opportunity to examine the qualifications of many other officers who had been appointed mainly because of their positions in the community, and the eventual departure of the director was accompanied by a general exodus of others adjudged to be unsuitable or too old for war service. Leslie Whateley was more blunt: 'Many of our senior officers were county ladies and it was difficult to get rid of them. They were simply there because of their titles.'

Helen was informed that she would be succeeded by Jean Knox who was to be joint director with her for six months from March until the changeover. Apparently she was outraged by the choice. For one thing, she could not understand how a major could be elevated to major-general in a matter of months. On that point Helen persuaded Captain Margesson to compromise and instead Mrs Knox was given the rank of controller (colonel) and made an inspector, with the duties of visiting units and studying conditions under which the girls served.

Leslie Whateley was emphatic that Helen, who was completely out of touch with the personal lives of her officers, did not know about Jean Knox's connections. For Leslie believed that the reason for her appointment was simply that Jean Knox had more influence in the War Office than anyone else in the upper echelons of the ATS at the time by virtue of a personal and very close friendship with a very senior member of the Secretary of State's staff.

Helen's ignorance is not altogether surprising because Mrs Knox was part of the Military Directorate concerned with recruiting and deployment of manpower, now far removed from Helen's sphere of operations. In that directorate she came into contact with men such as Sir James Grigg, who eventually replaced Captain Margesson as Secretary of State for War, and Sir Edward Grigg, Joint Under Secretary of State for War who later became Lord Altrincham.

Had the authorities searched every service in the world they could hardly have found two more opposite personalities than the first and second ATS directors. The daughter of G. G. Leith Marshall, Jean Knox was married to an RAF officer, Squadron Leader G.R.M. Knox, and they had a daughter. Apart from these facts, little seems to be known about her background. When approached to be interviewed for this book she refused

Jean Knox, who succeeded Dame Helen Gwynne-Vaughan as director, takes the salute watched by her deputy Leslie Whateley (*right*).

and her reluctance to talk about her period in office adds some credence to the suggestion of intrigue.

'I have deliberately kept myself in the background all these years,' she said. When the suggestion was put to her that she now had an opportunity to put the record straight, she added: 'Of course, there is much more than you could possibly know. I have written a book about it, which has been locked away.'

Helen's failure to nominate a successor who could carry on the traditions of the service in her style was not entirely due to her waning influence but also because the ATS needed an injection of new life, and a new image. The War Office devised a publicity campaign focusing on the glamorous young director who not only had the looks of a Hollywood actress but was rumoured to have once appeared on the stage. In fact, Jean Knox did take part in *We Serve*, a film depicting the work of the ATS and directed in 1941 by Carol Reed, in which she played beside Googie Withers, Celia Johnson and Ann Todd. While official photographs of Helen during her period as director are rare, there are many pictures in the archives featuring Jean Knox.

One of the first manifestations of the new régime was a re-styling of the uniform, inspired by the fashion-conscious director. To effect a compromise between the military cut and the female figure, a new jacket was designed with padded shoulders and a belt with a buckle. Skirts had four gores instead of two and the hemline was shortened by two inches to bring it more into fashion. Greatcoats were made semi-fitting, with a semi-lancer front, a military collar and no belt. Shoes were changed to the Norwegian pattern with an apron front. No longer were the old Lisle thread stockings an essential part of the uniform: the girls were permitted to wear silk stockings instead. Each recruit when she left the training centre was issued with a new uniform which was altered to fit and given another, not necessarily brand new. The lack of spare uniforms had in the past occasioned many complaints – it is said that one Sunday afternoon an ATS member came to the officers' mess at her unit with the request: 'Please, ma'am, may I take Mary Jane her tea from the cookhouse? You see, she's washed her clothes and can't go out.'

Whatever else Jean Knox may or may not have accomplished, she certainly smartened up the appearance of the ATS considerably. 'I give Jean Knox the credit entirely for changing the uniforms. She was herself very smart, very good-looking, and she made sure that everyone turned out immaculately on parade *and* off duty,' said Leslie Whateley. The official history of the ATS confirms this opinion: 'The uniform improved out of all knowledge: it was suitable for the purpose for which it was issued and it contributed greatly to the morale and efficiency of the Service.'

Jean Knox inspecting ATS girls on parade. The film star appearance of the young director lent glamour to the ATS at a time when its popularity was at a low ebb. Jean Knox smartened up the appearance of the ATS when she took over in 1941.

Coincidentally or not, after Helen's departure the government pressed ahead with plans for the conscription of all single women between 18 and 30 years of age and in December 1941 the National Service Act (No 2) was introduced to Parliament. It was a highly controversial step which, for the first time in Britain's history, compelled women to join the services. *The Times* reported, on 11 December 1941, a protest by one Member of Parliament: 'We are the first civilized country to propose that women should be drafted. The Nazis tried it and failed. How can we hope to succeed where the Nazis have failed?' In the same report another MP named Stewart raised again the issue of morality in the ATS:

> There is no doubt that the ATS has a thoroughly bad reputation. The conditions of the camps are bad, the physical condition of some of the girls is bad, and the whole service has a bad name. The War Office must take notice of the stories that are being circulated. There

> is a general impression that the ATS is not the sort of service that a nice girl goes into.

The War Office countered merely by stating that the pregnancy rate of unmarried women in the services was actually lower than in civilian life.

So desperate was the country's need for womanpower that the Act was passed despite opposition and a proclamation was issued on 5 March 1942. Recruiting was officially halted and the responsibility for drafting women into the services passed to the Ministry of Labour and National Service. Nevertheless, the implementation of the Act had been delayed diplomatically until the appointment of a commission which 'inquired into the amenities and welfare conditions in the three Women's Services'. The government called on Violet Markham, who had been a member of the First World War commission to inquire into the WAAC, to head the inquiry and Dr Edith Summerskill, a Labour Member of Parliament, became its leading spokesman. The report was published in August 1942 and, according to the official history of the ATS, did a great deal to strengthen the confidence of the general public, dismissing the allegations of immorality and putting forward a number of recommendations for improving the welfare of the women.

The appointment of Jean Knox provoked rumours, and the press, having picked up the gist of what was being whispered, persisted in badgering senior officers who, naturally, clammed up whenever the director was discussed. Jean Knox had been unfortunate enough to arrive amid controversy, and her retirement after a mere two years was equally contentious.

In September 1943 the ATS celebrated its fifth birthday with parades in Britain, the United States, Egypt, Palestine, Eritrea, Kenya and the West Indies. London was the focus of celebrations at home and representatives from groups all over the British Isles paraded at Westminster Abbey, where the salute was taken by the Queen. In recording this event J. M. Cowper, the official historian of the ATS, adds what can almost be described as a postscript: 'Unfortunately DATS [Director ATS], to whom this parade of the ATS at the time of its greatest strength was the outward and visible sign of the achievement of the Service, was not sufficiently well to be present.'

The malaise which was to lead to Jean Knox's premature departure a month later at the age of 35 has never been defined and the perceptive reader might be excused for detecting something more than ill health for her resignation. Cowper, just managing to mention Knox by name, goes on to explain: 'The hours of work and tremendous personal responsibility of the Director through these two years of rapid expansion had been a great strain that few women could have stood. The Service had by now reached its peak strength . . . it was perhaps inevitable that the reaction from these hectic months of building up and guiding the policy of the Service should now tell on the health of its leader, and on 31st October, 1943, Chief Controller J. M. Knox resigned on grounds of ill-health.'

The clue lies in the next paragraph: 'Senior Controller L. V. L. E. Whateley, CBE, who had held the appointment of DDATS at the War Office for over two years, was appointed to succeed her. During the whole of this time when DATS had necessarily been absent at conferences, on tour and visiting the women's services of the Dominions and Allies, her deputy had carried on the administration of the Service . . .' (Note that Jean Knox's CBE, which was awarded in 1943, is not mentioned, but that of her deputy is.)

In fact, for the two years of Jean Knox's appointment Leslie Whateley had effectively been running the ATS. Evidently this had been planned right at the outset when she was given a sufficiently senior rank to make decisions in the absence of the director. Jean Knox had spent most of her period as director on tour and had even managed to fit in a trip to Canada. It seems distinctly odd that her duty took her away so often during one of the most crucial and active periods in the ATS, when her 'hours of work and tremendous personal responsibility' had been such a strain, as membership expanded from a mere 40,000 to a massive 204,000. Not only that, but reading Leslie Whateley's book one is left with the impression that Jean Knox was very rarely able to attend the numerous official functions at which the director's presence was required.

The moment Jean Knox stepped down, Leslie Whateley sought permission to address a letter to each officer in the service – more than 6,000 of them. Paper was restricted but apparently such was the low morale of the service that she was granted the necessary authority.

> I am addressing this letter to all my officers, being the only method whereby I can contact you individually without further delay. I look forward, of course, to meeting you in person, but in view of the size of our Service and the area it covers, you will, I know, understand that personal contact must, of necessity, be a slow process.
>
> In this fifth year of war I realize how very weary many of you must be, and I think you should know that, as Director, I regard the welfare and well-being of my officers of primary importance. It is, I am sure, superfluous for me to say that the welfare and well-being of the Other Ranks is the first consideration for us all. This duty is delegated to you, but I realize that unless I have done everything possible, and I repeat possible, for my officers they cannot carry out this delegation.
>
> It is only human nature that you serving outside should feel that we in the War Office are blind to many of the worries and anxieties, both Service and private, with which you are

daily beset. To this I would reply that we (and here I speak specifically for myself) are far from blind. At this moment my thoughts and those of my staff are directed to seek the best ways and means to lighten your burdens and give you fresh hope and energy to carry on.

Without love of justice and a great human understanding no great work can succeed. I can at least assure you of both, and in conclusion ask you to believe that I am so very aware of how much your success *and* happiness depends on

Yours sincerely,

LESLIE E. WHATELEY

On the eve of the official announcement of her appointment, Leslie Whateley went to a party at Claridges with the Mountbattens, who, she said, 'were absolute angels to me'. It was there that the press laid siege to her, seeking the background to the whole affair. Mountbatten himself protected her from the reporters, telling them: 'You leave her alone,' and she was whisked away by General Sir Ronald Weekes, Vice Chief Imperial General Staff.

Ironically, the legend of Dame Helen grew during the Second World War and especially after 1945, so that today her memory is revered by those who knew her personally and also by those members of the present-day WRAC not yet born at the time of her death. Yet Jean Knox, who remarried after her retirement and became Lady Swaythling, is hardly remembered. She is the only director of this period who was not created a Dame of the British Empire.

In 1967, when the WRAC celebrated the Golden Jubilee of the WAAC, seven former directors of the ATS and WRAC were invited to be photographed with the then Princess Royal, Princess Mary, and the incumbent brigadier, Joanna Henderson. Dame Helen came to London from Sussexdown, the convalescent home run by the RAF Association. She was 88 years old, crippled and bent with arthritis, and very deaf. She dragged herself painfully up the stairs of Buckingham Palace to be presented for the last time to the Queen. There was only one notable absentee from the historic line-up – Lady Swaythling.

The achievement of the three war-time directors is summed up by a saying in the ATS which has become part of the folklore of the WRAC: Helen Gwynne-Vaughan dug the foundations, so deep that everyone fell in; Jean Knox put up the curtains, before the windows were in; and Leslie Whateley put on the roof, and finished the job.

9
ON ACTIVE SERVICE

One of the most significant features of British society in 1942, when the country was straining every resource to withstand the onslaught of the Axis forces, was its ready compliance with the need to conscript women. In 1939 a large proportion of women already had some experience of working, and certainly mothers who had served in the First World War were attuned to the idea of their daughters fulfilling a similar role in the armed forces. By 1943 four-fifths of the total addition to the British labour force since 1939 consisted of women, and the proportion of girls and women over 14 employed in Britain had risen from 27 per cent in 1939 to 37 per cent in 1943. There can be no doubt that this marshalling of womanpower gave Britain an enormous advantage in fighting the war: the country was able to rely on two armies – one composed entirely of men and one of women, both of which emerged in 1945 with equal battle honours. There were 214,420 girls in khaki when the ATS was at its peak strength in June 1943 and it was by far the largest of the three women's services. Of all combatant nations, Britain succeeded in utilizing its resources of man- and womanpower to the greatest effect and by 1945 almost eight million people were in uniform, half a million of whom were women.

Conscription was co-ordinated by the Ministry of Labour and National Service headed by Ernest Bevin. Recruits who opted for the ATS, or were directed to the ATS, had to undergo tests based on army experiments adapted for the ATS and administered by specially trained ATS officers and NCOs. These tests were designed to determine degree of general intelligence, ability to answer everyday mechanical problems, judgment of shapes and sizes, facility in spelling and arithmetic, fluency in written communication, and accuracy in carrying out clerical instructions. The results enabled assessors to grade candidates in six categories – Grade 1 was the top 10 per cent, Grade 2 the next 20 per cent, Grade 3 plus the next 20 per cent, Grade 3 minus the next 20 per cent, Grade 4 the next 20 per cent and Grade 5 was the bottom 10 per cent. Average attainment for all tests was Grade 3, plus being just above average and minus just below. More stringent tests, of a physical and mental nature, were devised by Professor Bartlett of the Cambridge University Psychological Laboratory for those who volunteered to serve with the Anti-Aircraft Command.

Irene Holdsworth describes being ushered into a small room marked 'School':

> Here we were made to sit at tables for two, with a partition between each person to prevent our looking at our neighbour's papers . . . We were each given a book, on the pages of which were various diagrams composed of numbered dots of various sizes, stripes of various thicknesses, and numerous squiggles which seemed quite meaningless. There was also a blank space on each page, and on a separate piece of paper we had to put the number of the dot, stripe or squiggle which would fit into this space and thus complete the pattern of the page . . .

After the tests the recruits underwent a medical examination:

> Heart; lungs; chest expansion; touch your toes; deep breathing; up on your toes; lie on the bed to have various parts of your anatomy prodded, and then pass on to another doctor – a man this time – who taps your knees; makes you kneel on a chair while he taps your ankles; looks at your teeth, ears, tests your eyes, and finally weighs and measures you. After that you are escorted by a motherly nurse in Red Cross uniform to a curtain at the far end of the room. She enters with you, points to a large tin pail and walks out again. 'What happens behind there?' whispered one of the girls when I came out again. I told her. 'But I can't', she said. 'I just have. . .'

Doctors also graded the recruits into five basic categories from AW1, a first-rate constitution, to EW, permanently unfit for any form of military service. The three sub-divisions of category AW were considered fit for service in any part of the world, the four sub-divisions of category BW fit for service in a temperate climate, but the CWs were suitable for home service only.

After all this the recruit waited for the call-up papers, which usually took about a fortnight to arrive, and was told to report to a training centre. The War Office notice suggested that the women might take with them: 'One housewife, with buttons, needles and thread. One towel. One sponge or equivalent. Six handkerchiefs. One pair gym shoes, food for the journey, National Registration book, ration book and civilian gas respirator.'

If there was one single factor which contributed most to the success of the ATS during the war, and indeed to the widening of opportunities for women in the aftermath of war, undoubtedly it was the intensive training provided.

Women had made significant advances into business and professional life by 1930 but the division of labour between the sexes was still, to a large extent, based on the Victorian principle that a man went out to work while

'And that means you!' *Left* Corporal Pat Cockrane, of Bolton, makes her point in front of the famous wartime ATS poster. *Right* an ATS girl proves that cleaning buttons can be fun.

his wife's place was in the kitchen and in the nursery. Musclepower and brainpower – two attributes which the majority of men considered women lacked – were the essential qualifications for earning a living wage. At the beginning of the war sufficient women were proficient enough in their respective employments to provide the core of the auxiliary services, and therefore training was rudimentary and designed merely to give recruits a superficial knowledge of army organization, drill, first aid, discipline and camp hygiene. As the need to employ more women in war work grew, and the ATS and its sister services expanded, a new approach was required and the training programme was adapted to cope with the large number of raw recruits being drafted into uniform.

For most of these recruits, straight out of school, those initial weeks were of primary importance as the protective mould of family life was shattered and they were exposed to a brand new world of military regimentation and strict discipline. It says much for the wisdom of the senior administrative staff, who were all in a sense amateurs, that the vast majority of girls who served in the ATS treasure memories of those hectic wartime years as the best days of their life.

At the height of the war in 1941 there were twenty basic training centres throughout Britain, a school for training NCOs, two Officer Cadet Training Units, a Junior Officers' School and a Senior Officers' School. In addition training schools had been established for specialist workers such as signallers, drivers, clerks, radio mechanics and electricians. The ATS had come a long way from its tentative steps at the outbreak of war when girls were thrust into service virtually untrained under officers unsure of themselves, the tasks they were required to perform, the means by which they could obtain supplies or the extent of their authority.

Mary Tyrwhitt had been one of the officers selected to devise the training syllabus, which in its early days was very much a hit-or-miss affair. The officers were not educators and they had no precedent to follow, except the vague knowledge of what had been provided for the old QMAAC. Mary was sent on a course for junior officers at the School of Military Administration in the New Forest before being posted to the War Office at Cheltenham, where she and three others settled down to prepare a training programme. By October 1940 they were installed at Aldermaston, having prepared lectures on drill, pay, documentation, military law, quartering, inspections, duties, responsibilities and privileges of officers and sub-officers.

'We had never done any instructing before and it was a case of the blind leading the blind,' she admits. 'We had about forty girls on that first course and in the middle of it came the most awful weather – deep snow at the beginning of November. The staff were living in the big house at Aldermaston but the student officers were in new huts with very little protection and they had to walk miles for their baths and the water froze.' Soon the school was moved to the training centre at Edinburgh where more suitable accommodation was provided. When the emphasis shifted to training NCOs, Mary Tyrwhitt was posted to Lichfield at the depot of the South Staffordshires.

'We were given the most terrible accommodation in the oldest barrack rooms you can imagine. The men did the instruction for us on the first course and I thought they were frightfully bad. They had no idea of adapting what they knew to women, and we all decided that we must do this ourselves and become independent.'

Apparently the Army was still not yet taking its women seriously enough, and the instructors and drill sergeants were not the best available. Not altogether surprisingly, it was quickly discovered that ATS recruits responded better to women NCOs than they did to men and as quickly decided that a cadre of trained women NCOs should be formed who could be posted to the training centres. So Mary and her team settled down to revise the syllabus, finally adopting the policy of creating a service background based on responsibility to the community, discipline, *esprit de corps*, welfare and team work between all ranks. Each student on the course was provided with notes covering all points of administration and there were demonstrations, individual tuition in the art of teaching techniques, discussion sessions and opportunities for criticizing performances. The aim was to build up in each student the necessary confidence in herself and in her power of leadership by means of practice in handling personnel while in temporary authority as duty student: 'We had to interview every woman as the students arrived on each new course and write reports on all of them. When we were training three hundred at a time it was a vast undertaking because we had only a week to ten days between courses. So it was fairly hard going.'

Very swiftly a new difficulty became apparent. During discussions the NCOs pointed out that while they were being taught the correct method of carrying out various regimental duties, when they returned to their units the officers under whom they would serve would largely be using different methods, which they themselves had devised. It would hardly befit an NCO to argue with officers and therefore she would have to follow instructions she knew to be incorrect. The problem was that the officers had been selected because of their specialized knowledge and were posted to units where they had few opportunities of gaining administrative experience or, indeed, of learning the precise duties of an officer.

Training for privates in the ATS did not end at the barrack gates when the girls marched out to take up their postings. In February 1940 the Motor Companies Training Centre was opened at Camberley for girls with previous driving experience. In the same month arrangements were made with the Central Telegraph Office to instruct teleprinter operators and with the General Post Office to train switchboard operators. By the summer of 1941, drivers were needed in such numbers that three Mechanical Transport Training Centres had been established with a total capacity of 1,900 students who underwent a ten-week course. Although male instructors were available, the ATS preferred to use their own because they considered the standard to be superior. But it was a difficult task to teach absolute beginners to drive heavy army vehicles. The idea of women drivers, of course, was received by men with some scepticism and indeed the accident reports at Camberley seem to justify some doubt:

> 'I knocked over a man,' one driver stated. 'He admitted it was his fault as he had been knocked over before.'
>
> Or: 'To avoid collision, I ran into the other lorry.'
>
> Or: 'A working gentleman offered to be a neutral witness in my favour.'

The ATS also organized and staffed a school to train clerks and shorthand-typists and in 1941, 62 were qualifying every week. By the end of 1942 the

ATS girls doing maintenance work on vehicles wield a tyre pump.

school in London would be expanded to admit up to 1,150 auxiliaries in training at any one time.

With the introduction of more skilled trades for the ATS, facilities for training fitters, projectionists, electricians and various types of mechanic also became necessary, and technical colleges were called on to adjust their courses to include women. The courses were slightly longer than those for soldiers because few women had as wide a knowledge of physics and mathematics as men. Except where the tests included some item of knowledge which was needed only in field force units, or where physical strength was required, the standards for the ATS were exactly the same as those for men.

By 1941 the supply of more mature women with working experience was exhausted and the recruits lining up for enrolment were younger and less sophisticated. The Army was preparing to employ women in more responsible jobs, beyond the traditional confines of canteening, cooking and clerking, and it was clear that training must become more intensive and more specialized. The intention was to bring the training of the ATS into line with that received by soldiers at a primary training centre. While the men's course lasted 42 days, women were allocated only 26 – not unreasonable because they would not be receiving instruction in weaponry. The first week was devoted to elementary drill, physical training, tuition in the care of kit, and other essentials such as inoculation and vaccination. The next two weeks consisted of theory, and the ATS was called upon to devise a suitable syllabus which would equip the young girl for the harsh realities of life in the Army. In fact, it was what today might be termed a 'pressure-cooker' course and its benefits were enormous: it provided a solid foundation for girls who were to play an essential role in the war effort.

Apart from technical training, auxiliaries were given the opportunity of attending civilian evening classes free of charge, most of them choosing to study commercial subjects. However, it soon became apparent that many soldiers and auxiliaries were ill-informed about the reasons why Britain was at war, so in September 1941 the Army Bureau of Current Affairs had started work with the primary objective of raising the morale of the fighting soldier by organizing discussions on suitable topics. In December 1941 an ATS staff officer was appointed to study the position in the ATS and she too reported that it was essential to concentrate on educating auxiliaries in national and international affairs.

At the outbreak of war, only eleven years had passed since the age of women electors was lowered to 21, placing them on equal terms with male voters, but amazingly many were still unaware that they had the franchise. Most working women in 1939 had not been subject to the stimulus of trade union activity – by 1938 the percentage of all women employees in trade unions had been only 14.7, compared with 37.8 per cent of men – and they had a decided lack of political consciousness, with no marked opinions except on matters of immediate concern to themselves. To them the idea that women should take an interest in public affairs was quite new. The ATS decided to encourage ABCA lectures and discussions on a platoon basis but it proved difficult for untrained NCOs and officers to stimulate the kind of debate the ABCA programme envisaged. A great disadvantage was that these sessions took place in free periods when the women were either keen to catch up on personal chores or to relax.

And so in the spring of 1942 Mary Tyrwhitt was transferred to command the resurrected Junior Officers' School at the Royal Holloway College, Egham. A hundred students, up to and including the rank of junior commander, were accommodated on each 26-day course, during which they received theoretical and practical training in administration. It was also hoped that these courses would increase the officers' sense of responsibility and broaden their outlook by allowing them to mix with fellow students:

> Many of these officers were the same people I had trained as NCOs and the difference between a good NCO and a good officer soon became apparent. Some were eminently suitable but others were self-conscious and thoroughly difficult. They were frightened of being found out and declared unsuitable as officers. They knew they had to be reported on and this made them less natural, especially if they thought they were in line for promotion.

The reporting system, carried out at the insistence of the War Office which demanded something in writing about each officer, was a bone of contention for several years and Mary Tyrwhitt was one of its main opponents. The reports were divided into three parts – paper work, practical ability and the opinion of the instructors during a general discussion among the directing staff. An officer was graded A, B, C or D depending on her score, A being over 75 per cent, B between 56 and 75 per cent, C between 31 and 55 per cent and D 30 per cent or below. But the last word on each person remained with the commandant, who could still grade an officer 'D' notwithstanding the standard of her paper work and practical ability. In other words, personality, character and qualities of leadership became the main criteria for ATS officers, all subject to one person's assessment. The ATS, which had begun by appointing officers in a haphazard way, was now refining its process of management selection and training. In so doing it was not only improving its administrative procedures and its overall efficiency but also ensuring that a large number of women were receiving sound managerial instruction and experience.

The recognition of the need for proper instruction for NCOs had come just in time to enable the ATS to cater for the large number of recruits flowing into the infantry training centres throughout the country. The NCOs were the recruits' first point of contact with military authority and the impression they made was a lasting one.

Because hers was a reserved occupation, Eileen Nolan had continued to work at Cadbury's until 1942, pursuing her interest in singing, amateur dramatics and Girl Guides during her leisure hours. Although she had seriously considered joining the ATS no opportunity had presented itself, but that year, like many other girls throughout Britain, she and her colleagues in the same age group were called into an office set aside specially by the company to meet Ministry of Labour officials.

> We were all interviewed that morning and at lunchtime I went home to tell my parents, who were completely taken aback, that I had signed on the dotted line to join the ATS. My call-up came a month after my medical and I was ordered to go to Halifax in Yorkshire on

> Friday, 27 November 1942. We weren't allowed to take any treasures such as books or photographs but I packed my prayer book and my Bible as well as a dressing-gown, slippers and all the necessary toiletries. I reported to New Street station in Birmingham with numerous relatives to see me off. It was absolutely bewildering. I was just twenty-two and had led a fairly sheltered life, never having been abroad.

For tens of thousands of young women conscripts this was a moment for tears as they said their farewells amid apprehension at the prospect of the new experience ahead. At dozens of railway stations up and down the country girls were gathering in their hundreds bound for destinations some had never heard of before. 'You seemed to be cutting yourself off from everything you treasured and loved, torn away from a familiar environment and shipped off to you-knew-not-where with hundreds of total strangers,' Eileen recalls.

At Halifax her train was met by NCOs, luggage was piled into an army truck while for the first time the recruits were ordered to fall in, draw themselves into three ranks and then: 'By the left, quick march. Left, right, left . . .' Dressed in a colourful assortment of clothes, ranging from Sunday best to informal wear and many in high heels quite unsuitable for marching, the girls were generally out of step and intent only on reaching the camp as quickly as possible. There was a babble of regional accents, perhaps a wave to curious onlookers and then, suddenly, ahead loomed the old Victorian barracks – grim, uninviting, immense, cold and demoralizing for raw recruits thrust into a foreign environment where lives were ordered from minute-to-minute by NCOs, who told them where to go, what to do and how to do it, even the speed at which they were to do it. 'You're in the Army now, Miss Jones . . .' 'Miss Jones' knew it and at this moment she was none too happy about it.

They were allocated barrack-rooms, which in most camps consisted of twenty rickety double-bunks with neatly-folded blankets and sheets and the usual 'biscuit' mattresses. 'I remember there were wooden floors,' says Eileen, 'and up the middle of the room was a piece of shiny linoleum and I learned to my cost, of course, that you never stepped on it because you had to polish it. So everyone always walked round the linoleum.' At the end of each bunk were two green boxes, known as soldiers' boxes, into which the girls could lock their possessions, and three pegs on which to hang a greatcoat and uniform. Then came a medical examination from which several girls emerged with towels round their heads, having had their hair washed to rid it of lice, while others were sent off for a bath. A corporal handed out a knife, fork, spoon and enamel mug to each girl, who had to sign for them. If anything was lost, its cost would be docked from pay: 'In those days you marched everywhere with knife, fork, spoon and mug and you held on to them like grim death, afraid to leave them anywhere for fear of theft. After that it was just one queue after another. We marched everywhere in threes – you weren't allowed to go anywhere on your own. That evening we received our nightwear – Winceyette pyjamas.'

As the recruits examined their strange surroundings, hemmed in on all sides by a host of unfamiliar faces and lectured by officious-sounding NCOs, the initial excitement of what might have begun as an adventure faded rapidly, replaced by a sense of foreboding which swiftly became acute homesickness. The bunks were uncomfortable, the blankets harsh, the lack of privacy embarrassing and the feeling of loneliness overwhelming. There were tears, plenty of tears, as many girls wept, some openly, others quietly into their pillows. After falling asleep at last, they were roused at 6 a.m. by the NCOs to a day which was even worse than the day before:

> That first weekend [Eileen recalls] seemed to consist of having one's arm jabbed with needles for tetanus, typhoid and smallpox. Many of the girls fainted. It seemed to be a mass reaction. Some, who saw others faint, would exclaim: 'Oh, I feel ill' and promptly collapse. Fortunately on the Sunday we were not worked hard because girls were recovering from their injections but we were handed lots of rules and regulations to read and digest. On the Monday we finished our kitting, and our uniforms were sent to a tailor in the Q Stores for alterations. We had a great deal of fun learning how to knot our ties, facing each other and trying out the technique in front of a mirror, and then adjusting our cap to the correct angle – absolutely straight and not on one side, checking that the badge was lined up with the nose.
>
> Once in uniform, all wearing coloured flashes on the shoulder to denote our company, we were paraded on the barrack-square to meet our drill sergeants and receive our first lessons in army drill. 'Now, I'm Sergeant Atkins,' the sergeant roared, 'and there's one thing I have to tell you. I'm the *best* sergeant in the British Army.' Then he walked up to an unsuspecting girl and, facing her, bellowed: 'What am I?' The girl thought for a moment as the sergeant glared down at her. 'You're the best sergeant in the British Army, sergeant,' the girl answered meekly.

Eileen later attended an NCO's course at Pontefract and recalls the importance of the NCO's role during initial training:

> Barrack-room corporals were almost God-like figures to us. They were the fount of all wisdom, helping us knot our ties, telling us when our hats were straight, handing out our mail, showing us how to fold our blankets and kit, teaching us the best ways of shining our

shoes or polishing our buttons, acting as mother-confessors in our depressed moments, instilling a sense of pride in our appearance and in our platoon – they were everything to us. We rarely saw the officers during the training course. They were there but were very much in the background.

She studied the NCOs with a critical eye, assimilating their good points and dismissing what she considered to be their deficiencies in handling the women, thus creating a standard of performance to which she would adhere. This analytical approach right at the outset of her career helped Eileen immensely during the following 35 years; in fact, it is typical of all the women who went on to become senior officers in the ATS and later the WRAC. The war gave them an opportunity to take a cram course, as it were, in woman management and the welfare of personnel, and there were lessons to be learned at every stage.

Of course, I was highly critical of the NCOs. I don't remember any really nasty ones but some shouted quite unnecessarily while others had a quieter and more effective approach which perhaps gained them more respect. When I became a lance-corporal I realized just how much the recruits depended on us. Apart from being their friend and trying to make them realize that we were there to help, we had to convince them that it wasn't going to be quite as bad as some of them at first thought. Some were older, married women whose husbands were at the front and who had left children in the care of their parents. For them there was a feeling of constant uncertainty, and they needed tactful handling and sympathetic treatment. Then there were girls who proved hopelessly inadequate. I remember one intake which comprised a very lively crowd of Geordies who all knew each other. Into this barrack-room came an eighteen-year-old who had been brought to the gates by her nanny. She had never in her life washed so much as a handkerchief, having come from a very wealthy family where servants did everything for her. For the first week she was totally bewildered as she tried to organize herself, her uniform and the rest of her kit, as well as cope with an ambience which was rough and in many ways crude. One big fireplace on the top floor of the barracks provided heat for fifty women and the girls had to fetch buckets of coal for the fire. It was amazing to see this girl knuckle down to the tasks of filling the bucket and carting it upstairs, ironing her uniform, polishing her shoes, shining her buttons and badges. Girls from this type of background needed gentle treatment and understanding.

The training began: how to recognize an officer; who to salute and how to salute; lectures on the organization of the Army and on the organization of the ATS; how the pay of 11*s* 8*d* a week was calculated and the procedure to be followed at pay parades on Fridays. The girls also had to learn the bugle calls, from Reveille to Last Post. The most welcome of all the calls was that announcing mail and, during the first week especially, the girls waited anxiously for word from home. For a few there was disappointment, which added to the burden of homesickness; then they were consoled by sympathetic NCOs. Evenings were spent pressing uniforms, polishing buttons and badges, and shining shoes to mirror brightness.

The 26-day training included a 48-hour weekend pass. Within the first 10 of the 24 days' practical work the girls underwent aptitude tests to select candidates for specific jobs. By the time the passing-out parade arrived the intake had been welded into a well-disciplined, well-drilled company with each platoon taking pride in its smartness and its performance on the barrack-square. Rapidly the class distinctions had disappeared, the toffee-nosed recruits being brought down to earth and the country girls given a new-found confidence by discovering latent abilities. They had marched together along highways and byways singing the popular songs of the day – 'You are my sunshine', 'Deep in the heart of Texas', 'Kiss me goodnight Sergeant-Major', 'Praise the Lord and pass the ammunition'. On the last Friday of training, the girls waited for their postings, hoping that their choice of work would not be disregarded, fearful that they would be separated from friends made during the days at the centre.

One problem encountered by Eileen Nolan perhaps more than anything else epitomizes her own character and also the personalities of the NCOs being drafted into the training centres at that time. She was a corporal by then and her bunk was at the end of the hut, curtained off from the 40 women in her charge to provide some measure of privacy and privilege; the only way the corporal could see round the barrack-room was to stand on top of a double bunk. In the first few days of an intake it was imperative that NCOs obtained a general impression of each recruit and kept an eye open for those who needed special attention and counselling. During the first days of one particular intake Eileen noticed one recruit, aged eighteen, who was shy and retiring and as the days passed it became apparent that the girl, instead of adjusting, was becoming more withdrawn and unhappy. Eventually Eileen found a moment to be alone with her.

'What is the problem?' she asked.

'Nothing, corporal,' the girl replied.

'Come on, I'm sure there is something wrong. You're not very happy here, are you?'

Eventually the girl admitted that she came from a very religious home where the family always knelt down together at night to say their prayers before going to bed: 'When I left home I promised my parents faithfully that I would do this in the Army but honestly, corporal, I find it impossible to bring myself to kneel down by my bed with all the girls around. They'll laugh at me and I couldn't stand that. I know it's wrong and that I should be able to rise above it but I can't.'

The girl paused for a few moments before continuing: 'I don't know what to do. I suppose I'll just have to work it out for myself.'

Eileen waited for her to finish and then said: 'Well, it's absolutely simple. When you're ready for bed this evening, just look up to my end of the room and we'll fix something between us.'

When the other girls arrived, they saw their corporal cleaning the area round her bed, from which the screen had been removed. Then, having finished her work, Eileen knelt down by the side of her bed in full view of everyone. There was a sudden silence as conversation in the hut stopped and then, in a quieter tone, everyone resumed talking. You didn't laugh at corporals who said their prayers at night and neither did you laugh at an eighteen-year-old girl who followed her example.

Of such were good NCOs made. They held the authority to make or break the recruits under them, to foster *esprit de corps* or to fester resentment.

In November 1942 the ABCA programme was extended under a 'Winter Scheme of Education' and the auxiliaries were lectured on 'The British Way and Purpose' which explained the machinery of national and local government and social services, and the status and interests of the dominions and colonies. Many of these ABCA periods were met with what one officer described as 'a wall of dumbness' or, as another termed it, 'a wall of deafness'. But their success depended very much on the enterprise and imagination of officers conducting the courses. Quizzes were held in some units, people engaged in public affairs were invited to form 'brains trusts' and mock parliamentary debates were held. In addition, visits to local places of interest were arranged in order to illustrate the practical importance of local and national government. Concerts of classical music, play readings and amateur theatricals were held, which widened the cultural background of thousands of girls who might never have dreamed of attending such functions in civilian life.

At a press conference in 1943 Leslie Whateley announced that nearly one-third of the 200,000 women serving in Britain were tradeswomen – that is, replacing soldier craftsmen in 80 trades. They included armourers, draughtswomen, fitters and wireless operators. There were more than 30,000 clerks, 9,000 technical storewomen in ordnance depots, more than 3,000 teleprinter operators and 4,000 switchboard operators, 4,000 cooks,

30,000 orderlies and 15,000 drivers. There were butchers, mess stewards, caterers and mess orderlies. By far the largest number of ATS girls, 56,000 in all, were helping to man the anti-aircraft defences, working side-by-side with the gunners, and operating searchlights. Unwisely, many recruits had initially allowed themselves to be persuaded to do jobs not of their own choice, and classification was difficult to change except on grounds of inefficiency. Some cooks, who were refused permission to switch occupations, served up a rice pudding which contained large quantities of mustard and was completely inedible. After a few similar occurrences, they were at last allowed to change their employment.

There were 116 categories of employment and when the Royal Electrical and Mechanical Engineers was formed in May 1942, members of the ATS employed by the Royal Army Ordnance Corps were transferred to become electricians, fitters, vehicle mechanics and welders. Vehicles of every description arrived in their workshops for servicing and the girls stripped engines, replaced brake linings, checked dynamos, ground new engine valves and repaired canopies and upholstery. In the autumn, teams of REME girls went into the fields to collect spiders which were placed on sticks. Then the auxiliaries breathed on the spiders to encourage them to start spinning, and passed a frame backwards and forwards to receive the web which was used to manufacture precision instruments. The average pass rate for the ATS taking REME courses was 95 per cent.

Eighty auxiliaries worked on a delicate operation code-named Tyburn, which was involved in the manufacture of vaccine to immunize people against scrub typhus, also known as tsutsugamushi disease, endemic in the Far East. During the Second World War this form of typhus was a more frequent cause of morbidity and mortality to military forces operating in the south-west Pacific regions and in the China-Burma-India theatre than was louse-borne typhus in the Middle East. The causative agent is a parasite of mites which attach themselves to wild rodents, and whose larvae crawl on to blades of grass and other vegetation. Operation Tyburn's vaccine was obtained by infecting cotton rats imported from the United States. Auxiliaries, dressed in cellular shirts and mosquito slacks, were charged with the care of the rats which had to be fed and watered, and with cleaning the cages daily. Other auxiliaries, wearing gowns, caps, masks and goggles, worked in the laboratory where 100,000 doses of the vaccine were processed for shipment to the Far East forces. ATS members also helped to select, check and issue thousands of items of medical equipment ranging from aseptic furniture to hypodermic needles.

In the Middle East a contingent of ATS girls came into contact with the more common form of typhus when they were sent to Aleppo in northern Syria to deal with Greek refugees streaming across the Turkish frontier.

Above 4.5in AA guns fire while ATS girls work on the range-height finder. *Left* 'Guns on target,' shouts an ATS lance-corporal in charge of the predictor.

They were called on to disinfect beds, clean floors and windows, and scrub paintwork in a desolate, 1914 Turkish barracks which was to be used as a disinfestation post. The refugees arrived at the rate of 1,000 to 1,500 every 48 hours. One sergeant-major and four nursing orderlies, wearing protective clothing against lice, had to persuade these protesting, indignant, hysterical and sometimes violently objecting refugees to strip off their clothing, which was then put into sacks and flung into an enormous cleansing apparatus to kill off the typhus vector. The girls were an object of curiosity in Aleppo, where uniformed women had never been seen before, and crowds of Syrians gathered whenever the auxiliaries went sightseeing, making it impossible for them to move around freely. All in all, it was a gruelling and hazardous experience, but they did manage to prevent what could have been a devastating epidemic of typhus in the region.

At quite a different level, 38 auxiliaries were employed as kennel maids at the War Dogs Training School, responsible for the feeding and hygiene and welfare of the animals. Food consisted of biscuits, meat and green vegetables; the dogs were groomed and exercised daily, and bathed every six weeks. The girls also assisted in the dispensary and in the dogs' hospital.

A novel departure was the drafting of women into the army bakery at Aldershot. The idea was received with great scepticism in 1941 by the master baker, Warrant Officer Randall of the Royal Army Service Corps. 'We have men, strong men at that, working full out stripped to the waist, doing a man's job, with a man's size plant, that was never made for female labour,' he argued. Nevertheless, on 23 February 1942, a vanguard of seven women reported for the tough trade test which would qualify them as Class 11 bakers. They had to work eight-hour shifts in temperatures up to 100°F wearing men's white jackets and trousers, supported by belts which they had to supply themselves, and a baker's cap (later to be replaced for women by a kerchief). Although the most modern machinery was installed, the girls had to learn to mix the dough by hand and knead it into loaves in case of mechanical breakdown. Junior Commander Ruth Sleigh (now Mrs Hicks of Farnham in Surrey), who commanded H Company of bakers at Aldershot, recalls that on one occasion the machinery did break down when someone tried to clean it with a knife while it was in motion. 'At that time the back-up machinery was being serviced and the hard manual work taught us all a lesson,' Mrs Hicks said. The only jobs the girls were not expected to do were tipping the sacks of flour into the chutes and loading the loaves on to the hot-plates.

By May 1942 the girls of H Company had developed into what was jokingly referred to as the Randall type – 'a high waistline, square shoulders, graceful and gentle curves where necessary, and a pair of hands that look as though they have been used for packing barbed wire'. Warrant Officer Randall had his own qualifications for candidates: 'They must be young, red-haired,

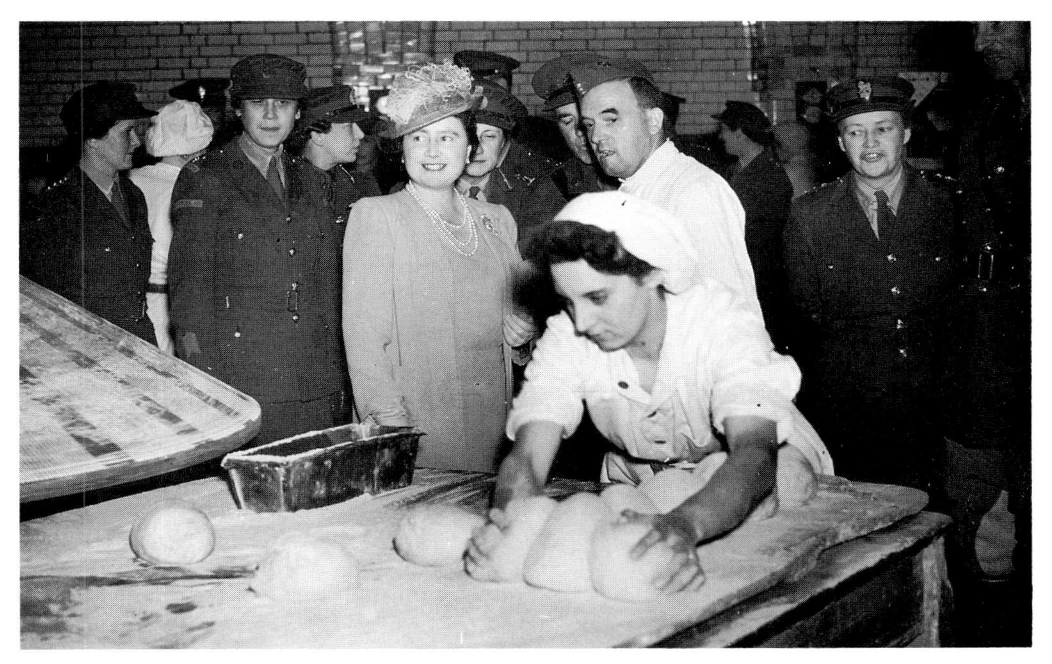

HM The Queen visits the Machine Bakery at Aldershot in July 1944, a month after D-Day. For ten days before the D-Day landings the girls baked non-staling bread for the invasion force. The ATS produced 77 million pounds out of the 129 million pounds of bread baked by the Army in the Second World War.

weigh 145 lb and have a surname beginning with Mac.' *The Sunday Times* reported on 13 June 1943 that 'The Army's Daughters of the House' were turning out 50,000 pounds of bread daily for the Army. They came from the Shetlands, the Hebrides, England, Wales, Ulster, Eire, Czechoslovakia, Germany, the Falkland Islands and Switzerland, and by the end of the war 436 ATS had registered for the course. The most successful was Marie Schnabel, a Czech who became an assistant master baker. Later ATS bakeries were established at Lingfield and at Leaton. Their greatest test came in 1944 when, for ten days before D-Day, the girls baked non-staling bread for the invasion force. In all, the ATS produced 77 million pounds of bread out of the 129 million pounds baked by the Army during the war.

Many ATS activities were cloaked in secrecy because the women worked in the Intelligence agencies. Betty Macfie tells of one clandestine assignment in May 1941 when, as commander of a motor company in Glasgow, she was asked to send a reliable driver to district headquarters with an ambulance for a very special detail. Told only that her patient would be a very senior German officer, the ATS driver recognized the man who was put into her ambulance at the designated rendezvous – he was Rudolf Hess, deputy to Adolf Hitler, who had flown to Scotland on 10 May and injured his ankle on landing. She duly delivered Hess to a mansion near Loch Lomond which had been converted into a hospital, and obeyed the instruction that she must not speak to her passenger. However, when she opened the door, Hess inquired: 'Where is this?'

'What did you say?' Betty asked, when the driver reported the incident.

'I just said aaaah . . .' she replied. During Hess's interrogation an ATS shorthand writer was present to take notes.

More than 10,000 ATS girls served in the Royal Corps of Signals, operating telephones, teleprinter, telegraph and radio services. In the largest signal office underground at the War Office, they manned two long rows of teleprinters connected with the huge network of teleprinter lines linking units throughout Great Britain. In the routing room they received and routed outgoing messages, and forwarded incoming messages to War Office departments in locked containers, by means of pneumatic tubes. Nine auxiliaries gave the world the news that D-Day had dawned. Soon after they came on duty on the morning of 6 June 1944, at Supreme Headquarters Allied Expeditionary Forces, a message was handed in at the receiving hatch of the signal office. Lance-Corporal Parry, ATS, picked it up, routed it and passed it to another for registration. Then it went to the teleprinter room, where seven ATS operators simultaneously transmitted it to the War Cabinet and to Allied headquarters all over the world. It was General Dwight D. Eisenhower's first communiqué and it read: 'Under General Eisenhower, Allied naval forces, supported by strong air forces, began landing Allied armies this morning on the northern coasts of France.' Within a few hours, auxiliaries in the War Office were connected by wireless-controlled teleprinters with the Normandy bridgehead.

It was the ATS motor companies – 30 of them by 1942 – which kept the wheels of military transport turning and made a vital contribution to the war effort, particularly during the spring of 1944 when Britain became a fortress, assembling the largest invasion force in the history of warfare.

On 28 July 1944 a small contingent of ATS clerks and two provost corporals joined the rear headquarters of 21st Army Group in Normandy. A month later reinforcements arrived to join their colleagues who were living in bell-tents, dug in for protection against bombing. By 1945 6,290 girls were serving on the Continent. They included staff officers in the Intelligence branch, Civil Affairs, Public Relations, Psychological Warfare, and Liaison with Allies, personal assistants to the chief of staff and his deputy, 120 cooks and mess orderlies, 113 drivers and 220 clerks.

Of all the many notable contributions made by the ATS, perhaps the 56,000 girls employed by the Anti-Aircraft Command received the most publicity and the greatest praise during the war. During the dark days in 1940 and

1941 it was imperative that air defences should withstand the onslaught of the Luftwaffe bombers which converged on cities and airfields with the object of destroying the RAF and also demoralizing the spirits of the people who were suffering the blitz. The man who commanded the AA defences during the war was Lieutenant-General Sir Frederick Pile, whose foresight enabled the ATS to play a major operational role in saving the country from defeat in the air.

As early as 1938 General Pile, who was recalled from the Royal Tank Regiment to organize the Air Defence system, had called in Miss Caroline Haslett, an engineer, to advise if any work on the guns could be done by women. The duties of a heavy AA battery consisted of locating the target and aiming the gun, which was controlled by highly technical instruments, and Miss Haslett reported that indeed a high proportion of these duties could be carried out by women. The first potential ATS radar operators arrived at the training schools entirely ignorant of electronics and wireless procedures, yet they had to learn not only how to operate the complex instruments but what went on behind the control boards. Radar for AA purposes was probably the most difficult of all types to operate because it involved teamwork requiring the identification of a hostile aircraft, tracking it, measuring its height, bearing and speed, and feeding all this information into a computer which regulated the aiming and firing of the gun.

The time during which the guns could fire was very limited and throughout that critical period the whole operation had to be flawless. The girls had to be able to distinguish their target from a multitude of other blips which could show up on the screens – flocks of birds, barrage balloons, hills and, of course, friendly aircraft. In simple terms the ATS were responsible for arranging a lethal interception for enemy aircraft with a salvo of shells which burst in the air, spraying a cloud of steel splinters. The shells took up to twenty seconds to reach their destination, during which time the aircraft might have travelled two miles. To score a hit required endless hours of practice and a degree of precision which could be achieved only by exceptional accuracy, deep concentration and extreme dedication to the task at hand.

On 8 September 1941 *The Times* reported that the first mixed battery had been in action but it was not until the night of 1 November 1941 that the ATS, together with the men actually firing the guns, could share the honours in bringing down six raiders. In these batteries the cooks and orderlies, no less than the plotters, telephonists, auxiliaries on the heightfinders and predictors, fire controllers and the spotters, felt that they were part of a team with the one and only object of playing their part against hostile aircraft. 'They knew their work was worthwhile; they brought down enemy planes and saw them hurtling through the sky; they shared dangers, excitements and disappointments with the men manning the guns and they knew what war meant,' historian J. M. Cowper wrote.

Inevitably the mixed batteries, where women were living in tents, caused some controversy. One member of an AA unit, Joan Savage Cowey, recalls:

> There was a feeling that we were sort of loose women living in tents with men. They called us 'officers' groundsheets' – we got that all the time. They didn't really know what intense training we went through; they just thought we were there to entertain the troops. The American soldiers were worse. They'd say the Brits had it really good, having us girls along to keep them happy. The whole thing – all the criticism of us – just had to do with sex.

The mixed batteries did create problems but not in the way the critics expected. Naturally some sexual indiscretions did occur – no matter how harsh the discipline, men and women could not be prevented from pairing-off when off-duty – but the greatest disruption was caused by couples who married. Army regulations still laid down that married couples should not serve together so wives and husbands had to be separated by posting one partner to a different battery.

Another controversial issue was the fine dividing line between plotting and predicting the course, height and speed of the target, and the actual firing of the gun. Officially the ATS was a non-combatant force but to all intents and purposes those serving in the AA were in the firing line, subject to attack by enemy bombs and fighters, and also, technically, they were handling lethal weapons. The argument raged over the moral question of whether women, as child bearers, should be in the business of taking life. The ATS maintained that although the girls were engaged on the instrumentation of a weapon, they never at any time physically pulled the firing lever of a gun. Yet stories persist to this day that on occasions they did, although officially these assertions are vehemently denied. Leslie Whateley gave an unequivocal answer when asked if the ATS at any stage had their fingers on the 'trigger'.

> Of course they did. They didn't pull the 'trigger' very often and not if they didn't want to – purely on a voluntary basis. Oh no, we know they did. I knew General Pile quite well and I talked it over with him and with my father. There was an awful row about it among some parents, and officers were instructed never to allow anything that would cause a public outcry. Girls on the batteries were all volunteers, remember, but if their parents objected they were posted elsewhere. It's more than forty years ago now and it's absolutely ridiculous not admitting what went on and trying to evade the issue.

As the war progressed the weaponry became more sohisticated and by 1945 automation was such that the guns were fired by remote control from the command post when on target, which made the distinction between aiming and firing almost negligible.

Controversy also surrounded the ATS searchlight units which were often located in remote areas and staffed by a troop of women, with one man, frequently a Home Guard gunner, to operate the machine gun which was mounted on a tripod. The official history of the ATS records that when the Luftwaffe started machine-gunning the sites in August 1942 the women were anxious to have an AA machine gun which they could use themselves, but this could not be condoned without alteration to the Royal Warrant. When the ATS had received full military status in 1941, the Secretary of State for War had told the House that this would include duties for searchlight stations and AA gun sites, and when the Conscription Bill was passed it stated: 'No woman should be liable to make use of a lethal weapon unless she signifies in writing her willingness to undertake such service.' However, she was subject to the Defence Regulation which stated that the Army Act applied 'in such manner, to such extent and subject to such adaptations and modifications as the Army Council deems necessary'. This appears to imply that it would have been relatively simple to change the rules to allow women to fire a weapon if deemed necessary, but no such alteration was ever made.

The ATS history adds that there was no operational reason for the installation of a machine gun in searchlight units and the provision of a gun manned by gunners would involve waste of manpower, additional building, and mixing the sites, none of which seemed practical politics. We are left to assume, erroneously no doubt, that many of the searchlight crews were therefore totally unprotected from air attack. Once again Leslie Whateley adopts a more realistic attitude:

> I can't remember at this distance whether the girls on the searchlights ever operated the machine guns. I think they probably did. If you are on a searchlight and the planes are diving down the beam at you, are you going to wait for them to shoot or are you going to take some action to stop them? I took all these things for granted when I was director, leaving it to the officers on the spot to take decisions in the best interests of the girls.

The experience of the first experimental ATS searchlight troop, formed in April 1941, had proved beyond doubt that the girls were capable of operating the sites without the assistance of soldiers. Fifty women were selected from units throughout the country and told to report to a camp at Newark under orders not to divulge any information to anyone. Tested for suitability, five failed the rigorous physical and mental examinations while the rest received preliminary instruction on aircraft recognition, sound location, map reading, and driving and maintenance of lorries. After being drilled on the barrack-square, they were sent on a fifteen-mile route march, wearing respirators and steel helmets. An indication of the fitness of the remaining 45 was that the squad swung back on to the barrack-square with no casualties. Their qualification for the task being no longer in dispute, the commander of 2 AA division at last disclosed the nature of their assignment and told them that they would receive the necessary technical training.

When the girls proved proficient in searchlight drill, they were moved to a site in Sherwood Forest. The move was carried out in the form of an exercise and instructions were issued by means of messages to simulate actual conditions. At dawn, dressed in male battledress and black tank berets with their kit at the ready, the troops waited for orders. The first signal arrived at 0800 hours, saying that there had been a raid on a certain site and reinforcements were required in the shape of a Mark IX sound locator and team. The team jumped into action. The driver of the three-ton lorry had never towed a vehicle before but she negotiated the 23-mile journey, her navigators locating the site by map references alone. To their dismay they discovered that the male troop had moved out leaving all their equipment in the pits, entailing the removal of the 'damaged' equipment before the girls could instal the replacements they had brought. The pits were deep and the towing chains rusty but they were able to man the winches successfully and achieve their purpose. The whole exercise took place under the critical gaze of instructors and senior officers who offered no advice or help.

From then on the girls ran the site in the same way as the men, digging, gardening, maintaining equipment and undertaking guard duties. When warning of an air raid was given, the spotter went out with her binoculars while other members of the team took up their stations at the sound locator and the controls of the light, keeping the lens in focus and controlling the current. It was bitterly cold in winter and 'teddy bear' coats and mittens were essential wear. The only complaints concerned the lack of sleep because they were roused for their tour of duty as sentries as well as for air raids. One can imagine the feelings of these women, alone at night, miles from friendly houses, unaccustomed to the darkness, exposed to the elements, nervous of the unfamiliar countryside sounds. Yet very soon they lost their fears and, rather than go on sentry duty in pairs and so lose more sleep, they opted to go alone. So successful was this first experiment that on 25 November 1942 the 93rd Searchlight Regiment RA, consisting of 1,500 ATS, was formed under a Royal Artillery commanding officer and an ATS adjutant.

One of the proudest parents of an ATS 'gunner' was Winston Churchill, whose daughter Mary (now Lady Soames) was the ATS junior commander

Prime Minister Winston Churchill and Mrs Churchill watch ATS predictor girls at work during the Second World War. Their daughter Mary, who was in the Ack-Ack, was not on duty at Slades Hill, Enfield during the visit.

of 481 Battery in Hyde Park. The Prime Minister once stopped off in his official car on his way from the House to Downing Street and the unsuspecting sentry demanded his identity card. Churchill produced the document with the compliment: 'You did quite right, my boy.'

The public took these girls to their hearts, although in Aberdeen, after a particularly heavy air raid, the girls of 128 Regiment were blamed by the locals for the casualties. The commanding officer requested the Lord Provost to arrange coachloads of businessmen and journalists to witness a demonstration. During the visit four raiders descended on the city and the girls were able to give a live performance of their skills, which led to praise for the city's 'gun girls'.

Casualties were inevitable. In May 1942 the first ATS member killed in action was Auxiliary J. Caveney of 148 Regiment, who was struck by a bomb splinter as she stood at a predictor on a south-coast site; she was actually on target when she collapsed. Her place was taken immediately by Spotter G. Keel, who continued to follow the raider, the guns firing without any interruption.

The greatest test and the greatest triumph of the ATS occurred during the flying bomb attacks, which began on 16 June 1944. They might have been thought an easier target because whereas piloted aircraft were able to take evasive action, flying bombs flew straight, but on the radar screens they were more difficult to spot because they were smaller and gave a weak signal. Gun emplacements were moved to the coast where the gun girls lived under canvas on the desolate mud flats of Essex and Suffolk throughout a cold and rainy autumn. They had to be on duty 24 hours a day, watching flickering lines and patches of light, but they had the consolation of knowing that the proportion of 'divers' or 'doodlebugs', as the V1 rockets were known, that were brought down was steadily increasing until nine out of every ten were secured; on some nights not a single flying bomb slipped through the defences. When the Allied armies cleared the Channel coast of France of German installations the attacks switched to the east coast, from Clacton to Yarmouth, and then the 21st Army Group in Belgium became the target. Accordingly, the gun girls were shipped across the Channel to set up an anti-flying bomb installation there.

They were not told where they were bound and boarded an old cattle ship at Sheerness for the journey to Ostend, which took three days, with minesweepers clearing the way ahead. No keys were available for opening the tins of Spam on board so they ate hard-tack biscuits during the voyage. On the day after arrival several girls were wounded when the newer version of the flying bomb, the V2, flattened the camp. This time there was no warning growl from the engine because the V2 flew faster than sound.

'All you heard was a rush of air and then a violent explosion,' Joan Cowey says. 'It was scary. They almost blinded you with a flash of light. The most frustrating thing was that we couldn't hit them. They were much too fast. We couldn't move the guns around fast enough.' Nevertheless the gun batteries did score some hits. By the end of January the score of flying bombs shot down was nineteen, and another was claimed in the first fortnight of February. Again, the main complaint was lack of sleep, and in the forward positions the gunners were unable to change their clothes for days at a time. They had to be withdrawn from the gun sites to catch up on sleep in hotels specially set aside for the purpose. To give some idea of the devastation, between 12 October 1944 and 15 March 1945, 5,960 rockets hit Antwerp, killing 731 soldiers and 3,515 civilians. The girls manning the guns lived an arduous life in Nissen huts and for six weeks one unit worked in solid frozen snow, eating iron rations and dehydrated vegetables out of mess tins. Icicles hung from the ceiling and there was no fuel for heaters. When the thaw came, roads collapsed and many sites were marooned. These girls proved to be the fittest of any in the ATS and the incidence of illness was very low.

In the later stages of the war the ATS instituted what was known as pre-OCTU wings where specially selected girls were taught the rudiments of the responsibilities they would assume as officers and given an opportunity to increase their confidence. From there they went to the OCTU establishment at the Imperial Services' College in Windsor. For most of the war Eileen Nolan remained in the training sphere of operations but in 1945 she attended a pre-OCTU wing at Pontefract and then was sent to Windsor for the six-week course designed to develop powers of leadership. It was at Windsor that the ATS established the traditions of officer training which was based very much on the Sandhurst model and which today is part of the WRAC experience at Sandhurst.

One practical exercise was an initiative test. Eileen's platoon was made responsible for decorating the Great Hall for the last dinner of the course. They were given ten shillings and told not to supplement it with any of their own money – a daunting prospect in view of wartime restrictions, particularly in early April when few flowers were available. The problem was discussed at a platoon meeting and in the middle of the brainstorming session one cadet, Mary Damer, suddenly exclaimed: 'Look, there's only one person in these parts who has the sort of flowers and shrubs we can use to decorate the hall.'

The others looked at her in astonishment.

'Do you know someone here?' asked one girl.

'Not really,' replied Mary. 'The person I'm thinking of is the King.'

It was a daring suggestion but in the spirit of 'nothing ventured, nothing gained', Eileen and Mary went to Windsor Castle the following afternoon. The policeman on duty at the gates listened patiently to their story and then telephoned one of the gardeners.

Next morning, during a lecture, Mary Damer was called to the telephone and when she returned she was grinning from ear to ear. In the coffee-break she explained that the call had been from the head gardener at Windsor Castle to say that the flowering shrubs were ready for collection and all that was needed was a vehicle in which to load them. They spent the ten shillings on hiring a taxi which returned to the King Edward Horse Hall laden with beautiful foliage.

'Of course, the staff were absolutely horrified when they found out what we had done and we all expected to be drummed out of the Army for our impertinence.'

Eileen was commissioned as a 2nd subaltern on Friday 13 April 1945, less than a month before the war ended. 'By then we had very smart uniforms and I remember the tailors coming to OCTU to do all the fittings for us. Practically every officer cadet who ever went through Windsor rushed out to a super shoe shop in the town, Derbys, who did a special shoe for ATS officers. This red-brown shoe became a mark of the Windsor OCTU and you could always recognize the officers who had been there by their shoes.'

To the Motor Companies Training Centre at Camberley in the spring of 1945 went the honour of training as a driver the 19-year-old heir to the Throne, 2nd Subaltern Princess Elizabeth. Leslie Whateley, who had known the two Princesses as children, tells how she was called to an audience with the King and Queen on 13 December 1944 to discuss the procedure for Princess Elizabeth joining the ATS.

> I was absolutely staggered because we had all taken it for granted that she would go into the Navy as a Wren. I was also proud and honoured that they had chosen the ATS. Looking back on the dark days in 1940, when adverse criticism was our only form of publicity, I realized that this official sign of appreciation and confidence in our service was evidence of how it had improved, and that when the actual enrolment of the Princess took place it would prove a very big morale boost to the whole service.

In March 1944 Leslie had attended an afternoon party at Buckingham Palace to be formally presented to the two Princesses. That evening she had dined with the Princess Royal, and during the following months they forged a lifelong friendship. Leslie believes that one of the reasons for the choice of the ATS was the Princess Royal's tremendous enthusiasm.

The announcement of Princess Elizabeth's commission as a 2nd Subaltern in the ATS was made on 5 March 1945. Leslie recalls:

> I heaved a sigh of relief when I read the news in the papers, because the actual work involved had been most intricate and there had been no precedent to work on. It had necessitated interviews with the Military Secretary to the Secretary of State for War, General Sir Colville Wemyss, and several of his staff, and finally visits to the Palace where the King himself went through the actual wording of the Gazette with me.

Maud MacLellan was the chief commander at Camberley when the Princess arrived to be trained as a driver. The instruction took place over three weeks in Windsor Great Park and she then became the twelfth member of a senior NCO's class to receive instruction on motor mechanics. The course included lessons on maintenance, map-reading and ATS administration.

When it was announced that the King and Queen would take tea at Camberley, Princess Elizabeth did her share of washing out the courtyard and cleaning the cars so that everything was spick and span for the Royal visit. Afterwards she remarked: 'You know, I never knew how much trouble we give when we go to inspect anything. I must tell the King and Queen what happens when they go visiting.'

Irene Ward in *F.A.N.Y. Invicta* says that during the visit the Princess's class was set the task of fault-finding in their vehicles. Princess Elizabeth soon found her fault and remedied it but the car refused to start, much to her embarrassment. However, the King was smiling: without the Princess noticing, he had disconnected the high-tension lead to the distributor.

During tea the King and Queen were asked whether their daughter talked about her work. The Queen replied: 'Well, last night we had sparking plugs during the whole of dinner.'

Maud MacLellan said:

> The King and Queen and the Princess herself insisted there should be no privileges or favours for her. She was to be treated as a junior officer. As such she called me 'ma'am' and was ever ready to open a door for me and to do other little services. She was there as a junior officer – no more, no less. As a driver we discovered she was considerate and kind. To old people on the road she gave first priority. On her last night with us I suggested she say a few words of good-bye in the mess ante-room. But the Princess insisted on shaking hands with every one of the thirty-seven officers. She was very upset at having to leave.
>
> The previous day, when talking about her departure, I asked if she was to become a regular officer in the ATS. She answered: 'I'd give anything I possess to be an ordinary person like some of my own friends and to be an ATS officer. But I cannot do that. I have to be always at everyone's beck and call. Therefore, I should be of no use.'

The Camberley centre gave her a clock as a parting gift, the frame of which was made in the workshops. On the front of the clock was modelled the three types of vehicle she had learned to drive – a utility, an ambulance and a saloon.

During the last two years of the war, many auxiliaries were posted far afield. In December 1943, 5,000 auxiliaries were serving in the Middle East under the command of Senior Commander Audrey Chitty. In 1940 Mrs Chitty had gone to Cairo to examine the possibility of enrolling all British Army wives or dependents and local women into the ATS. Returning to England aboard the *Empress of Britain* via South Africa, she spent seven hours in an open boat in the Atlantic after the ship was torpedoed. Undaunted, she returned to the Middle East in 1941 to take on what proved to be a particularly difficult

The Princess Royal (*second from the right*) and Leslie Whateley (*fourth from the right*) at a wartime briefing, *c*. 1944.

task. Eighty per cent of her command were locally enrolled, comprising Cypriots, Palestinians, Greeks and Czechoslovakians. To complicate the situation further, the majority of the Palestinians were originally European Jews. Apart from the clash of cultures, few of the auxiliaries spoke English and no British officer spoke Arabic, Hebrew, Greek, Czech or Slovak. With no lingua franca, all orders had to be transmitted through interpreters.

The girls were employed in large numbers at base ordnance depots and at General Headquarters or lower commands, responsible for all communications in Egypt as well as those in Palestine. The drivers of 513 Company operated convoy routes 2,500 miles long from Beirut to Tripoli in Libya. In the summer they endured searing heat and swirling sand, and in the winter suffered bitter cold as they crossed the desert at a steady 20 mph, sleeping on the sand in hastily erected tents, with kitbags as pillows. One of the minor scandals involving these drivers was that they wore trousers (their working uniform) when off-duty, much to the indignation of the Arab townspeople. This resulted in an order that all drivers of convoys must carry skirts for 'walking out' when off-duty, so that they would not offend Arab sensibilities.

The Turkish Cypriot recruits created another kind of problem. The idea of women in uniform was totally unacceptable to most Moslem parents and husbands. Some Cypriot girls viewed the ATS as an escape route from harsh domestic bondage. Consequently the recruiting office was besieged by pro-

In 1945 HM King George VI paid a visit to the Motor Transport Training Company, Camberley, to see his daughter, the Princess Elizabeth, who was training as a driver. *Right* HRH Princess Elizabeth learns how to change the wheel of an army truck.

testing parents or outraged husbands demanding the return of daughters or wives. On one occasion an infant was dumped in the porch of the recruiting office, to the consternation of the officer, who eventually ascertained that it was the offspring of a would-be auxiliary. The reluctant mother was packed off home with her baby.

The ATS also served in the Central Mediterranean theatre which extended from Algiers to Tunis in North Africa and across the sea to Italy. An ATS detachment of 1 officer and 36 other ranks, sent to Eighth Army Rear (administration) at Cesena in Italy in the winter of 1944-5, had to endure extreme hardship. They were flown to Forli and then transported the twelve miles to Cesena in coaches preceded by a police jeep with sirens screeching. The troops turned out in force to wave and cheer them on their way to the town at the foot of the Apennines. But there the cheers ended. Awaiting them were three small houses with no baths, lavatory basins or water closets. Sanitation consisted of trench latrines in the gardens. No water was laid on and every day the girls had to depend on filling a two-gallon jerrycan at the water truck. This had to suffice for washing, cooking and drinking. There was no lighting or heating and the girls relied on Tilly lamps (oil lamps) in the cookhouse and candles in their rooms.

However, nothing could compare with the experience in Italy of Junior Commander Goggin, who, in April 1945, was in charge of a Civil Affairs team serving with the headquarters of the Allied Military government for

Cremona province. Their task was to take over temporarily the administration of newly liberated areas until a civil government could be installed. On arrival at Parma, Junior Commander Goggin heard that Cremona had been liberated by the patriots and she persuaded the US Army to ferry her across the River Po to the city on the north bank where she discovered that her team were the first Allied troops to be seen in the province, which still contained a pocket of Germans being harried by the patriots. Despite the dangers, Junior Commander Goggin, aided by a Hungarian woman doctor, set to work reorganizing and running the public welfare, health, education and refugee systems in the province. Three days after their arrival the German garrison commander emerged from hiding and surrendered his force personally to Junior Commander Goggin, thus avoiding the risk of being taken prisoner by the patriots.

Further south, in Africa, 195 members of the ATS were stationed in Kenya and four were posted to South Africa. The ATS also served in India, in the United States and in the Caribbean.

When the war in Europe ended, an ATS signaller transmitted General Eisenhower's stark communiqué from Rheims to the combined chiefs of staff:

'The mission of this Allied force was fulfilled at 0241 local time, May 7, 1945.'

By the beginning of 1945 the war in Europe was nearly over and the ATS had established itself as an integral part of the Army, proving its versatility in coping with a variety of jobs, under the strain of falling bombs and in the severest climates. During the war 67 members were killed in action, another 9 died of wounds, 313 were wounded and 16 were posted as missing, making a total of 405 war casualties. Leslie Whateley became a DBE and was also awarded the CBE, the Croix de Guerre with silver star, and the United States awarded her the Order of Merit. Ten other members were awarded the CBE, 31 received the OBE, 123 the MBE, 275 the BEM and 238 were mentioned in despatches. Six received the US Bronze Star, and 3 the Bronze Star and Mentioned in Despatches (US). One also received the Czechoslovakian Medal for Merit.

It had taken another world war to prove that women did have the stamina and the versatility to adapt to almost any employment. If they had not demonstrated musclepower, they had certainly shown they possessed the brainpower and, indeed, the will and the enthusiasm to compete with men in almost every sphere of operation. There is no doubt that war experience in the ATS and its sister services also introduced a great number of women to the realities of economic life and did so more rapidly than might have happened in peacetime. This undoubtedly resulted in a widening of employment opportunities for females who emerged from the services not only qualified in a variety of trades but also equipped with managerial skills.

Although the First World War is usually accepted as sign-posting the way to female emancipation by permanently enlarging the numbers of women who went out to work and beginning the process of breaking down sexual exclusiveness in several areas, the Second World War consolidated the position of womanpower and in a significant way created the basis for another social revolution twenty years later. Post-war Britain, facing a decade of austerity coupled with the development of a welfare state, was not yet ready for a radical transformation in employment patterns. While some women were able to step straight into more responsible and challenging roles in civilian life, the majority resumed the traditional 'female' jobs and continued to play a secondary role to men in careers and public life. The old attitude – that women were primarily mothers and home-makers – had yet to be moderated by a society which now desperately sought a return to normality.

Sociologists who studied the position of women in this period point to a tendency for smaller families which allowed mothers to spend a greater part of their lives at work than hitherto, but most women did not think in terms of a career; they worked merely to supplement the income of the household. While the mothers of 1945 may not have initiated the liberation movement, they established a base from which their daughters launched the feminist revolution of the late 'sixties and 'seventies. Although it is difficult to pinpoint the wider social consequences of women's war service, one major development did result which, in a narrower but definitive sense, proved even more revolutionary because of its impact on a once exclusively male preserve.

Always the Army had been seen, as even present-day publicity attests, as a 'man-sized' job but it had become a 'woman-sized' job as well. When the ATS – and WAAF and WRNS contingents – took part in the Victory Parade, their presence was a reminder that the victory belonged not only to the army of men who had fought on the battlefields of Europe, Africa and Asia but also to the army of women who had served their country equally as well in a variety of roles at home and abroad. They were claiming a place in history, for they had broken down once and for all the sexual prejudices of the greatest male bastion of them all – the British Army. They had finally shattered a tradition of male exclusivity which had lasted for 284 years since 14 February 1661 when, on Tower Hill in London, Cromwell's army had laid down their arms in token disbandment and then lifted them again as loyal soldiers of King Charles II, thus founding the British Army.

When the ATS marched down The Mall, the women were demonstrating not only what they had achieved in the past six years but what they hoped to achieve in the future. They had proved their worth in wartime. Now they intended to prove their worth in peacetime. They wanted a permanent place in the Army.

10
THE WOMEN'S ROYAL ARMY CORPS

Although the end of the war in Europe bestowed a tremendous sense of achievement on the many thousands of women who had served in the ATS, this feeling was accompanied for some by a certain restlessness, generated by the uncertainty surrounding the future of the women's service. These servicewomen had been trained for war work and their doubts about whether they possessed the necessary qualifications for jobs in commerce and industry added to their personal anxiety. The euphoria of VE-Day quickly subsided to be generally replaced by a need to exchange service khaki for civilian clothes as the women prepared to welcome home their loved ones from the front lines in Europe. Six weeks after VE-Day, on 18 June, demobilization began with married women leading the way out of uniform. As a result the ATS numbers decreased rapidly, leaving obvious gaps in the Army in those trades which had been manned almost entirely by the ATS when hostilities ceased.

One very basic problem for those who had served for some time was returning to wardrobes of clothes which perhaps no longer fitted or had suffered during storage. When Leslie Whateley went to the Army Staff College as the guest of the commandant, General Gregson-Ellis, 'It was the first evening since the outbreak of war that I had worn evening dress . . . It was a bitterly cold night and the commandant's bungalow had been built without any thought regarding the elimination of draughts. At dinner I was acutely aware of its structural deficiencies. One of the reasons I had not worn evening dress before was that my entire civilian wardrobe had long been ravaged by moth. Little did my host and hostess know the difficulties I had gone through to collect an outfit for this dinner. Nor, I hope, were they aware that my evening shoes were my bedroom slippers.'

Fortunately the Army took account of the difficulties ATS members would encounter on demobilization. In place of the civilian clothes given to demobbed soldiers, auxiliaries when released from their duties received 56 clothing coupons and a plain clothes allowance of £12 10*s*, based on the first-grade utility cost of the following articles:

Hat	10*s*
Costume	£4 15*s*
Scarf	6*s*
Blouse of jumper	£1 –
Stockings	10*s*
Shoes	£1 5*s*
Raincoat	£3 10*s*
Alterations allowance	14*s*
	£12 10*s*

This allowance was scarcely sufficient to cover the increased cost of clothing and it was therefore raised to £13 16*s*. The women also received a fourteen-day ration card and were able to buy from Navy, Army and Air Force Institutes a fortnight's sweet ration and eight weeks' cigarette ration. Their release leave was 56 days, with an extra day for any completed month of service abroad.

The clothing allowance provides an indication of the current cost of living but, generous though the allowance undoubtedly was, it does not convey the state of the nation in that immediate post-war period. This was a time of austerity when not only clothes but food was severely rationed as Britain, for the first time governed by a majority Labour government, undertook the task of rebuilding its economy and its infrastructure. In waging war Britain had acquired debts of £3,000 million, had allowed domestic capital to deteriorate by about the same amount, had used up overseas investments to the extent of £1,000 million and had seen her exports decline by two-thirds since 1939. Large tracts of London, Merseyside, the Midlands, Plymouth and Clydeside, and many other towns and cities such as Coventry, had been devastated by bombing but, against this, entrepreneurs found tremendous opportunities to exploit the advances in science and technology by setting up new businesses in factories which were switching from weapon production to peacetime activity.

However, there was another factor which influenced the lives of the women who left the ATS during this period – the war had disrupted marriages and family life: there was a tenfold jump in divorces, which reached a peak of 60,000 in 1947. Nevertheless marriage remained popular and in 1951 731 out of every 1,000 women in the age group 20-39 were married, compared with 552 in 1911, while the 'baby-boom' sent the birthrate soaring to a peak of 20.5 per 1,000 in 1947.

With so many cities blitzed by the bombing, coupled with the sudden rush to get married, it was almost impossible for newly-weds to find suitable accommodation and by 1951 there was still a shortfall of one-and-a-half million dwellings, despite the government's attempts to solve the problem by creating estates of pre-fabricated homes. Many couples, particularly in working-class homes, stayed with parents, causing a corresponding increase in domestic tension, especially as many husbands insisted that the wife resume her role as homemaker and childrearer. But it is significant that a survey in the early 1950s discovered that many husbands were accepting a responsibility to help in the home if their wives went out to work. It was a pointer to what was to come twenty years later with the advent of the women's liberation movement, and provides another clear indication that war accelerates changes in society.

A large number of women in the ATS had become so attuned to service life that they could not envisage any other type of work. Fortunately, the Army did intend to retain a proportion of women, for a time at least, but only those who wished to stay in the service. A great many did agree to stay on, hoping that the ATS would become a permanent force, but the decision was difficult for young girls weighing up family commitments against an inclination to a military career. The attitude of Eileen Nolan illustrates the outlook of those who opted to remain in uniform. She thought long and hard about her future:

> I wasn't sure what I wanted to do. My parents were very keen that I should return home, so, although I knew that I didn't really want to go back to Bournville, I allowed my father to arrange an interview with the senior personnel officer at Cadbury's. I saw her when I went home on leave and she said that with my experience of management, undoubtedly I would get a management course with the firm.

Eileen, like hundreds of others wishing to remain in the Army, had tested her wings and discovered that the nest from which she had flown no longer had the same appeal for her, so she made up her mind that she would try to obtain a permanent commission in the regular service. The War Office had decided that, in the meantime, successful officer applicants would be granted a three-year interim commission and auxiliaries would receive a two- or three-year extra engagement. 'I said to myself that at the end of three years, if I proved not to be acceptable, I would be only twenty-nine and it would be worthwhile to have this extra experience.' After 28 days' re-engagement leave, Eileen returned to her post at the Leicester Training School and was promoted to junior commander (captain), having been commissioned for only fifteen months.

The momentous fact that women in peacetime would now have the choice of whether or not to serve in the Army had been suggested by the Secretary of State, J. J. Lawson, during a speech on the army estimates in

May 1946. After paying tribute to the ATS for its wartime work, he said: 'I hope that the ATS will remain, in one form or another, a permanent part of His Majesty's Forces, and I know that if they do, they will continue to render the same outstanding service to the country as they have in the past.' The statement did much to boost the morale of those who had chosen to remain in the service but it also emphasized the enormous responsibility of the director of the ATS, since her main task would be to transform what was in effect a Territorial Service into a Regular Force.

Leslie Whateley had no doubts about leaving the ATS. She and her husband, Raymond, had bought a farm in Devon and she was determined to retire as soon as possible so that they could restore the almost derelict 500-year-old property:

> The question now arose of who should be my successor. I dined with the Princess Royal one night to discuss the matter and, as was to be expected, she took great interest in the problem . . . Up to this time changes in the appointment of the director ATS had been sprung upon both the Service, and upon the public, after they had actually taken place. This, from the point of view of morale and prestige, was definitely a mistake. It was now necessary to weigh up in my mind all the pros and cons of possible candidates whose names I submitted to the adjutant-general for transmission to the Secretary of State.

In her own mind Leslie had no doubt who should succeed her and in anticipation of the final decision to be taken by Lawson on the advice of the wartime adjutant-general, Sir Ronald Adam, she began to delegate more and more work to her deputy, Mary Tyrwhitt, 'so that some continuity might be achieved when I retired'. Mary was by then in her mid-forties, sufficiently mature to take on the responsibility of heading the ATS and with enough experience of managing women to enable her to administer its affairs efficiently.

Mary Tyrwhitt had known for some time that she was being groomed for the post of director because Leslie had called her aside one day and told her of her pending retirement and preferred choice of successor. 'I nearly fell off my chair,' Mary admits. 'Honestly and truthfully, it was the last thing I expected. I hadn't even thought about it. Leslie told me she would be putting forward three names and we would all be interviewed by the Secretary of State and by the adjutant-general.'

The interviews took place at the War Office on 6 February 1946, the day on which Leslie Whateley received her DBE from the King at Buckingham Palace. Curiously, the War Office was concerned about ill-feeling among the candidates and in order to avoid the possibility of them encountering each other in corridors, directed them to three separate entrances. 'What they hadn't realized was that the three of us arranged to meet after the interviews to compare notes . . .' All three in fact reported on their interviews to Dame Leslie. Generously Mary suggests that her two rivals did not particularly want the position and that this counted in her favour. However, she did have one over-riding advantage: having spent most of the war years in the training sphere, she had not only met most of the ATS officers but knew them well. 'At that time I had a very good memory for names and faces, and they always used to come and talk to me about the courses they had been on and the work they were doing.'

Mary's appointment was announced on 14 March, by which time she had been told that her principal objective was to put forward a plan of operation to transform the ATS into a permanent force. Dame Leslie's last day in office was 3 May 1946. Next day Mary Tyrwhitt, with the equivalent rank of brigadier (during the war the rank of DATS had been equivalent to major-general but the peacetime complement of the Corps was substantially reduced and consequently the rank was lowered to brigadier), faced up to one of the most critical and demanding tasks in the eight-year history of the ATS:

> In the directorate I had three branches [AG15 – appointments of senior officers; AG19 – policy; and AG20 – training] and we all discussed what we wanted but there was a consensus that the priority was to get properly into the Army List. Until then we had a funny little book called ATS Regulations which was very good as far as it went but it wasn't regarded as authoritative by senior officers. If you quoted it, they said: 'What's that? Nothing to do with me.' That created all sorts of difficulties. We also felt that we must come under military law to enforce discipline more strictly. The worst punishment a commanding officer could give was fourteen days confined to barracks and fourteen days stoppage of pay. While the girls hated the idea of CB, the stoppage of pay did not make much difference to them because they could rely on their boyfriends to pay when they went out, so it really wasn't much of a hardship.

The question of maintaining discipline in the absence of a suitable penal code had been causing concern for a number of years. As early as 1942 the Markham Committee reported that complaints had been received from officers of the ATS and the WAAF about the inadequacy of their disciplinary powers:

> The principle of detention was pressed on us on all sides both by men and women officers who need further disciplinary powers to deal with women who prove incorrigible in the Service. The Committee are satisfied from the evidence given to them that the complaints

Mary Tyrwhitt, who succeeded Leslie Whateley as director of the ATS in 1946. She had the task of turning the ATS into a permanent peacetime force.

> under this heading are fully justified and in fairness to the officers it is necessary to deal with the difficulties so created.

The report stated that the War Office was considering methods of punishment other than detention. Generally it was felt that the relationship between the ATS officer and the women under her command was the key to the problem. Obedience was founded not on fear of punishment but on morale fostered by pure leadership, the theorists argued. The official ATS history states the case flatly:

> Although this proved to be adequate in the broader aspects of discipline for all but persistent offenders, it did little to diminish petty pilfering, which was as bad at the end of the war as it was at the beginning. Few group commanders were prepared to hand over cases to the civil police unless they were serious; civil courts were, in any case, loath to deal with them for they regarded such offences as military. Auxiliaries were therefore to all intents and purposes immune

> from punishment and there was some ill-feeling among soldiers who were awarded heavier punishment than auxiliaries in a similar position could receive.

This anomaly was even more apparent at the end of the war when the ATS followed the troops into Germany and where they formed part of the British Army of the Rhine. The absence of any power to deal with offences overseas which, in the United Kingdom, should have been handed over to the civil authorities, now created a major problem. Controller Cowper says that a number of currency offences were committed by auxiliaries and the only possible action was to return offenders to the United Kingdom, presumably far wealthier than when they had left. No wonder soldiers, who faced a court martial for similar offences, felt that the Army was applying double standards.

The subject of detention had been raised time and time again but was always dismissed because it would have entailed the establishment of a detention barracks and the provision of staff skilled in the treatment of delinquents. By 1944 three sociologists had been engaged to advise on personnel management and to provide counsel for units on particular problems. This progressive step paved the way for a more enlightened and scientific approach to woman management and laid solid foundations for the modern-day WRAC. Auxiliaries had been detained at the two Absentee Reception Centres in London and Manchester, and Cowper tells of incidents where the guards managed to prevent serious damage by spotting a fire started by one desperate auxiliary, and intervened when detainees began to cut up the bedding, rip their clothing to pieces, break gramophone records and ruin the books and games provided in the recreation rooms. A more serious incident occurred when auxiliaries removed the covers from an electric light switch so that the piquet or any member of the permanent staff would receive an electric shock when feeling for the light.

An auxiliary was well aware that she could not be placed under lock and key 'except in her own defence' and therefore reasoned that the best way of avoiding war service was to gain a reputation as a persistent defaulter. Consequently some ran away as often as they could. ATS unit commanders tried many ways of holding these delinquents, including confiscation of clothes, but the girls escaped from camps and barrack-rooms clothed only in shirts and knickers and without their shoes. 'They squeezed through lavatory windows which appeared small enough to preclude the passage of anything bigger than a cat; they scaled walls and dodged guards. Those who preferred to remain with their units where they were housed, fed and paid, were sometimes greater problems,' Cowper concedes, because of the damage they caused and their refusal to obey orders. Three recruits made history when, clad only in pyjamas, they mobbed a male regimental sergeant major on parade. This outrageous behaviour proved too much and, contrary to all orders, they were locked up. To the astonishment of everyone, the trio then went on the rampage, tearing down the walls separating the three cells in which they were confined. Cowper comments that the three partitions had proved strong enough to restrain generations of male offenders in the past. So much for the army contention at the beginning of the war that 'women were gentle creatures who did not need coercion'.

Mary Tyrwhitt established a policy committee to investigate all the matters which would have to be put before the Army Council. Painstakingly, her staff collected the evidence needed to convince the authorities that it was necessary to amend the penal code but once again opposition arose to detention for women. The Labour government of the day felt that the whole concept of detention would have political repercussions: by that time the image of the ATS was shining so brightly, due to its wartime exploits, that the public could hardly conceive of the idea that there were delinquents within its ranks, still less that they should be treated like common criminals and put behind bars. This was by far the most controversial subject which the committee was called on to tackle, but in the end a memorandum setting out the advantages and disadvantages, together with evidence collected from around the country, proved convincing and the principle of detention was reluctantly accepted and implemented. However, by 1968 detention was no longer in use although the principle is under review again.

Two other aspects of the reorganization, seemingly less important but of major consequence to the women themselves, were the ranks held by the ATS and the recognition by the male army that ATS officers should be saluted. 'The Army used to pretend they didn't know what our ranks meant and they called us "Miss" and refused to use our titles,' Mary Tyrwhitt says. 'The same applied to saluting between men and women. While we saluted them, for a long time they wouldn't accord us the same courtesy. You can't blame them, I suppose. The men were able to recognize instantly a male officer as either a lieutenant, captain, major or whatever, but the sound of junior commander, senior commander, even chief controller, was strange to the rank and file.'

Mary was adamant that her officers should have the same ranks as the men. Such matters were routinely discussed with her opposite numbers in the WAAF, the WRNS and the Queen Alexandra's Imperial Military Nursing Service, and her temerity in demanding rank parity was questioned. She remembers especially the director of the WAAF, Air Commandant Felicity Hanbury, exclaiming: 'You must be mad. They'll never do it!' Mary told her: 'It matters very much and I am going to go ahead bald-headed for it. I think we may get it.'

The WRAF (the name Women's Royal Air Force, used in the First World War, was re-adopted on 1 February 1949) had to wait until 1968 before achieving rank parity and the WRNS have still not achieved it, but Mary's stubbornness was rewarded in 1949 when the WRAC was brought formally into existence.

In March that year she was invited to an interview with the Chief of the Imperial General Staff, Field Marshal Viscount Slim, who had succeeded Lord Montgomery in 1948. Slim had commanded the 14th Army in Burma, 'the Forgotten Army' as it was called, and had gained enormous popularity when he succeeded in pushing the Japanese out of the country, taking Mandalay in late March 1945 and reaching the capital, Rangoon, on 3 May.

> He was my pin-up soldier of the war [Mary admits] but, more important, he was a man you could talk to. As I sat in his office he had my memorandum on the ranks and saluting before him. He said that he wanted me to put my case again. 'I know it's been made hundreds of times but I'd like you to present it once more.' I stated it as best I could and he listened patiently. At the end he paused and then said: 'I approve.' And that was the end of that.

One is left to wonder whether Monty, with his more rigid attitude to army tradition and his domineering personality, would have conceded the point quite so readily.

With the principle of a permanent women's army approved in November 1946, one of the more pleasant decisions which had to be taken concerned the uniform the future Corps would wear. Here there was no lack of co-operation from the men. To Mary's consternation

> All the chaps threw themselves into it heart and soul. They would have liked to choose it, you know, and that would have been absolutely terrible. I'm not anti-man but at the same time the design of the uniform needed a more professional approach. We had meetings with the other services – the WRNS and the WAAF were also to be an established part of the armed services – and the nurses, so that we could keep in step with each other. I decided in my own mind that, provided I had the necessary finance, our uniforms would be designed by really first-class designers.

Her main adversary was the Board of Trade. Its responsibility for such matters was entrenched in army regulations and it insisted it had excellent designers who were particularly anxious to undertake the task. One can imagine the enthusiasm at the prospect of tackling such a new concept as producing a uniform for women, as opposed to the rather humdrum tasks which normally occupied the board's time. At a meeting which included the matron-in-chief of the QAIMNS, the Board of Trade officials put their case. Mary was ready for them, having prepared her strategy in advance. She countered with the suggestion that if the Board of Trade designers were so good, surely they would not object to some competition. 'I told them that if I were given permission to interest civilian designers in the project, we could see prototypes of all the designs and decide which was best.' The board could hardly refuse this challenge to its expertise and Mary won her argument.

The designs were paraded at a fashion show coinciding with a conference attended by the QAIMNS who were also seeking a new uniform and a change in name. Norman Hartnell's lovat green uniform won unanimous acclaim and was formally adopted, after the King and Queen had been given a preview. Over the next few years khaki, worn since the WAAC had been formed in 1917, was gradually phased out and by 1963 the WRAC had totally discarded it. Hartnell's original design was reviewed constantly to keep it in

A WRAC recruit fitted with her uniform

tune with changing fashions: the classic suit comprised a single-breasted jacket with cut-away fronts, neat epaulettes and flat, slit hip pockets. The buttons carried the monogram of the Princess Royal, who during her lifetime associated herself so closely with the Corps. A slim skirt, a white shirt and collar, and bottle-green tie completed the outfit. One of the Savile Row tailors appointed by the Army to produce the uniform was Bernard Weatherill, the present Speaker of the House of Commons. The hat was designed by Aage Thaarup, and the King, whose personal interest in the ATS headgear extended as far back as 1943 when Leslie Whateley had been called to Buckingham Palace to display it, approved the new version which was becomingly high-crowned, with a patent leather peak. Mary Tyrwhitt recalls that when she went to receive her DBE in 1949 the King asked: 'Have you got your cap all right yet?'

The WRAC No. 1 dress, also designed by Hartnell for formal occasions, consisted of a lichen-green poplin shirt and collar, with a bottle-green woven tie, a skirt and jacket of bottle-green serge, bottle-green knitted gloves with satchel in matching leather and nylon stockings in 'Silhouette' shade. Black leather gloves were worn by officers. The WRAC uniform of today has more than 80 items and includes a green Melton greatcoat and a dark green shoulder bag; for tropical wear, servicewomen wear a lightweight beige linen dress. Mess dress was described by E. Ewing, in her book *Women in Uniform through the Centuries*, as the ultimate in the apotheosis of uniform into contemporary fashion, a bold step forward in a trend which has been growing steadily. Designed by Owen Hyde-Clark, formerly of Worth, it is a slim cream and gold brocade Empire gown, with small sleeves, square neck and a fish-tail pleat at the floor-length hem; a long green silk sash, fastened to the shoulder by a single rank-marked epaulette, falls to the ground, ending in a gold fringe. Ewing comments: 'It is also that most rare and enviable of feminine fashions – a couture creation at less than half couture prices, made by Hilliers Couture.' All the WRAC uniform is planned to be fashionable, smartly cut yet efficient and military in style.

The most contentious debate during the establishment of the new Corps concerned the name, which was to be honoured with the title Royal. One of the first suggestions, the Royal Army Territorial Service, was rejected immediately because of the unfortunate acronym. In fact, acronyms were a constant bugbear since no one in the Corps wished to be saddled with a nickname derived from the initial letters of its title, for which reason Royal Army Women's Corps was also dismissed. The name had to be acceptable to the Army Council and ultimately had to be approved by the King. Mary and her senior officers discussed all the possibilities and when they finally settled on what they thought a suitable name it was put first to the Princess Royal who had the ear of her brother. In this way the name evolved: the Women's Royal Army Corps. Nevertheless there is still a tendency to call the women of the WRAC 'Racks', something which is firmly discouraged and frowned on.

When the debate ended on 5 February 1948 the then Secretary of State, Emmanuel Shinwell, made a formal submission to the Crown for permission to raise a corps of women for the Regular Army and the Territorial Army. The WRAC, according to its charter, was 'to provide replacements for officers and men in such employment as may be specified by the Army Council from time to time'. The legislation which brought it into existence also included a charter for the present-day WRAF and the Queen Alexandra's Royal Army Nursing Corps. The Royal Navy, as always, elected to act independently and the WRNS had separate legislation. For the WRAC, the Queen assented to the appointment commandant-in-chief, actually colonel-in-chief, a role which she has retained as Queen Mother. The Princess Royal, of course, continued as controller commandant, and after her death the Duchess of Kent succeeded her in this position.

And so on 31 January 1949, the proud ATS ceased to exist, its end understandably accompanied by a feeling of sadness among the more than 200,000 women who had served in its ranks during the previous ten-and-a-half years. It had graduated from the sheer amateurism of the early war years into an efficient, indispensable part of the services, a regiment which had built its own traditions and had secured a permanent place in military history. Next day its members exchanged their ATS badges and buttons for the gleaming new WRAC symbol of a laurel wreath surmounted by a crown; within the wreath a lioness rampant. The corps motto, *Sauviter in modo, fortiter in re* – Gentle in manner, resolute in deed – retains a vital, womanly element and yet emphasizes an inflexible devotion to duty.

11
AN ARMY CAREER

For thousands of women the formation of the WRAC was a watershed in their lives, forcing them to reconsider their future. Many realized that the Army offered them a varied career with the opportunity to gain experience in management and in carrying considerable responsibilities which they might never encounter in civilian life, where many women had to be content with jobs as typists or clerks and where executive positions invariably went to men. Besides, Britain still had an empire and there was always the chance of a posting overseas. At home and abroad the opportunities were there to be grasped.

In 1949 Major Lucy Anwyl-Passingham had just returned from three and a half years in Egypt, where she had commanded the first unit of 100 servicewomen to be drafted abroad. Originally the ATS had posted overseas only those who volunteered, and Lucy remembers the near-mutiny of the girls in 1945 when they found themselves on a train to Glasgow where a ship was waiting to transport them to Suez:

> At Preston all the girls got out on to the platform and I had to listen to their complaints. Mostly they were concerned about what their parents would say. I managed to pacify them and when we arrived at Glasgow we discovered that the Airborne Regiment was sailing with us. From that moment I had no more trouble with the girls.

Lucy's experiences in the Middle East were hardly typical of service life for women since they were usually stationed in areas far removed from trouble spots, but they aptly illustrate the hiccups which could, and did, happen. In September 1945, while commanding a Palestinian ATS company just outside Cairo, she received orders to report to a transit camp for demobilization. 'I rang the adjutant in Cairo [Junior Commander Betty Busby] and asked what I should do. "Send your release book back and just go on serving," she said. And so I did. I certainly wouldn't have continued in the Army if I had been home in the UK but in Egypt I was having a much better time than I imagined others were.' The following year she was caught up in a violent demonstration by Egyptian students and political activists in Alexandria.

The army police post near the barracks was surrounded by a rioting mob who hacked two policemen to death and severely wounded three others. The angry mob then advanced on the barracks and for seven days Lucy and 30 male officers barricaded themselves in their offices, living under siege conditions until the riot was quelled. When she returned to England and the newly formed WRAC, Lucy learned that in order to remain an officer she would have to attend the Regular Commissions Board then based at Fernhurst in West Sussex:

> I realized that I had quite a worthwhile career ahead of me in the Army. The prospects of further promotion in the WRAC appeared to be very good. Nevertheless it was a difficult decision because I was then thinking of marrying a Royal Army Medical Corps officer I had met in Egypt and, besides that, my parents lived in Ascot and I was keen to return home. Mary Colvin, who was my commandant and who went on to become director of the WRAC, persuaded me to continue and eventually I went to the RCB.

In 1946 the Leicester training school was closed and moved to Guildford (which became the new headquarters of the ATS and later of the WRAC) and Captain Eileen Nolan went with it, serving under Betty Vetch who shortly afterwards resigned her commission in order to resume her peacetime career in Edinburgh as a kindergarten teacher. Eileen stayed at Guildford until 1948 when she was posted to B Company 12 Battalion in Prince's Gate, Kensington, one of the largest companies in the service at the time. The 300 women under her command worked mainly in the War Office, then in Hobart House, as clerks and secretaries but some were ambulance drivers at Millbank Hospital. The women lived in nineteen requisitioned houses in the area of Sloane Square and Sloane Court Gardens. Having been in training units for most of her army career, this was a totally new experience for her, as was living and working in a revitalized London, beginning to regain its bustling pre-war reputation. One unexpected assignment was being selected to command the contingent taking part in the Remembrance Day service in Whitehall:

> Both the years I attended it was extremely cold and, as everyone knows, the service lasts for several hours and the atmosphere is highly charged. My contingent consisted of twelve women who were standing behind me. The first year people were fainting in front of me and I became anxious about the girls drawn up behind. I could hear movements in the crowd at the back but I couldn't turn round to see if any of my troops had toppled over after standing for so long. I had

> to go through the entire service in a constant state of apprehension and not until we received the order to march off could I turn round and make sure that all twelve were still on their feet.

For two consecutive years she also commanded the contingent taking part in the Festival of Remembrance at the Albert Hall:

> People who see the ceremony on television may not realize the difficulties involved. The steps in the Albert Hall are very shallow and it is enormously hard to maintain the rhythm of marching. If anyone gets a tiny bit off beat, they instantly lose their step and when they reach floor level they must adjust very quickly. Nowadays, when I watch, I am still willing them to get it right.

In 1949 Eileen had been delighted to welcome to her company a young lieutenant, Audrey Williamson, who had originally been a physical training instructor in the ATS and had been selected to represent Great Britain in the 200 metres at the 1948 London Olympic Games. Then she was very much an unknown quantity and very few athletics commentators expected her to win a medal in an event being run by women for the first time at any Olympics. To everyone's surprise Audrey reached the finals and when she lined up at the start almost the entire ATS in Britain held their breaths for the twenty-odd seconds of the race. That was the year Fanny Blankers-Koen of the Netherlands swept all before her, but at the tape, to the delight of the crowd, Audrey Williamson inched past the American finalist, Audrey Patterson, to win a silver medal for Britain. Fanny had clocked 24.4 seconds, Audrey Williamson 25.1 and Audrey Patterson 25.2.

'When I heard that Audrey had been posted to our company I knew that sport in our unit would certainly improve. I reasoned that my company would be able to win everything in the inter-battalion sports and of course we did, with Audrey always in the forefront.'

But that year, like Lucy, Eileen and Audrey had to undergo the gruelling tests of the RCB if they wished to stay on in the WRAC. Once again Eileen had to take stock of her situation. 'I think today we talk much about career women but in 1949 I doubt whether the expression was even known. I was 28, I wasn't married, and I thought I would lose very little by going to the RCB and gain an awful lot if I was successful.'

Looking back on the two days she spent at Fernhurst, Eileen recalls that the experience was very similar to the War Office selection board she had attended at Hampstead in 1944 before going to OCTU, the main difference being that the girls now underwent a modified physical programme to test their initiative and leadership qualities in outdoor exercises. This marked the start of the highly sophisticated course later developed at Leighton House which all would-be WRAC officers now attend.

> Perhaps my lasting memory of Fernhurst is the dividers in the rooms where we slept. They had used hessian to give each of us some privacy and whenever I think of that RCB, it is the overpowering smell of hessian that comes to mind . . . Within a few days of completing the course I was told that I had passed the board and had been offered a regular commission. That, really, was the moment of decision for me and I knew that I wanted to stay in the WRAC.

In 1949 Dorothy Humphery was one of three senior WRAC officers on the RCB and she recalls how she and her two colleagues, Jean Rivett-Drake and Molly Railton, both of whom became directors, agonized over whether or not the candidates should be offered regular commissions:

> You bent over backwards to be absolutely fair. An awful lot depended on the age group and one knew all these officers personally. They had all done a wonderful job in the war and it was extremely embarrassing to adjudicate on their suitability to go on serving. Thank goodness there were male officers on the board who didn't know any of them. They helped us to relax and also demonstrated to the candidates that they would be judged by independent examiners.

Dorothy vividly recalls her battles during this period with obstinate Guards officers who refused to welcome women into their mess. 'I used to sit somewhere near the door and after the first port had gone round, I'd slip out quietly. After one such occasion, a very senior visiting general called on me the next morning: "Humphery, I notice you came out of dinner before we did." I told him I always did and why. "Well, you won't do that again when I'm here."'

In later years, when commandant of the WRAC officers' training college at Camberley, she was able to chuckle at the irony of the situation when a group of her officer cadets visited the command headquarters at Salisbury, where they lunched in the officers' mess. 'Afterwards I asked for their impressions. One of them told me: "I was surprised not one of the men stood up when we came in." Well, I mean, senior officers standing up when a little thing comes in with a white cap! That was a very good lesson for the young girls to learn. They couldn't be part of the show if they expected all the men to get up and offer them the best chairs.' Echoes of Helen Gwynne-Vaughan.

Dorothy also had her share of travel abroad. She had been one of three ATS officers to attend the US Army Staff College at Fort Leavenworth, Kansas, crossing the Atlantic on the *Queen Mary* in August 1944 with Pamela

Wilson and Barbara Davey, who had enrolled in the ATS from Cape Town in South Africa. They were amused to be called 'sir' by a bewildered New York taxi driver who was thoroughly confused by the sight of women officers in uniform. Later she commanded the WRAC contingent in Singapore during the emergency which began in 1948 and remembers escorting the director, Frances Coulshed, who succeeded Mary Tyrwhitt in 1950, round the British Colony. 'If we went outside Singapore itself we always had a Gurkha guard and a driver. On one occasion Dame Frances and I strayed off the safe route on to the red route. When we arrived, the garrison almost had a fit.' It was a period of particular tension after Sir Henry Gurney, the High Commissioner, had been assassinated so two senior women army officers driving through an area where there was guerrilla activity caused something of a stir.

Also serving in Singapore at the time was Sergeant Elaine Anton who says that nowhere in the country was safe: travellers risked ambush on the winding roads and trains were targets for derailments. Elaine returned to Singapore in 1959 as a warrant officer and in 1965 was posted back to Malaya as administration officer Cameron Highlands garrison with the rank of captain. The garrison consisted of a military hospital, a Change of Air Station (holiday centre) and two training camps. Not long after she arrived, Lieutenant-Colonel Charles Dobson became ill and after his evacuation, Elaine was appointed garrison commander with the rank of acting major for about sixteen months.

Few women had had the chance to travel abroad and the Army offered many their first experience of living in a foreign country. One person who will never forget her posting abroad is Irene Ludlow. She had served in several British messes but in 1947 she heard the exciting news that she was posted to Austria. 'That was a wonderful experience – beautiful! I really *lived* in Austria,' Irene recalls. Almost every event was a new adventure for this country girl who admits had it not been for the Army she might never have crossed the Channel or even ventured beyond the county boundary of Wiltshire.

She was sent to Klagenfurt to work in the garrison dining-room and at weekends she and her friends travelled to Vienna, which was still a divided city, territory of *The Third Man*. One day they lost their way and strayed into the Russian zone. The Cold War was at its height, following the breakdown of the four-power conference on Germany in December 1947 and the Berlin Airlift, when the American, British and French zones were supplied by air during the Russian blockade.

> Heavens, were we scared! We kept walking and all we could see were these Russian soldiers pointing guns and chasing after us. We were in a state of near-panic until, to our intense relief, we spotted an American GI and rushed over to him. He grabbed us and pulled

> us over into the American zone before the Russians arrived. That was the scariest adventure I ever had.

The following year Irene stood in an office in Klagenfurt taking the oath to serve King and Country in the newly formed WRAC, and in 1950 returned to Guildford where she began her career as a batwoman, cleaning officers' buttons and shoes, tidying up the officers' mess and generally 'looking after them to make sure they looked smart and were comfortable'. Seven years later she went to Cyprus to bat for Colonel Lucy Davies (née Anwyl-Passingham) and then began a remarkable sequence of caring for the needs of six successive directors of the WRAC. The first was Mary Colvin, whom she describes as 'a very horsy lady. Every weekend she used to say: "Corporal Ludlow, I've had a nasty bump again. The horse stopped and I kept on going!"'

Irene had reluctantly accepted a 'stripe' after first refusing it because 'I'd rather have my friends and belong to the junior rank. You lose some of that friendship when you have a stripe on your arm.' Corporal Ludlow gained another distinction. Her greatest love in the Army was marching and her tall figure was a familiar sight at most WRAC ceremonial occasions. 'They used to ask for volunteers and the RSM would say: "I've got your name, Corporal Ludlow. No need to volunteer."' She took part in 21 Remembrance Day services in the Albert Hall, a record unlikely to be surpassed.

At home in London Eileen Nolan was saying her farewells to countless officer friends embarking for overseas postings and hoping that she might be the next. In the meantime she was kept busy organizing the transfer of her scattered unit from Sloane territory to a hutted camp in Richmond Park. It was mid-winter and she had pored over huge charts, showing the destination of furniture, of workers and of their possessions. The idea was that the 300 girls would go to their offices as usual in the morning and that evening be driven in hired coaches to their new accommodation where all their belongings would be waiting for them.

> It was an absolute pantomime. At one time the whole of Sloane Court was crammed solid with green steel lockers. Pedestrians complained that they couldn't get by and one lady telephoned to say that she was terribly sorry but all the ornaments on her mantlepiece were jumping up and down because of the thuds from the boots of soldiers who had been called in to make the move.

But the worst part of the day was yet to come. A party of 40 girls from Claims Commission in Piccadilly went missing, and Eileen spent hours on the telephone trying to find out what had happened. Yes, they had duly been

One of the last parades inspected by Dame Helen Gwynne-Vaughan, who is talking to Major Marjorie (Tootsie) Yeates. Lt-Col Mildred Millington can be seen between them. Standing tall on the right is Irene Ludlow who enjoyed marching and always volunteered for parades. *c.* 1951. *Below* Out of step! One of the most embarrassing moments for Captain Eileen Nolan was seeing this picture in a newspaper in 1951.

collected by the coach. Yes, they had left their offices on time. Nevertheless they had not been heard of since, having apparently vanished into the murky grey of a London winter. By 8.30 p.m. the situation looked serious but then, to the enormous relief of the guards posted at the gates, a procession of bedraggled and weary girls was seen approaching the camp. Their coach driver had deposited them at the gates on the opposite side of Richmond Park in the mistaken belief that the camp site was only a few yards inside the fence. By the time the error was discovered, the park gates had been locked behind them and the girls set out to walk, with no lights to guide them and deer wandering at random in the darkness. Dressed in office frocks and unsuitable shoes, the group was led by the intrepid Sergeant Docherty, who ordered them to scale fences and stumble across soaking fields until the distant lights of the camp loomed ahead. It proved an exhausting, four-mile hike, the equivalent of an ill-equipped route march through open countryside in pitch black.

Eileen's most embarrassing moment came during an army parade in London in 1951. She had been detailed to lead the WRAC contingent of 100 girls drawn from all four London companies.

> We marched in threes, which was not at all easy because the unit proved unwieldy. I was marching at the head, with a warrant officer who was marker, behind the Sandhurst contingent. It was a long, three-mile march which at the end stretched up The Mall to Buckingham Palace and round into Bird Cage Walk. We were all pretty tired by that time and a daily newspaper took a photograph which was splashed across the entire centre-page spread. It showed me, the officer, in one step and the 100 behind me in the other! I still have the newspaper cutting as a reminder. I'm afraid I was teased unmercifully, especially by my father.

Shortly afterwards and entirely unrelated, Eileen's dream of an overseas posting came true; at the end of March 1952 she embarked from Liverpool on the *Empire Test*, bound for Kingston, Jamaica. The ship was carrying about 450 personnel, among them reinforcements for the Royal Welch Fusiliers accompanied by their mascot, Billy the Goat. Unfortunately the passenger list described Eileen simply as Captain E. J. Nolan. 'You're a woman!' one of the movement officers exclaimed when she reported to him. 'Crikey, we've got you berthed in a cabin with five male captains!' Eileen was moved to another cabin which she shared with two army wives.

Standing on the deck of the *Empire Test* as it steamed away from home waters, she had very mixed feelings about travelling 4,000 miles to take command of a company of locally enlisted women. Although naturally excited at the prospect of going abroad for the first time, she faced a daunting task, for there would be no woman more senior than her to whom she could refer. Decisions would have to be made in isolation. It would be the first real test of her leadership and management qualities. After settling into her quarters at the officers' mess of the QARANC in Kingston, she was introduced to her company. Among them was Corporal Small, tall and absolutely immaculate in her uniform, who in 1953 would receive the BEM on Eileen's recommendation in the Coronation honours and had the distinction of being presented with the medal by the Queen herself during the Royal visit to Jamaica in November that year.

At the Queen's Birthday Parade in 1953 Eileen and her staff sergeant were on parade as keepers of the ground, positioned on each side of the saluting base. That year the Jamaica Regiment was trooping the colour and as one of the officers passed Eileen, he leaned towards her and whispered: 'Pardon me, ma'am, did you know your slip is showing?' For a WRAC officer on parade, or anywhere else for that matter, it was almost the equivalent of a Guards officer with a strategic button undone.

> I was in absolute despair. Here was I on the parade ground in my uniform, not daring to look down and wondering if it could be possible that my slip *was* showing. This made it an extremely difficult parade and I felt exceptionally uncomfortable throughout. After we had marched off the square, my staff sergeant came to me and gasped: 'I have had the most terrible time, ma'am. As one of the officers passed me, he said: "Pardon me, staff sergeant, do you know your slip is showing?"' So we had both stood with our hands firmly pressed against our skirts, terrified that our petticoats would come down at any moment. I can tell you we made that officer suffer when we met him later!

Eileen quickly discovered that the Jamaican girls were expert needlewomen, a skill which came in handy after she attended her first big function at King's House, the official residence of the governor, Sir Hugh Foot. It was a reception for the Queen's Birthday and she was driven to King's House by her escort, a male army officer, in an MG well past its prime. As the sole WRAC officer on the island Eileen was representing not only her company but the entire Corps and she was determined not to let the side down: she chose a long, pale lavender evening dress, worn for the first time. At the end of the evening she discovered, to her dismay, that a long line of oil had seeped from the MG on to her beautiful dress. 'You can imagine my horror, believing then that it was totally ruined. But the women of the company reassured me. "Oh, ma'am, don't worry, we'll put it right." They cut out a panel of material and patched it so exquisitely that no one was able to see the meticulous repair work.' The following year her Jamaica company virtually scooped the prizes in a worldwide WRAC handicraft competition in London, winning three firsts, two seconds and two thirds in the categories in which their work was entered. Eileen found numerous opportunities to exercise her own talent for amateur dramatics. She produced *Lady Windermere's Fan*, and in the cast was a young lieutenant from the RWF, William Roache, who later became well-known to television viewers as Ken Barlow in *Coronation Street*.

One of the great tragedies of the Army in peacetime occurred during her stay in Jamaica. A York aircraft, carrying families of the regiment and including about twenty children, was lost after refuelling at Reykjavik in Iceland on its way to Kingston. Eileen heard the news as she prepared to go to the airport to meet a replacement WRAC warrant officer aboard the plane. 'You can imagine what a ghastly time it was for everyone – husbands who were devastated by the news of wives and children lost. And the frightful part of it was that nothing more was ever heard about the aircraft – no one ever knew exactly what happened.'

Eileen sailed home in March 1954 aboard the *Empire Clyde* to attend the WRAC Staff College near Camberley in Surrey with other officers from the United Kingdom and an Australian, Dawn Jackson, who eventually became director of the Women's Royal Australian Army Corps. Eileen's next posting was as a staff captain Q (Quartering Branch) at the War Office, where she was responsible for moving freight to and from the Middle East. At the time of the Suez crisis she worked round the clock in the operations room, constantly in touch with the Great Western or London Midland, requisitioning trains for troop transportation.

In 1957 she was promoted major and posted to Chester. The following year she flew to Tripoli in Libya, to take command of the 90-strong WRAC unit there and to do a staff job at the British Army headquarters. The first lessons to be learned in Libya were the strict Muslim rules regarding the behaviour of women in public. The Islamic code posed enormous problems for WRAC servicewomen, who were surrounded by potential escorts, not only in the British garrison but also at the United States Wheelus Air Force base.

> As you can imagine, there was no lack of boyfriends for the girls and so the rules had to be explained carefully to them. They were not allowed to show any form of affection in public. This meant no holding hands, or walking arm in arm, or kissing or even flirting in the mildest possible way. It was tough on the girls but vital that they observed the local customs.

Many of the girls were still teenagers and although intially all were thrilled to be posted overseas, they often found that conditions were very different from what they had expected, and they became bored and disillusioned. The heat was intense and if the girls did not enjoy swimming or sunbathing, they had to be encouraged to occupy their spare time in other ways. Tours were organized to the ruins of Roman cities and educational functions were arranged in an attempt to stimulate interest. Shopping in Tripoli was confined to two streets which had no big department stores, and if the girls went to the Arab *souk* they had to be escorted by soldiers. Under these conditions homesickness was rife and it fell to Eileen to console girls who missed their families and longed for the freedom of life back home.

Inevitably there were numerous romances. If under 21, the girls had to seek permission from their families to marry; frequently Eileen had to write to parents, informing them of their daughter's decision and formally requesting their approval. In most instances there were no objections but occasionally permission was withheld and this caused considerable distress. Parents in any case very seldom managed to attend the ceremonies in the garrison church, so Eileen frequently played the role of mother-of-the-bride with a senior male staff officer to give the bride away. If the husband was a member of the British Army Eileen's responsibilities did not end at the church door: her staff job included quartering, which involved renting accommodation for families and married couples. Here again she clashed with Muslim tradition – Libyan property owners were not accustomed to dealing with women who had this kind of authority, and negotiations were conducted reluctantly.

> They wouldn't say anything, but from their expressions I knew that they were finding it difficult to accept. This job made me very popular in some quarters and exceptionally unpopular in others, depending on whether the wives were allocated the houses they especially wanted in the area they themselves would have chosen. We tried to follow the rules absolutely fairly and used a points system, based on the size of the family, the ages of the children and whether they had been without a quarter at home.

It proved to be a lesson in diplomacy and a supreme test of her resourcefulness but she quickly developed a flair for soothing the ruffled feathers of indignant Libyans and disgruntled Britons.

Eileen returned home in April 1960 and was posted to York where she served in the recruiting and liaison department. Then, in 1963, she moved to the WRAC postings branch at Stanmore under the command of Colonel Joanna Henderson, another who later became director. During this period the WRAC was refining its system of planning long-term career paths for women. Eileen's task was to plot the postings of officers, sending them on specialized courses to qualify them for work in specific areas such as signals or ordnance, and generally ensuring that they were equipped for a wide variety of jobs in the Army. Here she came up against the enormous conflict which every member of the WRAC faced when she decided to marry. In those days most women took it for granted that if they married they left the service.

> It was a constant nightmare for us. Posting plots can be ruined in this way because you would set up a chain of about five people to take over from each other. Then, suddenly, you received a message to say that Captain X had just announced her engagement and would soon be getting married. It meant starting again from square one.

At that time the WRAC was pressing for wider acceptance in the Army and suggesting new areas in which the girls could be employed. National Service was ended and defence budgets were being cut back and gradually the Corps had dwindled in numbers as the overall peacetime army strength was reduced until it reached a strength of approximately 5,000. Ironically, with the number of men drastically reduced, new opportunities were opened up for women.

Joanna Henderson envisaged that eventually WRAC officers and other ranks would find a permanent place in signals or other army corps and would remain there until retirement instead of returning roughly every three years to the WRAC stream and new postings. But here again marriage clashed with military priorities and there were instances where it was obvious that the Army was discriminating against women. Sending a soldier on a specialized course is an enormous investment and senior male officers often excluded women on the grounds that should they marry in the near future the money might be wasted. In an era of tight budgets this was perhaps excusable but it penalized career women who were justified in complaining to headquarters that they were being overlooked.

Nevertheless two notable breakthroughs occurred which offered hope that perhaps higher military echelons and masculinity were not as inseparable as some had imagined. In the early 'sixties the RAOC promoted R. M. (Billie) Hill to full colonel to fill one of their own vacancies and in 1969 the Royal Army Educational Corps promoted Jill Hands to lieutenant-colonel. These were the first senior promotions of women beyond the limited confines of the WRAC itself and they demonstrated that at last women were becoming more acceptable to the Army as a whole. In 1963 another milestone in the WRAC was reached when the first two women nominated for the Army Staff College at Camberley wrote the examination and passed the required level.

It was a triumph for the WRAC as a whole because the women had started the course with the handicap of not having had training in military tactics and fieldcraft, and therefore they had had to study independently the basics which every male officer had learned at Sandhurst.

Perhaps it was her awareness of this gap in the WRAC officers' experience which caused Eileen to take a long, serious look at the existing courses when, in 1965, she was assigned to command the WRAC officer training wing at Camberley which had been moved from Hindhead two years before. She took over from Major Bridget Forbes Adam, whose father had been the wartime adjutant-general, Sir Ronald Adam. Colonel Humphery was the college commandant.

One of the advantages of the new location was its proximity to Sandhurst; the officer cadets were already attending all the main lectures at the Royal Military Academy, although they did their training separately. The outdoor exercises of the officer cadets were still very restricted and almost immediately Eileen sought permission to devise a scheme which would allow the cadets to live under canvas for a weekend from Friday night to Monday morning. Colonel Humphery readily agreed and they chose a camp site in Tweesledown, near Aldershot, on the edge of the racecourse.

Inevitably news of the girls' first venture under canvas leaked out and on the first Friday night Eileen received a telephone call reporting that the camp had been raided, presumably by Sandhurst cadets, but that fortunately little damage had been done. Next day Eileen arrived with a group of senior WRAC officers to observe the exercises:

> When you are outside with cadets under such conditions, you see a totally different side of their characters. Youngsters who have tended to remain in the background during lectures suddenly come into their own and those you imagined would turn out to be *the* leaders retreat into the background.

That night, after campfire, Eileen retired to her tent and tucked herself into a sleeping-bag. Half-an-hour later the tent collapsed around her. As she struggled to extricate herself she heard cries and screams as tents came down all round the camp. She had been half-expecting another incident and had not undressed, so was able to run immediately to her car and turn on the lights, revealing a group of young men disappearing into the bushes. Bent on revenge, the girls took after them and managed to apprehend several of the culprits. They were from the Mons cadet wing, near Aldershot, where short service commission officers were trained.

> I remember well taking one of them back to Mons in my car and he was sitting in the back seat, quite obviously upset about being caught.

> When we arrived at Mons a startled guard sergeant confronted me at the gate. After I had explained the circumstances, the sergeant peered into the car and said: 'Into the guardroom, *sir*!'

The incident was generously treated as a little bit of fun by both WRAC and Mons, and when the brigadier wrote to Eileen to apologize for the incident he explained that he had given every miscreant a good talking to. 'However, I did also tell them that if it ever happened again, as efficient officers they should ensure that they were not caught.'

Part of the course at Camberley consisted of an afternoon with a beauty counsellor.

> I realize this may sound strange [Eileen says] but obviously it is important for the girls to retain their femininity and so we arranged for them to be taught make-up and coiffure. There was also one session of flower-arranging, which might surprise many people. I always believed that this was necessary because in any officers' mess it will always be the female officers who are asked to arrange the flowers for big functions. Wherever I was, I always took great pride in doing the flowers in the mess, but naturally some women disagree.

Two women who did disagree were the first American exchange officers. They were so disgusted at attending a lecture on flower-arranging that they stood up at a WRAC conference and said so, feeling it was beneath the dignity of an army officer to receive instruction on this task. Captain Barbara Kent of the US Army was even more strident in her condemnation: 'If they tried to do that in America, the girls would throw up.'

Coming from an American servicewoman it was perhaps a rather strange remark, considering the situation that had existed across the Atlantic less than ten years before. The Marine Corps demanded that its women marines 'be the most *attractive* and useful women in the four line services'. Naturally this had led to inter-service rivalry and the US Air Force chief of staff ordered the commander of the recruiting services to get 'better looking WAF'. Major-General Jeanne Holm, a former director of Women in the Air Force, says that physical appearance became the chief criterion in the selection process: each applicant was required to pose for four photographs – front, side, back and full-face. Civil rights leaders assumed the photograph's purpose was to determine race, but this was not the case.

The Women's Army Corps also joined in 'the beauty contest' and servicewomen's indoctrination courses more closely resembled ladies' finishing schools than military programmes. From then on, courses were heavily sprinkled with lectures on feminine appearance and bearing. 'Even

Private Carol Edwards, a courier and postal operator, at work in the British Forces Post Office in Aden.

in the combat zone [in Vietnam]', General Holm tells us, 'where they were regularly diving for shelter in bunkers, the women were expected to uphold the image.' So meticulous were the Marines that they required their women marines to wear lipstick and nail varnish to match the braid on their uniform hats – Marine Corps scarlet. According to General Holm, skirt lengths were the grounds of constant skirmishes as the young women attempted to follow the extremes of civilian fashion: when hem lines were rising, women rolled up their skirts at the waist when their female commander was out of sight. It went without saying that all the services selected the most attractive women as receptionists and secretaries. 'More than one attractive technically trained enlisted woman found herself decorating the outer office of a general or admiral with nothing more challenging to do than to look pretty, answer the telephone, and be pleasant to visitors.'

In 1967 Eileen was promoted to lieutenant-colonel and after six months in Scotland she left for Singapore, arriving there in May 1968. Her main command in Singapore comprised about 150 WRAC servicewomen working in almost every branch of the Army, but it also extended to Malaysia,

WRAC girls attached to the Royal Signals, Hong Kong, work with Chinese civilian girls in an army telephone exchange.

Saigon, Bangkok, and Hong Kong, where small detachments of women were stationed. During her tour Eileen visited all the areas under her command. Her arrival in Saigon coincided with the second Tet offensive by the Viet Cong. Three WRAC sergeants were working for the military attaché at the British Embassy in Saigon and although an effort was made to dissuade her from going, Eileen insisted on visiting them. Despite the tense situation she remembers attending an evening of Scottish dancing at the British Embassy, but her greatest impression was seeing the wives of British Embassy staff making clothes for Vietnamese orphans.

The WRAC has seen service in many parts of the world and has gone out of its way to assist countries who wished to form their own women's service. In 1964 Major Daphne Clark was selected to go to Ghana with a warrant officer, Sheila Wolstenholme, to join the British Joint Service Training Team in Accra and to advise President Kwame Nkrumah on the enlistment of women into his army.

My manifold duties were to include setting up recruitment and

> selection procedures and to organize basic and future trade training. However, while brushing up on procedure at the WRAC records branch at Winchester on 24 February 1965, someone rushed in with the evening newspaper. I was astounded to read that President Nkrumah, then on a visit to Peking, had been deposed by a group of army officers who had staged a coup. You can imagine the confusion. No one in London seemed to know what the position was – neither the Ministry of Defence nor the Foreign and Commonwealth Office could give us a definite answer to the question of whether or not I should go. Then one day, out of the blue, I found a packet of papers on my desk containing a ticket for a slow boat to Accra. It had come to me direct from Ghana and the consensus was that I should set off on my tour which was to last eighteen months.

Major Clark sailed on the Elder Dempster line vessel *Aureole* and was met at Accra by Major Patricia Norman, whom she was replacing and who was due to leave within two days.

> The next two days were a blur of activity in a hellish heat and really there was very little time to talk and to catch up on the situation. The confusion in London was nothing compared with the muddle which reigned in Ghana. At a farewell lunch for a Ghanaian officer leaving for somewhere in the Far East shortly after my arrival, I met many important people and the other officers of the BJSTT. The person I remember most was a large Ghanaian matriarch, swathed in her colourful robes, who chatted happily until she suddenly asked if I had any children. I told her I had none. She gave me a hard and disdainful smile and said: 'Woman no piccins, no good.'

Worse was to follow. Within days Daphne Clark was politely but firmly told by a Ghanaian army staff officer to go home because there had been a bad blunder, but officials at the British High Commission and Brigadier Angus Irwin commanding the BJSTT intervened on her behalf. She was permitted to stay, with her tour of eighteen months cut to seven, but Warrant Officer Wolstenholme was sent home. However, the chaos which existed in Ghana in any case prevented Daphne from performing the task which she had been sent to do. Brigadier Irwin tried unsuccessfully to obtain a decision from the new military authorities about the position of the small corps which had been set up under Nkrumah's régime.

> I faced the prospect of having no real job to do. The Ghanaian commander of the Women's Army Corps, Major Christine Debrah, had been stripped of her post as director yet she remained in place as

commanding officer of six officers, 50 NCOs and privates who occupied a small group of buildings and offices in the camp headquarters. Then Major Debrah went to Nigeria, supposedly for a weekend but she stayed away for three months until a series of investigatory commissions set up by the then president, Lieutenant-General Joseph Ankrah, had reported. I was grandly titled adviser but did not know who I had to advise. The power struggles in the army were then beginning and obviously it was affecting the whole structure of the military . . . I found myself the only British servicewoman in Ghana, without a proper job, and ahead of me stretched months with seemingly nothing to do. To make matters worse a six-week-long seamen's strike in the UK stopped our fortnightly supply of provisions and when a ship did come in at last I had to find cold storage space for three consignments of supplies. Fortunately the team found me other work and I kept strict office hours. In the absence, or with the 'escape', of Major Debrah I embarked on what could be termed 'damage limitation', endeavouring to maintain the morale of a corps which was existing in very trying conditions. It was extremely difficult for me to keep neutral and friendly in an atmosphere which changed from day to day.

Daphne attended a commissioning ceremony at the Military Academy at Teshie and during the rehearsal discovered that they had copied Sandhurst in drill and dress, even to the extent of the adjutant riding a white horse up a flight of steps into the officers' mess after the parade. On the day the six officers of the Ghana WAC stunned Daphne into dowdiness. They wore their No. 1 dress of scarlet tunics tightly belted over short blue serge skirts, white gloves, ginger knee-length nylons and high-heeled court shoes. Their tightly plaited hair was topped by high black horsehair wigs and crowned with peaked caps smothered in a profusion of gold braid.

To get to our places we had to pass before all the assembled company of politicians, diplomatic corps and the military, as well as wives, cousins and aunts. We exchanged greetings all along the line. When I reached Brigadier Irwin I saluted and said 'Good afternoon, sir.' He sat there, immaculate in his best white tropical uniform and, remaining stoicly expressionless, said in a good carrying voice: 'Mother Carey and her chickens!' The horse misbehaved itself in public, too.

Later Brigadier Irwin managed to extricate her from a grim predicament when she was formally invited to attend the state execution of two young Ghanaian captains found guilty by court martial of organizing another abortive coup.

I volunteered swiftly to act as courier on behalf of Brigadier Irwin

> and to give a lecture to BJSTT members at Takoradi. I arranged for the ex-president's Hawker-Siddeley 125, with an RAF pilot, a Ghanaian co-pilot and engineer, to leave the capital very early on the day of the execution and stayed away until the last possible moment . . .

During her last month in Ghana Daphne at last managed to make what she considered to be a useful contribution by finding a permanent home for the corps. Cash had been made available for refurbishing a disused detention camp at Labardi and she turned herself into a 'work gang leader', the work being done by hefty labourers with enormous grins overseen by a gnarled foreman in an outsize pith helmet.

> Came the day, near to my own departure, when in a marvellous muddle of transport, including a Mammy Wagon with 'The Original Chandler' painted in curlicues all over its cabin, army trucks and my beaten up private car, the Women's Army Corps moved in. The WAC senior NCO led the way with the CO's desk, drawers still in place, perched on her head. After a short break we held a ceremony of dedication which was performed by the Anglican army chaplain, the Muslim army Alhadji and an awe-inspiring witchdoctor in full feathers and ornaments who solemnly took my bottle of best duty-free gin and poured it out 'as a libation to the gods'. I joined in the tribal dances, the fou-fou pounding ceremony and the general fun until sunset. At least I had managed to do something to help them get started by establishing them in a camp of their own.

In August 1969 British troops were sent to Northern Ireland after a serious escalation of violence in the province. The violence began in Londonderry, culminating in a battle between the residents of the Bogside, the Catholic area of Londonderry, and the Royal Ulster Constabulary. A few days later the violence spread to Belfast and in an attempt to put down the unrest the British Army sent troops to the aid of the hard-pressed RUC. Quietly and unobtrusively the WRAC despatched a contingent of servicewomen to support the army operation in Ulster.

Captain Audrey Purton of the WRAC Provost (military police) and eight NCOs arrived in Belfast to assist the newly formed Public Protection Authority. There Captain Purton was eventually to encounter conditions which matched almost exactly those she had experienced twenty years earlier in Egypt and Cyprus where her task had been to search illegal Jewish immigrants to Palestine detained by the military authorities.

> The PPA, as it was known, was formed by the Home Office (Northern Ireland) to counteract intimidation to both Protestants and Catholics.

A member of the WRAC on patrol in Northern Ireland with troops.

We took over a disused police station as our headquarters where civil servants answered telephone calls from people who felt threatened. A team consisting of a WRAC policewoman, a military policeman and one RUC constable or woman constable would proceed to the address in order to investigate, comfort, or in some cases escort frightened people to relatives. In the Catholic areas the RUC were not welcomed and so it was left to the military police to visit those who felt they were being intimidated. The majority of such persons were elderly women, some feeling so threatened that they were forced to leave their homes. One elderly lady I visited, the grandmother of a serviceman, had petrol-soaked rags pushed through her letterbox and then set alight. Fortunately there was little damage. During the first few weeks we received as many as 400 calls in 24 hours. We worked sixteen hours a day, managing about five hours sleep. The only serious problem was the shortage of accommodation. Thousands of extra troops were pouring into the province and it was a case of having to put up with many hardships. For my first few nights I slept on the floor of a sitting/duty room. I later found that a cell at the police station was more comfortable.

Early in 1970 violence against the security forces began to increase and after a summer of hostility the role of military policewoman changed to searching women and children. Because there were insufficient policewomen to carry out all the tasks, volunteers from all trades in the WRAC were called on to go to Northern Ireland. The volunteers were carefully selected and were sent to Northern Ireland on a four-month tour but, despite the hardships they had to endure and the abuse to which they were constantly subjected, most of them volunteered for another four months.

On 1 October 1972 the Army launched 'Operation Segment', with the object of securing Belfast city centre against persons placing explosive devices while at the same time maintaining reasonable access for commercial purposes. Barriers were put up across certain streets and pedestrians and vehicles were directed to entry gates, one for men and another for women, the latter controlled by WRAC policewomen. Other WRAC search teams worked with the infantry at border check points in areas which became known as 'Bandit Country'. For some time it had been suspected that women were being used to carry concealed arms, ammunition and explosives so they had to be searched thoroughly.

> Searching was a far from pleasant task [says Audrey Purton] and the WRAC girls, whose average age was nineteen, had to suffer a lot of aggression. One NCO had her tie pulled tight round her neck and was almost strangled so after this incident ties were no longer worn. The biggest problem were the teenagers from the Bogside in Londonderry and the Falls Road in Belfast. They would place pins under the collars of their coats and when the searcher ran her hands down the garment they would sustain nasty scratches. I recall one particular incident when a girl placed fish hooks at the side of her coat to keep a belt in place and when the searcher frisked her both hands were severely torn. Another favourite trick was putting razor blades at the bottom of handbags and, if not spotted by the searcher, this resulted in very badly cut hands.

Colonel Anne Clissitt, who commanded the WRAC in Northern Ireland from 1973 to 1975, said she used to marvel at the endurance of the girls.

> They had to put up with an enormous amount of abuse from those people who were not terribly friendly towards them. Fortunately most girls were able to switch off when they returned to the barracks. 'We have the NAAFI and our boyfriends to take our minds off the hard times we get', one WRAC private told me. I remember another person telling me: 'I know it's Sunday because the newspapers change, otherwise every day is the same.' And those

> days sometimes stretched into fourteen or more hours on duty. We had to organize social functions for them and ensure that there was plenty of recreation, such as pony treks and hill climbs, but always, of course, maintaining the strictest security.

By the middle of 1973 nearly 200 WRAC searchers were in Northern Ireland. The Armagh platoon of 30 women were always conveyed to and fro by helicopter and they worked alongside the various regiments on duty in Ulster. Audrey Purton recalls that 'one NCO leapt out of the helicopter and made a run for cover. One never knew, of course, if there was a sniper about and so the transfer was always a risky business. On this occasion the NCO clambered through a hedge and managed to leave part of her skirt on the barbed wire, much to the amusement of the waiting soldiers.'

When each volunteer arrived in Ulster, she attended a week-long course which equipped her to cope with and understand the background to the troubles. The girls were taught first aid, self-defence, arrest procedures, the handling of evidence, the recognition of explosives and the techniques of searching women; their only protection was a flak jacket, a helmet with a visor and a truncheon.

The bravery of WRAC servicewomen in Northern Ireland has been recognized by the award of one military medal for outstanding devotion to duty, several Mentioned in Despatches and General Officer Commanding commendations. A searcher at a check point in Londonderry took control of the situation when a sniper opened fire and wounded all three soldiers on duty there. She administered first aid, kept cool under very difficult conditions and took the correct action. An NCO also came under fire while travelling in the rear of a vehicle with a soldier who was shot. She administered first aid to the wounded man and comforted him. When the vehicle arrived in a safe area, she got out and discovered that her skirt was soaked in blood from a wound in her thigh. Both these servicewomen were mentioned in despatches.

On another occasion a WRAC corporal was besieged with other members of a search team in a house in the Ballymurphy area. Swinging her truncheon, she led the way out of the house and all members of the team escaped without injury. Another WRAC corporal raced into a derelict, booby-trapped building after she heard an explosion followed by screaming; a soldier lay seriously injured and a second was hysterical as a result of shock. The corporal's prompt action in dealing with the situation and administering first aid saved the soldier's life. Both these corporals received GOC commendations.

Captain Purton says that despite the conditions under which they worked injuries received by the girls were never serious. During rioting some were hit by stones which left one with a cut in her head needing thirteen stitches and another with a broken nose while a third nursed an injury to her leg from a table fork embedded in the flesh. 'Many were kicked and punched but this never stopped any of the girls from returning to their duty.'

Audrey retired as a lieutenant-colonel in 1984 after serving for 39 years 4 months. She was the last member of the ATS to leave the WRAC.

Later in the 'seventies the WRAC was asked by Sri Lanka to assist in setting up a tri-service company and Major Janet Lawson, a captain and a warrant officer went to the island to take command of the young corps and to help train recruits. Apart from the usual difficulties encountered in a foreign country, Major Lawson received a few strange requests – on one occasion she had to ask headquarters for assistance because 'now they want a pipe band'. The problem was passed to Anne Clissitt, then in command of the Guildford Centre, and she consulted the WRAC's director of music. Between them, they managed to collect pipes and tapes which were sent to Major Lawson who within six months had duly set up a pipe band.

Brunei also asked the WRAC to assist in the formation of a women's company after a feasibility study by a team including Major Sue Wing, who visited the sultanate on the northern coast of Borneo in 1980. A recruiting campaign begun in October 1980 resulted in more than 800 applications for posts as officers and NCOs and in March 1981 three Brunei women were selected to attend the WRAC College at Camberley to undergo training as officers. Major Rowena Patrick, Captain Prunella Samson and Warrant Officer Sheila Murray were sent to Brunei to organize the recruit training; Rowena says the problems she encountered were mainly cultural and religious. For instance, one of the chief areas for women in the military is driving but Islam forbids women being in a one-to-one situation with men to whom they are neither married nor engaged. As women in the motor transport section would be required to drive staff cars occupied by senior male officers, this type of employment was ruled out in Brunei.

As Rowena discovered, the strict rules caused other dilemmas:

> Muslim women do not swim, nor do they reveal their bodies in bathing costumes to anyone save their immediate family. To prevent them drowning in the Bruneian jungle when crossing rivers, or travelling in boats or in flash floods, they had to be taught to swim. The swimming pool was closed to the public, all male lifeguards were asked to leave and we prepared for the first lesson. Every girl duly appeared in her swimming costume worn over a track suit and a T-shirt . . .

It took much persuasion before some of the girls compromised by wearing shorts instead of a track suit but most continued to wear T-shirts and some even borrowed pyjamas from fathers or brothers.

The syllabus included weapon training and here Rowena faced another problem.

> Brunei servicewomen are often very small and the M-16 rifle is quite heavy and long. On occasions weapons drill proved very difficult and we had to exercise much patience in training them. Care also had to be taken at the firing range. I recall the time when they had to stand in a slit trench with the rifle resting on the top before firing at the target. When we looked along the trench there was no sight of one girl, just her M-16 poking out at the top. She was only 4ft 5in tall and was unable to see over the top of the trench. So we fetched a sandbag for her to stand on and she scored very well.

The fourth intake passed out in April 1983 carrying weapons for the first time at the personal request of the Sultan. The women are now employed in the Brunei army as clerks, including work on word processors, pay clerks, logistic accountants, storewomen, electronic technicians, avionic technicians, computer operators, medical assistants, physical training instructors and cooks.

The WRAC also serves in the Falkland Islands. The first contingent of nineteen women under the command of Captain Di Foster was sent on 19 July 1983, after being acclimatized to South Atlantic conditions by a week-long intensive survival course in the Welsh mountains round Tywyn. Selected from volunteers, the girls are clerks, cooks, postal and courier operators and supply specialists at locations round Port Stanley, and serve tours of five months.

12

UP IN ARMS?

Although the early 'seventies was dominated by a series of events at home and abroad which had enormous economic and political impact on Britain, one particular development – the emergence of the feminist movement – was destined to begin a complete revision of the structure of society. Its repercussions were so powerful that even the Army, which in the past had tended to remain coldly aloof from progress in civilian working conditions, was forced to take notice.

In America, and indeed in many European countries, the feminist movement was exerting tremendous pressure for change in attitudes, and as a result women's role in the labour force was expanding. In Britain the Women's Liberation Workshop was established in London in 1969 as a co-ordinating centre for local women's groups, but its influence was small and its protests muted until the publication in 1970 of Germaine Greer's book *The Female Eunuch*. This not only endorsed the women's liberation movement but provided dramatic impetus to a social revolution, the seeds for which had been sown before and during the First World War when women were first admitted into traditional male occupations in large numbers. Referring to the suffragettes, whom she called 'the first feminist wave', Germaine Greer said: 'Then genteel middle-class ladies clamoured for reform, now ungenteel middle-class women are calling for revolution . . .' It was time for 'the second feminist wave'.

Coinciding with the feminist movement was an increasing belief in meritocracy – people should be chosen for positions of power and influence not by birth or virtue of their wealth but for superior talents or intellect. A new generation of Britons resented the values society had placed on the old school tie, the unfair privileges bestowed by wealth and the inbuilt advantages of being born on the right side of the tracks. In the 1960s Britain had witnessed a liberalization of higher education resulting in the upgrading of many colleges, the development of what became known as polytechnics and the creation of new universities so that more school-leavers could enjoy further education. All this led to a greater awareness in society of student activity, culminating in 1971 in the recognition of their political rights by the lowering of the voting age to eighteen.

Appropriately, at the head of the WRAC in 1970 was a woman well qualified to foresee the direction in which she should steer the Corps and sufficiently tactful to nudge her superior officers into a re-examination of women's role in the Army.

Sheila Heaney, the daughter of a doctor, was an academic in the same mould as Helen Gwynne-Vaughan. At Liverpool University she had read for a general arts degree which included sociology and economics

Colonel Sheila Heaney, who became director of the WRAC in 1970.

before attending Loughborough College of Technology in Leicester where she took a course in engineering, with the idea of becoming a factory inspector. Instead, her army career began in January 1939 when, at the suggestion of a friend, she joined the ATS in Merseyside. Like Lucy Davies, her decision to remain in the ATS after the war was largely influenced by a posting abroad. Sheila was sent to East Africa and when she returned to Britain in 1949 attended the RCB 'merely to see what happened'. With her sociological background, she was interested especially in the methods which the Army was using to select officers.

> I remembered going to an ATS conference some years before and making an impassioned plea for some form of scientific selection. By the time of conscription we had instituted a rough and ready system of selection which improved as the years went on. I was fascinated in 1949 to see what procedure had been adopted and I must admit that I was really impressed by the RCB, although I wasn't sure they had reduced subjective value judgment to the minimum. That may be partly because, being such a smallish corps, everyone was inclined to know everyone else and under those circumstances I believe objectivity was more difficult to achieve. But the technique was certainly there.

After becoming head of the WRAC personnel and selection department, AG16, she was appointed director in 1970, working very closely with Eileen Nolan who had succeeded to her previous post. In her new position Sheila was confronted with the view, being put forward by senior women officers, that the WRAC should develop and expand job opportunities. To a large extent the increasing clamour for equal pay for work of equal value was at that time also exacerbated by Britain's impending entry into the Common Market and the eventual signing of the Treaty of Rome:

> A lot of thought was given throughout the country to equal pay for equal work. Industry had been developing the exercise of job evaluation and when the Army came to consider its pay structure, naturally job evaluation was also examined and a major review of all trades was instituted. We had never had equal pay for the women nor had we expected it, because although the women's services of other armies – such as the Israelis and the Americans – had begun to handle weapons, we had not yet reached that stage.

In America, 1970 was what has been described by Jeanne Holm as 'the watershed year for women in the armed forces, the year in which important national events converged to force the issue [of equal opportunity]'.

Before 1970 the defence establishment was 'incredibly insensitive' to the presence of military women, as demonstrated by the publication in August 1969 of the Department of Defense Human Goals paper, promulgated in response to civil rights pressures and concentrating largely on the elimination of racial discrimination – astonishingly, the document, which was distributed worldwide and lettered in calligraphy on parchment in full colour, did not take women into account. However, in 1970 a new version corrected the omission. Now the relevant paragraph read: 'To make Military and Civilian service in the Department of Defense a model of equal opportunity for all regardless of race, *sex*, creed, or national origin, and to hold those who do business with the Department of Defense to full compliance with the policy of equal employment opportunity.' (Author's italics)

1970 was also the year when women in America began to attack military sex discrimination in the courts. In December First Lieutenant Sharron Frontiero of the US Air Force challenged in the Federal Court the rule that married servicewomen were classified as single officers and therefore did not qualify for on-base family housing as did married servicemen, nor were their husbands entitled to medical facilities routinely available to the wives of male members. Although a three-judge court rejected Frontiero's argument she eventually won her case in the Supreme Court. As a result of the judgment, the Department of Defense directed that women were to be treated equally with men in all matters of dependency and entitlements, and the word 'spouse' in such matters was to replace 'wife' or 'husband'.

Frontiero's attack on the sexual discrimination embodied in military regulations roused the feelings of servicewomen in the US and throughout the Western world, but not until 1979 were the rules changed in Britain. When Dr Jane Orr was in the RAMC in 1979, she was married to a civilian and innocently applied for an army house, not realizing that only husbands were entitled to married quarters. As the application form did not require her to specify her sex, she did not say she was a woman and her application was successful. More than a year later the Army discovered its mistake and gave her a fortnight to vacate the house. Fortunately for Dr Orr, and for every other servicewoman, the press and television featured her story and after a parliamentary question the rules were changed. Today servicewomen can apply for housing on the same basis as army husbands. The feminist movement in Britain had made four basic demands – equal pay, equal educational and job opportunities, free contraception and abortion on demand, and 24-hour nurseries. Typically, the popular press highlighted the more bizarre demonstrations by the fringe groups who gave expression to the liberation movement by publicly burning bras, but in 1970 parliament did pass the Equal Pay Act. This Act, however, did not include the three armed services though Sheila Heaney was finding that some young officers joining the WRAC were, as she puts it, 'articulating a greater independence of spirit'.

> The principle had been rammed down their throats by the people in the feminist movement and although feminism entering the ranks of the Army sounds aggressive, it wasn't. The average recruit joins because she wants to live in a structured community but with the Commission of Equality being set up, and the entry into the Common Market, there was a greater public awareness of the need for more opportunities for women. Certainly the graduates coming into

> the Corps suddenly felt that their horizons would be broadened in the near future.

In 1972 Sheila had visited the USA in order to study developments in the WAC and the move towards integration of the women's services into the regular army, air force and navy. She realized that the Americans were being forced to 'jump off the end of the diving board before learning to swim'.

Major-General Holm says that events in the last half of the 'sixties and early 'seventies had combined to end the long period of stagnation and regression in the women's line programmes. Just as had the British Army in the First and Second World Wars, the American military were facing manpower problems generated by the Vietnam War, and the situation was aggravated by mounting opposition to the draft, by the expanding role of women in the labour force and a new, more aggressive tide of feminism. 'The synergistic effect of these forces challenged the services' traditional attitudes towards women and forced change upon a reluctant military establishment.' Brigadier-General Mildred (Inez) Bailey, who became head of the WAC in August 1971, says:

> We were seeing tremendous changes, some of them good and some of them not so good. We were entering the period of equal opportunity between the sexes and among the races. I think the pressures were far more intense and the agitation far more vocal than anywhere else and the armed forces was the focus of attention of civil rights organizations, who demanded changes almost overnight.

Until 1965 women in the US military had been virtually a token force – 'typewriter soldiers', as General Holm describes them. But, she says, even with the Department of Defense frantically seeking a solution to the manpower problem, 'It was symptomatic of the military mind-set that the decision to use more women came after all other options had been considered. One is reminded of the observation in 1941 that they would probably have preferred "dogs, ducks or monkeys" to women if they could have used them.' However, there was no alternative, and Inez Bailey was instructed to expand the WAC.

> It was almost like being back in World War Two again as far as training, clothing and quarters were concerned, because we moved so rapidly that the supply system couldn't cope and the training system became clogged with recruits. We doubled our strength of 12,200 women in a year, tripled it in another. It was rather chaotic and at the same time we had to address all the problems involving equality.

Sheila Heaney returned to Britain with a clear idea of how the problem of equality between the sexes ought to be tackled.

> I felt we must be cautious – it had to be evolution rather than revolution. We had already been planning career paths for women outside the regular postings of the WRAC [i.e. in the British Army generally] and we had to ensure that this did not in any way affect someone on the regimental pyramid. I felt strongly, however, that the chance should be there if we had someone of the right quality. The Army had to give us the opportunity for people of the right quality to be promoted outside the WRAC and not merely fill an appointment with a woman because certain ratios had to be fulfilled, in the way that they had tended to do these things in the United States. In other words, it should not be discrimination but merit which decided the appointment.

Later Inez Bailey visited the United Kingdom and was able to bring Sheila and Eileen up to date with events in the US. As she reported,

> We had begun to talk about disestablishing the WAC as a separate corps and integrating women completely into the army in their administration, training and billeting and, while I knew this was a desirable thing to do, I felt personally that this should take a period of years to be implemented and should be accomplished very carefully and very slowly. I felt we had to deal with a multitude of sociological and cultural problems first.

It was the sort of language Sheila thoroughly understood. One of the most useful consequences of Inez's visit was the initiation of an officer exchange scheme which took the form of two-year appointments for captains. In 1974 the first two WRAC officers, Captain Prunella Samson and Captain Claire Montanaro, went to Fort McLellan, the headquarters of the WAC in Alabama, for the first year and were posted to military units in the United States for the second year. This scheme continued until the WAC was disbanded in 1978 and the Americans admitted that they could no longer guarantee to send women.

In 1973 Eileen Nolan succeeded Sheila Heaney as director of the WRAC and in September that year the British Army appointed a working party under Brigadier Arthur Stewart-Cox to investigate the Future Employment of the Women's Royal Army Corps. It was a reaction to Sheila Heaney's determination that women should be given greater opportunities and demonstrated that the Army could no longer resist the pressures society was exerting. Its terms of reference were to consider career opportunities with a view to improvement for both officers and servicewomen of the WRAC, and in particular to study constraints and the possible takeover of civilian posts. In 1975, while the working party was still investigating, the Sex Discrimination Act was passed by Parliament but, once again, its provisions did not apply to the Army, Navy or Air Force.

Almost parallel with the appointment of the working party had come pressure from the Committee of the Senior Service Women Officers of the [NATO] Alliance set up on an informal basis in Copenhagen in June 1961 at the instigation of Colonel Elsa Martensen-Larsen, director of the Women's Royal Danish Air Force.

The aim of the Copenhagen conference had been to collate information on the status, organization and conditions of service in the women's services of NATO member countries, and to examine future possibilities and prospects for the employment of women within the military forces of the Alliance. Although the committee met twice more during the 1960s, it received no formal recognition from NATO. The turning point arrived in November 1973 when the fourth conference, sponsored by the NATO

Brigadier Eileen Nolan with her opposite number in the United States, Brigadier-General Inez Bailey, director of the Women's Army Corps.

Information Service and co-ordinated by Colonel Martensen-Larsen, took place at NATO headquarters in Brussels. The delegates represented 28 women's services comprising more than 100,000 servicewomen and they came from Britain, the United States, Denmark, France, Canada, Norway, the Netherlands and Turkey, with West Germany sending an observer. For the first time the nursing services were also included.

Eileen Nolan was the WRAC delegate.

> I remember well the three Turkish girls. At our first session, we all stood up to introduce ourselves and to identify which service we were representing. When it was Turkey's turn, the girl representing the army spoke first, followed by the representative of the navy. Then the youngest of the three got to her feet and said in halting English: 'I jet pilot, combat ready.' This absolutely astonished us because the women's committee at that time was not in any way considering a combat role. Yet here was a woman, coming from a country which one would not normally have associated with that kind of progress, announcing that she was trained for combat! No one else present could match her achievement – our main concern at that time was just to get the committee recognized officially by NATO!

With this object in view the delegates appointed an *ad hoc* committee and, after a meeting with the deputy secretary-general of NATO, notification was received that in future the women's committee would be sponsored by the secretary-general. It was the first step on the road to official recognition. The 1973 conference spent much time discussing the future role of women in the armed services and adopted a unanimous resolution agreeing that women should share fully the obligation to defend their countries and that in so doing should have, or shall have, equal rights with men as well as equal pay. They called on NATO countries to take action to widen the military employment of women within their military services.

Appropriately the next conference in London was timed to coincide with International Women's Year and was held in the Ministry of Defence itself. It began with a group photograph of delegates lined up on top of the steps leading to the Ministry's main entrance. Then a male officer suggested that the delegates reassemble at the bottom of the steps for another picture.

> At the time it seemed rather an odd suggestion [Eileen admits] but we duly complied and the photograph was taken. When at last we were escorted inside, we learned that there had been a bomb scare within the MoD itself and the male officer in charge of us had cleared the

> main entrance by the rather unorthodox method of herding us down the steps out of harm's way until the all clear was given.

With International Women's Year very much in mind, the conference discussed its objectives – peace, development, equality – as they applied to women in the services: by now the delegates were representing the interests of 145,000 servicewomen. Once again it was stressed that every effort should be made to attain official military status within NATO rather than just sponsorship by the secretary-general and it became the task of Eileen, who had been elected chairman, to achieve this. In April 1976 she flew to Brussels with Elsa Martensen-Larsen to see the chairman of the NATO Military Committee, Admiral Sir Peter Hill-Norton, to discuss the matter.

> He gave up an enormous amount of his time to listen to us and was very sympathetic. He asked me to prepare an official paper which I did that weekend. We didn't have long to wait and after the proposal was approved by the secretary-general the military committee agreed on 19 July 1976, in document MC 249. I felt that if I hadn't done anything else in my tour as director, this had been a great step forward.

From that moment, too, as chairman of the committee Eileen became the senior ranking woman in the NATO Alliance. Her last major task as director of the WRAC was to attend the 1977 Brussels conference of the women's committee. Among the 34 delegates from 10 member countries, Belgium and West Germany were represented officially for the first time, both having recruited women into their armed forces in 1975; in Germany's case it was in a limited capacity as surgeons in the Medical Corps.

The most important development reported at the conference was that which had taken place in the United States, where separate women's detachments or units had been or were being disestablished and women were being integrated with men in the units to which they were assigned for duty or training. The delegate declared that women in the United States were now on an equal footing with men in uniform, having the same opportunities for promotion, the same pay scale and the same privileges and benefits. Equality had been achieved at last for women who served around the clock and around the world in virtually every military career field except those categorized as direct combat or close combat support.

In summing up the conference Air Commodore P. J. Tamblin of the WRAF, who had succeeded Eileen as chairman, said that discussion rightly centred on the difficulties women faced in trying to extend their contribution to their national forces and thus to NATO, and how they were tackling them:

> I think it is fair to say that all the delegates felt that women could play a larger part in their particular services if it were not for men's misgivings about employing them extensively in the military sphere.

The WRAC had, however, made some progress towards breaking down discrimination. During the early 'seventies the first two women lieutenant-colonels had been accepted for the Joint Services Staff College at Latimer in Buckinghamshire; courses which became open to the increasing number of graduates included the degree course at the Royal Military College of Science at Shrivenham. A huge effort had been required on the part of many people to obtain permission for a woman to attend but unfortunately, in her third year, the first candidate married one of her fellow students and left the service before graduating. This confirmed the reluctance of senior military officers to send women on training courses of this nature: quite justifiably, they pointed out that the investment of a considerable amount of time and money was involved, and that a male officer had been denied the opportunity of attending the course.

'It appeared we had taken one step forward and several steps back,' Eileen said. Undeterred by this enormous disappointment, she successfully argued the case for a second girl to be allowed to go on a course. To her utter dismay this girl, too, fell in love with a fellow student and announced her engagement. However, this girl did graduate and after the ceremony, which Eileen attended, the couple sought her out and told her that they intended to honour the agreement that the girl serve at least five more years.

One remaining bastion which the WRAC still had to storm was the Royal College of Defence Studies, normally reserved for selected colonels and brigadiers. Because these are the most senior ranks attainable in the WRAC, attendance at the college, with its chance of higher promotion, became the ultimate ambition. Achievement of it required the appointment of a director young enough to continue in the Army after serving at least three years as head of the WRAC. At the time it appeared to be a remote possibility. Although Eileen was requested to stay on for a fourth year as director she had reached her retirement age and knew, too, that her successor, Anne Field, would also retire after her tour as director. However, waiting in the wings was Lieutenant-Colonel Helen Meechie, only 39 when Eileen retired in 1977, who was destined to make history by becoming the first woman brigadier to attend the college in 1986, when she was succeeded as director by Shirley Nield. In 1987 Helen Meechie was the first woman in the British Army to be appointed to a senior staff role outside the Corps. At the age of 49 she became director of army service conditions at the Ministry of Defence with responsibility for the standard of everyday service life, pay, accommodation and pensions – a major step forward for women in the military.

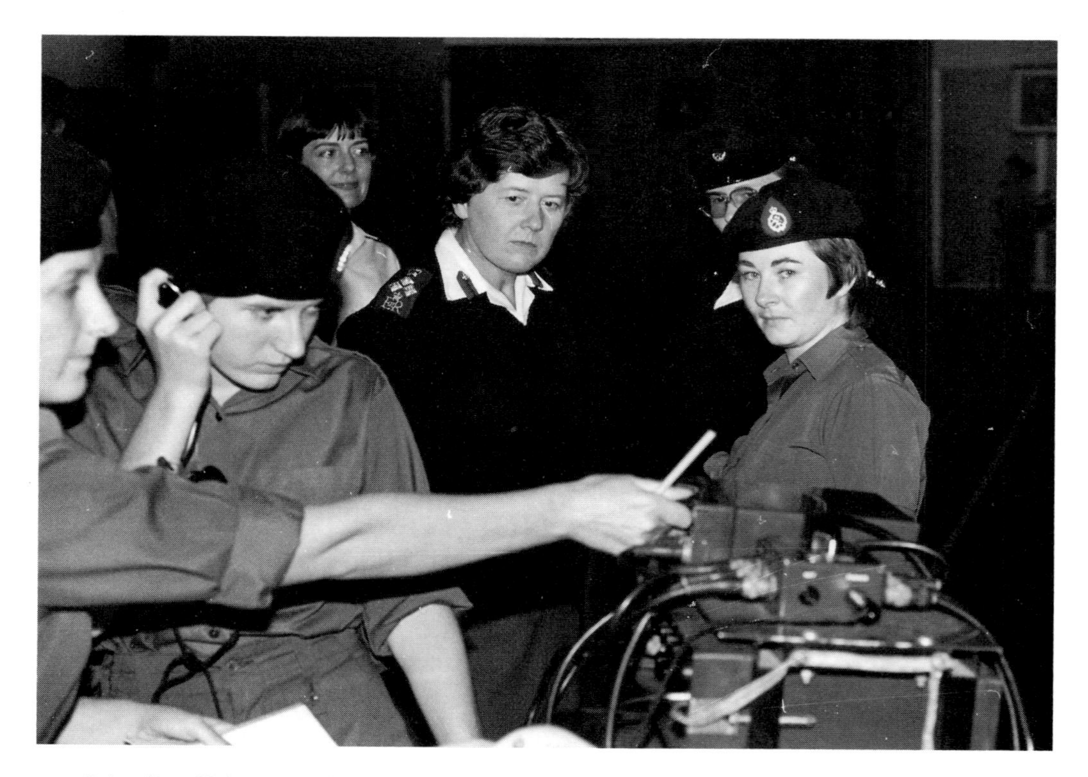

Brigadier Helen Meechie watches as Privates Breach (*left*) and Fletcher are taught operating procedure by Corporal Elder (*right*).

In 1976 the working party into the Future Employment of the WRAC had completed its first report which, in some respects, exploded like a bombshell in military circles. Ever since the foundation of the WAAC in 1917, the status of women in the armed forces had been assumed unequivocally to be non-combatant. Even during the Second World War when the controversy over the ack-ack units raged, the government and the War Office had emphasized that the ATS remained non-combatant: they were not permitted to handle offensive weapons and therefore would not be allowed to fire them. It is quite remarkable that no one thought to clarify the position of the ATS at that stage by re-reading the Geneva Convention, drawn up by 35 states in March 1906 and amended in 1925, which covered the care and protection of non-combatants, wounded troops and prisoners-of-war. The working party, faced with looking at the long-term future of careers for women in the Army, discovered that there were only two specific references to women in the Convention, which had been amended again in 1949. These appeared in the Prisoners of War Convention and required that women were to receive treatment as 'favourable as that granted to men' and that separate compounds should be available in mixed prisoner-of-war camps.

Non-combatants were discussed in the context of the Wounded Convention and referred specifically to doctors, medical orderlies and chaplains – in other words those people who were responsible for the caring effort, either physical or spiritual. Apparently international military law did not recognize any other type of non-combatant. Legally, therefore, the WRAC was neither *de jure* nor *de facto* non-combatant, and the status accorded to female soldiers was purely a matter of usage or custom rather than of law. Ironically, one person had appeared to recognize the situation for what it was – Dame Helen Gwynne-Vaughan who, in May 1918 when eight members of the QMAAC were killed in an air raid in France, had soothed the emotions of outraged press reporters by saying: 'Since we were replacing combatants, the enemy was entirely in order in killing us if he could.'

The clarification of the legal position had enormous implications, for the working party now recommended that the WRAC be recognized as a combatant corps, albeit a non-belligerent one. *Ipso facto* the WRAC had become, virtually overnight, a combatant unit of the British Army. While recommending that WRAC personnel be precluded from fighting tasks within the Royal Armoured Corps and the infantry, the working party recognized that women could henceforth be deployed in any role, in any arm within the regular army or TA Volunteer Reserve, other than in those employments involving the use of direct fire methods. A complete review of the definition of the WRAC's role was required.

When the WRAC had been formed in 1949, King's Regulations for the Army required that: 'The WRAC provide replacements for male officers and men in such employments as may be specified by the Army Board of the Defence Council from time to time.' This was now thought to be inadequate because it failed to recognize WRAC officers and servicewomen as part of the operational, training and administrative machinery of the service. It was therefore proposed that the new definition of the WRAC's role should be:

> The WRAC is to be organized and trained, as an integral part of the army, to carry out those tasks for which its members are best suited and qualified so that it will contribute to the maximum efficiency of the Army as a whole.

Almost immediately the working party was faced with another dilemma. If women in the Army were to work alongside men, they must be expected to contribute on the same terms as those men. That seemed logical enough but, since the WRAC was not armed, the women required male escorts for protection in lethal or potentially lethal situations. In fact, in the past there had been instances when women had carried arms – Lucy Davies admitted that while in Egypt she had been instructed unofficially in the use of a firearm and had at times carried a pistol for her own protection. Other women officers, too, had undergone weaponry training and most of them had declared their willingness to protect themselves rather than depend on the men. But such incidents were never acknowledged officially and generally women were restricted to areas where they could be easily defended by men at all times, necessarily resulting in the diversion of valuable manpower and effort and in limiting the employment and deployment of WRAC personnel.

The key to the future of the WRAC lay in deciding whether or not to recommend that the WRAC be allowed to bear arms. There is no record of the working party's discussion of this highly controversial subject but they had some idea of how it might be received by the public because in 1975 weapons training had become *de rigueur* for servicewomen in America. Apart from instruction in basic rifle marksmanship, some US servicewomen had even gone on to advanced individual training with light anti-tank weapons, M-16 rifles, grenade launchers, claymore mines and M-60 machine guns. America had come a long way from the days when the obsessions with appearance had caused the WAC to drop all activities considered too masculine, such as bivouac training, map reading, rigging tents or living in the field. With the demand for equality in the United States forces, weaponry training had become not only necessary but obligatory, and the American public had accepted the change in policy almost without demur.

But would the more staid and conservative British public, who had protested so vigorously when their daughters were transferred to the ack-ack units in wartime, be as unperturbed as their American cousins in peacetime? They would soon find out. The working party dropped its second bombshell by recommending that the WRAC 'should be permitted to contribute to their self-defence and local protection and should therefore carry and use the appropriate defensive arms'. The weapon considered most suitable for defensive purposes was the 9mm issue pistol. The working party envisaged that eventually WRAC personnel would receive defensive weapon training during basic instruction and that in future WRAC applicants would be required to sign an undertaking to be trained in the use of, and to carry, defensive weapons when ordered to do so.

One officer who welcomed the move was Captain Gael Hammond, who in January 1974 had been posted to Cyprus as Staff Captain Personnel Services. On the night of 14-15 July when the Cypriot National Guard overthrew the government of Archbishop Makarios, Captain Hammond was in Kyrenia with a party of Royal Scots officers and their wives.

> We wandered slowly home not knowing what had happened but curiously aware that the island was particularly quiet. We had a meal about midnight at Limassol on the way back to the battalion

mess at Episkopi. Only when we got back to the mess did I realize something was wrong.

During the next five days Captain Hammond and a sergeant clerk worked on average twenty hours a day locating the whereabouts of Army, RAF and United Kingdom-based civilian families. Also, schoolchildren were due to fly out to parents based in Cyprus for the summer holidays so she had to stop flights and arrange for children to go to relatives at home instead.

My first experience of coming under fire occurred during that hectic period. A car park at the telecommunications centre had been designated a reception area for tourists and Colonel John Groom sent me there to ascertain what nationalities we were dealing with. As I got out of the car I heard the battle and bloodbath taking place in Episkopi. I don't remember much more except eventually wandering round the car park and coming back to the car to be faced by the Royal Scots RSM who apologized profusely for the string of swear words he was using. 'Ma'am, if I hadn't sworn at you, I'd never have got you moving. I have never in my whole life seen hair standing on end as yours was, ma'am' . . . We did not carry arms in those days and bullets were flying across the roads.

We then started to evacuate tourists and I tried to calm wives who were stuck in quarters with bullets flying through their windows. I talked to them on the phone and on the radio, listening to the sound of the bullets, keeping them lying flat.

During the Turkish invasion on 20 July Captain Hammond was at St John's School in Episkopi where the Army had opened up an evacuation centre.

I was sleeping during the day and was awakened by the roar of planes. Heart in mouth, I rang the operations room and admitted I was petrified. Others were as terrified as I was – we had 39 WRAC servicewomen in Episkopi to start with but it grew to about 100 – and I remember one little girl who was particularly frightened and who I had to calm. Eventually she became a very good member of the team. The emergency went on until August and we had to organize armed convoys but I didn't know what that meant because we weren't trained in tactics in those days as we are now. Somehow I got this armed convoy together. I don't know how I did it and I remember my first convoy arriving at 5 a.m. and the staff sergeant reporting: 'Ma'am, we're all here.' I said: 'Did I get it right?' and he assured me that I had. Eventually I ended up becoming a kind of immigration officer

> checking the passports of Cypriots flooding into the reception centres and deciding whether they were entitled to go to Britain. It was exceptionally difficult and on one occasion I was attacked and held up against a wall with a knife against my throat. Fortunately Colonel Leo Macy, the paymaster, walked in at that moment and from then on I had an armed guard with me all the time. That, of course, was a waste of manpower. Had I been trained in arms I could have looked after myself. I believe, too, that I would not have experienced the fear I felt in Cyprus had I been fully trained.

The recommendation that WRAC personnel should use and carry defensive weapons was a radical departure from the original concept of the ATS and the WRAC but it allowed the working party to consider future tasks for servicewomen far more freely and on a wider front than hitherto. Of course, there were constraints which it took into account, such as not placing the WRAC in field units or airborne forces which, loosely, are considered to be those forward of main divisional headquarters where there is a possibility of being overrun by enemy forces or where their primary role would be killing by direct fire. Also the physical limitations of women in handling heavy equipment had to be borne in mind.

In retrospect, the working party was dodging the issue by being overcautious and pandering to what it thought public opinion would be. The real issue was whether women should be freed for limited duty in combat areas. Even in 1976 the working party must have realized that modern warfare had advanced to a stage where any position along the lines of communication was vulnerable to attack. Brigadier Helen Meechie argues this way:

> What is any enemy going to do? They are not going to sit back and let you work all your ordnance units and transport units; they are going to take them out. It is ludicrous to say that women sitting at the rear are in safe areas. Equally, it makes no sense to define a theatre of war and only train women in the use of weapons in that area because a parachute drop can come anywhere in Britain – Luton, for instance. It would be ridiculous to say: 'Sorry, we didn't expect you in Luton so we haven't trained anyone in Luton.'

One must conclude that the working party decided discretion was required in pronouncing on what, after all, seemed to be a delicate and highly controversial subject. With a history of conservatism in military judgments, it must be conceded that their report already had more than a degree of audacity in defying long-standing traditions.

This report laid down that women in any task must be able to carry out the full range of training required for the employment and fulfil all aspects of the employment laid down in a job specification, gain an adequate range of experience for the efficient carrying through of the task, and thereby have the opportunity for a full career. In this way, the working party believed, a more challenging range of careers could contribute to the will of women to remain in the service rather than become bored with the endless routine to which many had been subjected in the past. It even foresaw women being considered for special duties with the Special Air Service or the Intelligence Corps. There were eight recommendations:

1. A new role be promulgated for the Corps.
2. The WRAC should formally be recognized as a combatant Corps, but employed in non-belligerent tasks.
3. WRAC officers and servicewomen be authorized to carry pistols as defensive weapons.
4. WRAC personnel should be given access to a wider range of employments and appointments.
5. Some WRAC officers and servicewomen should serve on combined rolls or Career Employment Groups in competition with men.
6. Training of the WRAC, for identical tasks should, whenever possible, be undertaken jointly with men and this to include the training of officers at RMA Sandhurst.
7. Terms of service for WRAC be brought closer to those governing male service.
8. Commanders of either sex be authorized to administer discipline to male and female subordinates.

The working party had delivered a document which was to have far-reaching effects and which stimulated considerable argument in senior military circles, where there was still heavy opposition from officers in the more traditional mould: for them, the very idea of women marching through the portals of Sandhurst was almost sacriligious. There was no doubt about the report's revolutionary nature, for although it fell short of the ideals expressed by the feminist movement, which still demanded equal pay for equal work, it did go a long way towards guaranteeing women a far better deal in the Army, reflecting the changing values of society which now recognized that women would play a more demanding and strenuous role in the workplace.

In June 1977 the Army Board accepted most of the working party's recommendations, agreeing that the WRAC should be recognized as a combatant corps but rather pointedly remaining silent on the question of women carrying arms. Not until 1981 did the then Secretary for Defence, Francis Pym, announce that the WRAC was to fall into line with other NATO forces and undergo weapon training with small arms. He also made it clear that in certain circumstances they would carry sub-machine-guns or pistols. The weapons chosen were the Sterling sub-machine-gun and the Browning 9mm pistol. It is now compulsory for women joining the WRAC to train in arms, though those who have a genuine objection may be excluded in special circumstances.

The decision was greeted with hardly a murmur of protest from the public. Perhaps they had been conditioned by the sight of policewomen in the front line in the war against crime. Also by that time there had been considerable publicity about weaponry training for women in America and other NATO countries. In 1977 two additional protocols had been added to the Geneva Conventions agreed in 1864, 1906, 1907, 1925 and 1949. The first contained 120 articles and the second 20 articles but nowhere was there a reference to women serving in the armed forces. Lieutenant-Colonel Dr E. L. Gonsalves, a specialist in military law, summed up the Geneva Convention thus: 'There is no restriction to the combatant activities of women serving in the armed forces and there exists in this respect no adverse distinction nor discrimination between men and women serving in the armed forces.' Therefore well-informed people would have expected British servicewomen to follow the trend. The move brought protests from some senior WRAC officers and praise from others. Brigadier Helen Meechie, who was director of the WRAC when weaponry training was introduced, believed it was necessary.

> But it wasn't easy to implement because we were told that the weaponry training had to be on a no-cost basis. This is clearly difficult because even firing one round costs something. What they really meant was not building armouries, issuing weapons or training every servicewoman to the task. What followed was an identification of those areas in which it was deemed essential that women be weapon-trained and the training initially followed on an individual basis. Then in 1984 weapon training was introduced into the student officers and officer cadets programme at Sandhurst.

While the WRAF went ahead with weaponry training from 1981, the WRAC had to wait until 1988 before beginning courses at the Guildford Centre. In the early months of 1988 the first women instructors qualified in weaponry and from July all recruits were trained in arms. The WRNS are not yet armed.

How do the women themselves react to packing a holstered pistol or possibly strafing a potential human target with a sub-machine-gun? *Soldier* magazine, a Ministry of Defence official publication, conducted a random survey of WRAC opinion in 1981 and published the reactions of the ten whose views were sought.

The girls were asked to imagine two hypothetical situations. In the first,

Quartermaster Sergeant Instructor Cairns demonstrating the essential parts of a pistol at the Royal Military Academy Sandhurst to senior officer cadets. *From left to right* Diana Nash, Jennie Heap, Phillipa Wright and Bridget Collin.

three armed infiltrators burst through the door of an installation where they were based. In the second, a fresh-faced boy of twelve stands in that same doorway, his arm arched back, preparatory to lobbing a grenade into the room. They had to assume they were alone and had the initial responsibility to act. Would they panic . . . fire blindly . . . freeze . . . or surrender?

Private Jo Starczewski, aged 18: 'If I had to shoot, I suppose I would. If it was him, me, her or whoever, I suppose I would shoot them on instinct. I would defend myself but I hope that the case will never arise . . . I might just back down. I don't think I could shoot a twelve-year-old boy.'

Sergeant Beryl Jones also hesitated about killing the boy. 'I would try to wound him or talk him out of it,' she suggested. But what about the three men? 'I would only open fire if they opened fire.'

Private Viva Rose, a 20-year-old stewardess, said she would shoot to wound but not to kill: 'Yes, I could shoot but it would have to be a quick look and a bang . . . If the boy were over sixteen, I think I could. People like that know what they are doing. I don't think I would panic and I don't think I would surrender.'

Driver Davina Mills, aged 22: 'I haven't got the heart to kill the boy. I love children. But I don't think I'd lose my nerve if it came to the crunch. Yes, I think you could, perhaps, rely on me.'

Lance-Corporal Dee Riley, aged 27: 'To me, it is quite simply either me or them. As for the boy, I would shoot at his arm. Someone older, I might shoot to kill.'

Lance-Corporal Alison McClelland, aged 18: 'I couldn't kill anyone – no way! I think I would refuse to carry a gun. I won't do the training – I shall object.'

Staff Sergeant Win Carnegi, aged 41: 'In a defensive situation I think I could shoot . . . As for the boy, I would try to distract him or talk him out of it . . . I cannot bring myself to shoot a child let alone kill him . . .'

Private Stefanie Humphrey, aged 21: 'I think I could turn my hand to shoot someone. I think one would remain absolutely calm or hysterical . . . I would stay calm – and then go to pieces afterwards . . . I would try to maim the boy . . . I might even try to talk him out of it.'

Private Lesley Davies, aged 21: 'No one wants to die and if it's a question of living – him or me – then I would probably shoot. And I would expect all my female colleagues to do the same.'

Cook Noelle Hutchings, aged 25: 'I think if it was a case of my mates getting killed then I would have to shoot to kill . . .'

These answers were obviously impulsive responses by women given little time to think out a logical reply. In retrospect they might have pondered the distinction between a woman in the REME who repairs a tank gun and the man who actually fires it; between the girl who tracks down an enemy aircraft and the gunner who pulls a lever to shoot it down; between the woman who handles the electronics controlling a cruise missile and the man who launches it. Morally there is no difference whatsoever. Senior officers in the WRAC concede that point, which is why they are already beginning to face up to the day when women's role in warfare will undoubtedly be enlarged to include combat.

One of the remaining controversies of life in the Army for women is marriage and the natural desire of many women to become mothers. There has never been any overt restriction on women in uniform marrying but in the early days of the WRAC there was, as Eileen Nolan described it, 'almost an automatic reaction that if you married, you left the service. We hadn't reached the age of women's lib and I don't think any of us would have thought twice about it. Many girls married army officers and certainly in those days there was no such thing as posting husbands and wives together.'

Lucy Anwyl-Passingham, who married Lieutenant-Colonel David William Davies in 1955, was one WRAC officer who was torn between her husband, who was in the RAMC, and her own career when posted to Cyprus in 1957.

> The director, Mary Railton, asked me what my husband would think. I telephoned him and his immediate reaction was: 'I think you'd better go.' The posting meant promotion to lieutenant-colonel, my husband's rank, and he made the point that I should not allow someone else to be promoted over me. And so I went, rather hesitantly. I was one of the first wives to be posted away and by 1959, when I was due to return, the RAMC had agreed to post my husband to wherever I went. Sadly, he died before I returned home.

These days the Army is far more accommodating when posting personnel and every effort is made to ensure that serving husbands and wives stay together. However, in many instances wives choose to go abroad even if it does mean living apart from their husbands. Colonel Nan Robertson, commandant of the Guildford Training Centre, spent three years in West Germany commanding the WRAC attached to the BAOR while her civilian husband remained in England. The decision is always left to the individual but very few decline the opportunity, which usually carries with it promotion.

Gael Hammond married Lieutenant-Colonel Michael Ramsay in 1977 and although they were posted together to Hong Kong they spent a long time separated when Michael went to Germany and she remained in England.

> The more senior one gets in the Army the more difficult it becomes to get postings abroad together. We have coped but with great difficulty – we ran up enormous telephone bills speaking to each other every evening, sharing our troubles and our cares over the satellite that links us.

Colonel Gael Ramsay, who is deputy director of the WRAC, is adamant that she would have re-enlisted had she had children.

In today's Army marriage will not prevent a woman becoming director of the WRAC if she is in line for the top job, despite the fact that it is 45 years since the last married woman was appointed to this post. A quarter of the 400 WRAC officers are married, many of them to other serving officers, so the chances are high that one of them might become director. Marriage, however, is as far as they can go. The 'right of retirement' on pregnancy grounds was one of the 'liabilities', for so it was described, discussed by the Working Party into the Future Employment of the WRAC. The policy in 1975 and the policy today is that WRAC officers resign their commissions and servicewomen are discharged after four months of pregnancy, in or out of marriage. The woman may be permitted to rejoin the service six months after the birth if she can prove that adequate arrangements have been made for the welfare and well-being of the child, but in practice this rarely happens. And one can understand why, because the Army takes a lot of convincing that, even if a childminder is employed or a suitable crêche is organized, the responsibilities of motherhood will not impinge on a woman's duties. The Army expects its personnel to be ready to travel anywhere at any time and believes that mothers would not be able to pack up and go without first making protracted arrangements for the care of their children.

While this rule remains rigid for mothers, the Army takes a different line with its fathers. There are many soldiers with children in the British Army, a fair percentage of them single parents who, one can assume, are also weighed down with family responsibilities; yet men are not required to prove that adequate arrangements have been made for their children.

In fact, there *are* two mothers in the WRAC but both are exceptional cases, suggesting that only very occasionally might the Army be prepared to bend the rules. One is a widow whose officer husband was killed in Northern Ireland, and the other is a divorcée whose children were not living with her at the time she joined the service.

Brigadier-General Inez Bailey summed up the viewpoint of the US Army in 1974 and the points she made then roughly echo the opinions of the WRAC now: 'Mothers have a role in child-rearing that is different from fathers and we have to think about what effect this has on mission readiness and our ability to be available for world-wide assignment.' Commenting on the rising number of unmarried women becoming pregnant, she added: 'It is unthinkable that a pregnant woman should continue to live in troop billets, sharing rooms and facilities with her peers during the advanced stages of pregnancy; yet should she be put out in the civilian community without an adequate capability of caring for herself?' That dilemma is shared by all directors of women's services in Britain yet the rule remains as rigid as ever: if you are pregnant, you go. And there the matter rests. Or does it?

In America, Canada, the Netherlands, most other NATO countries and Australia, servicewomen with children do have the right to stay on in their jobs, although the Reagan administration has had the policy under review. Curiously the matter was first raised in America in 1949, long before the emergence of the feminist movement, when the chief of the US Navy's Bureau of Medicine and Surgery, Rear-Admiral Clifford A. Swanson, argued that pregnancy 'is a normal biological phenomenon in women in the military age group'. He maintained that there appeared 'to be no reason for terminating the service of personnel who are pregnant but physically able to perform their duties'. President Truman was not convinced by the admiral's reasoning and in April 1951 signed an Executive Order permitting the services to terminate the employment of any woman who was pregnant, who had custody of or adopted a child under eighteen, or who by marriage became a step-mother of such a child living in the household.

Women could apply for a waiver to this rule but it was rarely granted until the late 'sixties when the military began to take a more liberal view, forced on them by the frequent litigation brought by servicewomen. An applicant for a waiver had to prove that she could provide for a child without it hindering her duty. In 1967 Major Eleanor L. Skinner of the US Air Force applied for a waiver to adopt a boy. The air force told her to first adopt the child then apply for a waiver but gave her no assurance that the waiver would be granted. Because formalization of the adoption depended on the waiver, she found herself in an impossible situation until Major-General Holm stepped in to argue her case and the waiver was granted. The press rightly contrasted Skinner's position with that of two men, one a sergeant who was praised for accepting a Vietnam assignment despite being a widower with several children, and the other a single chaplain who was applauded for adopting two Vietnamese boys.

General Holm took up the cudgels on behalf of servicewomen to change the inconsistencies of the policy. Although she received support in 1970 from the judge advocate general's office, which counselled that while the policy was legal they concurred with her proposals, she was vociferously opposed by Colonel Elizabeth P. Hoisington, then director of the WAC and later promoted to brigadier-general, and by Captain Rita Lenihan of the navy. Holm won her case on the waiver issue when the deputy chief of staff for personnel, Lieutenant-General Robert J. Dixon, arguing that 'we should be doing things *for* people, not *to* them', ordered his staff to rescind the minor children discharge policy. But the veto on pregnancy remained.

However, the US Army ignored the ruling on its waiver policy, in spite of several cases brought against it, even when the Department of Defense instructed the services to drop the waiver policy and rules on pregnancy by 15 May 1975. The continuing litigation caused one major to explain the position of the WAC thus: 'Many women are company commanders in parades and you couldn't have a pregnant woman leading a parade.'

By 1975 the WAC had a new director, Brigadier-General Bailey. She was of the same opinion as her predecessor, Brigadier-General Hoisington, and with the support of the army secretary, Howard H. ('Bo') Calloway, implementation of the new policy was delayed. In 1976 the courts ruled that the Marine Corps regulations requiring the discharge of a pregnant marine as soon as pregnancy was discovered violated the Fifth Amendment. That decision should have settled the issue but the US Army continued to baulk at the change of policy until 1978 when Bailey's successor, Brigadier-General Mary Clarke described the policy as 'discriminatory', adding that it failed to recognize pregnancy as a temporary disability and violated the principle that the army takes care of its own.

It is interesting that a Department of Defense study in 1977 concluded that the differences in lost-time for men and women were insignificant: men lost much more duty time on average for absence without leave, desertion, alcohol- or drug-abuse, than did women for pregnancy.

In 1980 the American magazine, *Soldiers*, refuted a suggestion that pregnant women were a detriment to the army's ability to mobilize and deploy by stating: 'If you take all personnel who are considered non-deployable within units required to fill unit readiness reports, you'll find both men and women. Less than 10 per cent of non-deployable soldiers are in that category because of pregnancy. The other 90 per cent of non-deployables would appear to be the main detriment to readiness – much more than pregnancy.'

Brigadier-General Hoisington, now retired, still maintains her original stand on the pregnancy issue. Interviewed in 1986 about her views on women in the US Army, she declared:

> I worry more than anything else about the children that the women are now having. Of course, they have the problem on the male side, too, with the single parent, and I think it is and will continue to be a bigger problem as time goes on.
>
> Who is going to take care of these kids, or the babies, when the mother or the father has to go off to duty? A single parent father might be able to arrange for a neighbour to look after Johnnie if he is

> ill, but the mother who is a military woman and single calls in and says I have to stay at home and take care of him. Who does the job in the office when we let all these women have time off for pregnancy and for looking after their sick children? This is a problem that is getting bigger and bigger and I personally feel that the US Army and other armies in the world have not been able to come to grips with it.

In many ways the US Army *has* come to grips with it. American servicewomen are allowed to stay on for several months during their pregnancy, wearing special maternity uniforms. When they return to work after confinement, crêches are provided for the children at military bases at home and abroad. However, it is officially estimated that 75 per cent of the married women in the US forces are mothers, a rather startling statistic and one which certainly begs the question whether all these women are ready at a moment's notice to be posted away from home.

Although there is no move yet in Britain to fall in line with other countries, the possibility is very strong that in the future the Ministry of Defence may have to yield on the pregnancy issue for servicewomen, not only because society may insist, but because of the enormous wastage of highly skilled personnel.

Brigadier Sheila Heaney raised this very question in 1986 in the course of an interview for this book. While agreeing with the policy that pregnant women should be discharged, she forecast that the Army might have to weigh up the costs involved in losing permanently women with high-grade technical qualifications.

> An increasing number of women in civilian life are having their families and then returning to work. With technology which requires expensive and extensive training, the Army might wish to encourage more to resume their careers. I will applaud that decision if that is the way society at large has moved. Social attitudes are bound to be reflected in the Army.

Brigadier Helen Meechie believes the pregnancy issue is perfectly straightforward.

> If you are a commercial venture and you can afford to bring people in part-time to substitute, then you can also afford to allow women to have six months' maternity leave. The system in the Army does not allow you to do that and when you look at the American experience, they are at any one point ten per cent undermanned. What happens

> during that time? They operate without that ten per cent. It makes no military sense whatsoever.

It makes even less military sense if one considers that in the British Army doctors advise that women should leave in the fifth month of pregnancy and only be permitted to apply for re-instatement six months after the baby is born, thus requiring an absence of at least eleven months. Brigadier Meechie points out that after six months the servicewoman in the United States still has the right to say she is not returning to duty:

> So you have done without that individual only to find that you have kept the job there for her and she might not want it. All that we in Britain are saying is that we are not going to do that. We need to be 100 per cent manned and therefore we discharge a girl when she is pregnant.

She also believes it is reasonable to demand that provision is made for the child's care before the mother applies for re-instatement.

> It's not for us to look after the baby. We've had someone with three children but she had a nanny to look after them. It's not a case of saying officers do not have children, it's a case of saying officers should be employable, which means worldwide at the drop of a hat. It is something the military have thought through. I was director just short of five years and I did not have one application for re-instatement in these circumstances. I think the realities of what service life means, combined with husbands' commitments and the commitments of family life, are arguments against any idea of rejoining the service.

A young lieutenant who was due to be married the following week echoed the feelings of her former commanding officer: 'I intend to have a family and I shall not apply for re-instatement, because I feel the Army is a twenty-four-hour commitment. Under no circumstances could I be a mother and also a member of the WRAC. The demands on my time at work are far too much.' Of four NCOs questioned about the pregnancy policy, only one thought it was unfair: 'Civilian women are allowed time off by their firms. Why can't the Army do the same for military women?'

There just might be hope, though, that eventually the Army will re-think its present policy on pregnancy. In 1987 the government changed the law to give servicemen the right to sue for compensation if they are injured on duty and a court of appeal ruled that an ex-soldier, who claims to have contracted cancer as a result of nuclear tests in 1967, could sue for damages. These are significant digressions from policies which have remained rigid for a long time and they suggest that unless conditions for women are reviewed they too could come under attack in the courts. It may take twenty or more years but eventually the Army will have to move in step with the changing values of society. In the meantime the WRAC, and its sister services, continue to insist: 'No children, please.'

Marriage, quite apart from motherhood, may also be an inhibiting factor for a career in the WRAC. Apart from her duty in the Army, it is still usually the responsibility of the wife to organize the household, prepare the food, take care of the cleaning and laundry. Unless she employs domestic help, she finds herself with the strain of what amounts to a dual job, in much the same way as do civilian women in employment outside the home. A wife in the WRAC faces enormous strain in holding together a marriage and some of their unmarried colleagues maintain that sometimes it shows. 'Obviously they are thinking ahead to the time when they can go home and what they might be doing that evening. You can't afford to let your mind wander when you're in the Army. It requires intense concentration all the time.'

Despite the numerous opportunities for leading a fairly full social life, the British Army frowns on intimacies outside marriage: what you do outside the perimeter of the barracks is your affair obviously, but we make the rules for what is done on our property – that is the attitude. Officers have their own rooms which are very comfortably furnished, and when they reach the rank of major they also have a sitting-room. There is no rule against entertaining male guests but the careful woman officer may consider it discreet to have a colleague present to maintain visible propriety. Also, of course, some of the rooms in messes are very small and close together, so that any indiscreet behaviour would be instantly noticeable. If promiscuity is suspected it is likely to bring a reprimand or even a request to resign a commission, depending on how gravely the offence is viewed.

The same conditions obviously apply to NCOs who may also have single rooms, and to the privates who will be sharing rooms with up to three others, effectively ruling out any possibility of entertaining men alone. The permissiveness which now is fairly standard in civilian courtship does not seem yet to have permeated the corridors of the Ministry of Defence, which keeps a very stern eye on the women in the three services. Dennis Barker in *Soldiering On* sums it up this way: 'The women of the Women's Royal Army Corps lead lives balanced between the permissive society and the nunnery – with a slight bias, if anything, in favour of the nunnery.'

13
SANDHURST

There is something like 250 years of tradition behind the Royal Military Academy although the site at Sandhurst itself was chosen only at the end of the eighteenth century by the man recognized as the academy's founding father, John Gaspard Le Marchant. The move of the Royal Military College to Sandhurst took place in 1812 when the Old Building was completed for the training of 'gentlemen cadets to be future officers of the cavalry or infantry'. In 1940 the RMA at Woolwich, which had trained officers for the artillery, engineers and signals, amalgamated with Sandhurst to educate and train all army officers on a common basis. Unfortunately the Second World War interrupted the plan and for the next seven years Sandhurst became an OCTU location. But, on 4 January 1947, with the intake of 328 officer cadets, the RMA Sandhurst began its new life.

Through its imposing portals have passed such distinguished soldiers as the young Churchill, Haig and Montgomery. No wonder Sandhurst is held in such awe and the thought of women being drilled on the parade ground in front of the Old College was as abhorrent to some men as the prospect of girls being enrolled as pupils at Eton and Harrow. Perhaps the sentiment is best summed up by a one-time sergeant-major at the Royal Military Police stables at Aldershot who very definitely preferred horses to women: 'What I say is, put a woman in charge of anything and there's always a cock-up.' Little did he dream back in 1977 that within nine years his company would be commanded by a woman, Major Pepi Simpson, at Aldershot, home of the British Army.

The move by women to Sandhurst took place over many years and began early in the 'sixties when the WRAC College was established at Camberley, virtually across the road from the academy. At first the women joined the men for social events only but during the period when Anne Field was commandant of the WRAC College, civilian instructors from Southampton University were replaced by the academic staff at Sandhurst. This resulted in a gradual process of integration and it seemed obvious that the next step would be total incorporation of the college into Sandhurst, but despite in-house discussions the move was resisted. In 1975 the Working

Party into the Future Employment of the WRAC discussed the issue and its recommendation that the girls should live at Sandhurst was accepted by the Army Board.

During the discussions at the Ministry of Defence, it had been suggested that the limited fields of employment for WRAC officers stemmed from the narrow breadth of experience open to women in the Army and their subsequent limited training. The most obvious way of giving them a basic grounding in army education was to allow WRAC officers to receive instruction with the men from the outset of their careers. The Army Board ordered the working party to examine the proposal in depth and to report on the feasibility of training WRAC at Sandhurst; in October 1978 its report disclosed that the commandant, at that time Major-General Sir Philip Ward, and his staff were concerned that the introduction of WRAC into their student body would have a detrimental effect on 'the essential tempo of courses because of the female physical and endurance limitations'. Unfortunately, the women on the receiving end of that allegation will not disclose what their initial reaction was. The Army, diplomatically, reported merely that the WRAC College staff at Camberley were 'more optimistic'.

Brigadier Anne Field, who had succeeded Eileen Nolan as director, discussed the situation with Major-General Sir Michael Gow, director of army training, and decided that the obvious way forward was to make the WRAC College the fourth college at Sandhurst, and this took place in October 1981. Colonel Daphne Clark was at Camberley at the time and overnight her title changed from commandant of the WRAC College to commander of the WRAC College of the Royal Military Academy Sandhurst.

By 1984 the decision to move the WRAC College to Sandhurst had finally been made and the move took place under the direction of the adjutant-general, Sir George Cooper, the director of military training, Major-General Jeremy Rougier, the commandant at Sandhurst, Major-General Geoffrey Howlett, the director WRAC, Brigadier Helen Meechie, and the commander of the WRAC College, Colonel Shirley Nield, who had succeeded Daphne Clark. At the time the Camberley college trained student officers (graduates), officer cadets (non-graduates), warrant officers and non-commissioned officers with a through-put of about 600 women a year. The length of the graduate course was nine weeks whereas the non-graduates had a 28-week course, in line with Sandhurst. The warrant officers and NCO training moved as a package to the WRAC Centre at Guildford, and then Shirley Nield settled down to take a fundamental look at the officer training to try to match it with Sandhurst standards.

Major-General Howlett instructed Shirley to develop a course which was suitable for both graduates and non-graduates, but when she floated this idea at Sandhurst there was concern from the academic staff, who argued that they would be confronting two entirely different levels of intellectual capacity and training, and doubted whether they would be able to address them simultaneously with equal success.

Their argument was based on experience with the system at Sandhurst which separated the two streams – non-graduates taking the courses at Old College and New College, and graduates receiving their instruction at Victory College. Intense rivalry exists between the colleges, because non-graduates enter as cadets whereas graduates arrive as student officers with one star already on their shoulders, denoting second-lieutenant status. So, technically, the graduates are officers in training, a subtle but significant difference.

As it happened, Shirley Nield was well qualified to adjudicate on the problems which the academics anticipated. She had read psychology at Sheffield University and before joining the WRAC on a full-time basis in 1961 had been commissioned as a member of the TA. She was one of the first graduates to attend the WRAC School of Instruction, as it was then called, at Hindhead in Surrey.

> So I arrived at Hindhead as a second-lieutenant and this caused all manner of difficulties because I was living in the officers' mess, with the instructors, and they had to work out special ways in which I would be treated, what I was to be called and with whom I could go shopping. I found myself being called by my Christian name by the other officers but was not permitted to use theirs and had to address them as ma'am. I was called ma'am by the cadets and I wasn't permitted to refer to them by their Christian names and had to call them Cadet This or Cadet That. I was an officer to the cadets but a cadet to the officers. I knew one of the cadets very well because we had worked together as probation officers but we suddenly found ourselves in a curious position with neither of us allowed to use our Christian names. When it came to shopping on Saturdays, discussions took place on how this could be arranged. In the end it was decided that we should not travel on the bus in each other's company but could meet discreetly in the town if we wished. The instructors promised to look the other way if they spotted us together. I often say to people that during the six months I was at Hindhead the only creatures I could refer to by their first names were two dogs – a Jack Russell and a little spaniel.

On a more serious note, when Shirley put forward her views at Sandhurst she was drawing on her own experience. She contended that while the graduate was older, had a trained mind and a little more experience, the basic intelligence level was not that much different from the non-graduate who, in any case, had already attended the RCB and was therefore the élite of the prospective candidates for commissions. Besides, both categories of student at Sandhurst would be learning new subjects and this would put them all on the same level. She also pointed out that combining the two courses would mean dealing with only one group of women who would all have the same length of training.

Eventually a 25-week course was agreed with a good mix of academic and military subjects, ensuring that WRAC officers of the future would have a sound tactical knowledge to enhance their professional credibility and ease their entry into the Junior Defence Staff College later in their careers. Throughout the initial discussions Brigadier Meechie had the full support of Major-General Howlett and it was decided to have a trial run at the Camberley College with the final switch to Sandhurst taking place in January 1984. To everyone's delight the solution to the class-mixing problem was vindicated at the end of the first course when a non-graduate was awarded the academic subjects prize, adjudicated by the academic staff at Sandhurst.

The hearts of the traditionalists sank when they realized that the girls really were moving into a wing of the highly prestigious Old College, the very heart of Sandhurst, with the magnificent splendour of its high-arched ceilings, huge oils of military heroes, solid brass locks and the grand Mess Hall echoing with memories of the famous who had dined here during its 170 years. Shirley Nield believed that

> the men were horrified at the thought of us treading on what was regarded almost as regimental holy ground and there is still a *frisson* in some of the old officers when they find that Old College is occupied – half of it, anyway – by the WRAC. We chose the carpets, the curtains, selected all our pictures and photographs and one highly polished trestle table which dated back to the Windsor OCTU during the war.

Senior officers who might remember a rather spartan Sandhurst are inclined to shudder at the modern comforts. Wall-to-wall carpets soften the wooden floors which once rang to the stamp of heavy army boots and the clank of cavalry spurs; well-sprung mattresses replace the straw palliasses; cosy duvets add colour to beds which were once covered with coarse blankets. Flowers decorate the ante-rooms and housecoats hang on hooks which once supported heavy greatcoats and polished Sam Brownes. In Shirley's estimation,

> Initially the sergeants' mess viewed us with suspicion but accepted

> us as soon as they realized how keen the girls were to learn. Remember we had to prove ourselves and so there was a remarkable enthusiasm among the girls. We found that the NCO instructors, even those teaching fieldcraft, were especially eager to teach them and it wasn't merely because of the natural attraction between the sexes but because the girls were bright and attentive and really wanted to be taught everything.

The impact the girls made was far greater than many of the Sandhurst stalwarts had expected.

> They envisaged a handful of women in some small corner of Sandhurst who would be brought out only on special occasions – in other words, we would be invisible most of the time. However, when we moved, the requirements for WRAC officer training increased and we were looking for something like 80 young women in training. And, of course, we not only had the cadets but more women taking up positions as clerks, drivers and on the administrative staff. Approximately 80 women marching about on Old College square and appearing in church in hats and at Sovereign's Parade is a force to be reckoned with. We were always treated with great courtesy and at no point did I have any trouble that suggested animosity. There was the usual banter between male and female students and rivalries between the colleges, and I'm not going to say that there wasn't the odd untoward remark but, on the whole, the transfer took place in the most gentlemanly way, however painful they may have found it.

Among the first girls at Sandhurst was Catherine Wilson of Plymouth. 'The men treated us extremely well, but perhaps we were lucky being something of a novelty,' she said. Another trailblazer was Anne Gow, who enthused about the social life. 'With so much contact, it was only natural that couples should become friendly.' Her only complaint concerned the king-size blisters she developed on her feet during the 36-hour outdoor exercise in the New Forest.

Known as 'Passing Cloud', this exercise requires the girls to cover 22 to 25 miles using night navigation. They are dropped off in the New Forest in the middle of the night and so their first task is to orientate themselves. They have to live off their rations and carry a full pack of combat kit. Shirley Nield devised this modified exercise after studying a similar one for the men, who have to endure far more rugged terrain at the famous Brecon Beacons. 'I thought running up and down the Brecon Beacons was just a little too much for the girls to bear. I saw young men weeping with fatigue and I really thought it would not be sensible to subject the girls to such strenuous exercise.'

After the trek through muddy fields during some of the coldest months of the year, the girls must be ready for the assault course which is as tough as the men's. Faces blacked with camouflage cream and lugging heavy vehicle tyres, they scramble over and under obstacles and beneath wires to reach a set goal. They also have to face the confidence course, designed to sort out the stronger-willed from the timid. The girls have to climb trees, balance precariously on high wires twenty feet above the ground, scale twelve-foot walls, cross rivers on logs and swing on ropes over deep streams. Many take a ducking and emerge covered in mud, and invariably it rains. But, wet weather or sunshine, the girls must take it in their stride, always conscious that they are under the critical scrutiny of instructors. Watching the girls finish the punishing course for the first time, Shirley commented: 'And to think we gave up flower arranging for this!'

Develop character first and military leadership will follow, is the rule Sandhurst applies. During the first five weeks, therefore, character-testing is most in evidence. It is the period when marching is the order of every day, when spit and polish is applied to shoes and boots and when irons are wielded until the arms ache from fatigue; when bull-and-bluster initiation is at its most strident, when buttons must be perfectly in line on uniforms, when discipline is instilled into the most obdurate; when abuse is frequent and praise rarely if ever given. On the other hand, criticism and complaint are not stifled. If justified they are encouraged, listened to, acted upon, and wrongs are righted. Sandhurst must move with the times, stay in tune with the mood of society, adjust when necessary, but always within the strict parameters of what will be good for the Army.

The girls are taught skill at arms, firing pistols and sub-machine-guns. They could also find themselves canoeing down the Thames or rock climbing in the Welsh mountains. In the classrooms they study military technology, army history, politics and sociology, warfare and international affairs. Always they are aware of the Sandhurst motto, Serve to Lead, which embodies the spirit of all that an officer must experience and learn. It is leadership that counts here and that means being able to command a body of men or women who will respect you and trust your judgment. Someone once said that respect can never be bought, it must be earned – a lesson Sandhurst cadets must absorb early in their careers.

They learn it on the parade ground where drill sergeants may, even with the girls, exhibit a vocabulary rarely heard in drawing-rooms. 'How do you face up to Guards drill-sergeants?' one course of women cadets was asked. 'We love them,' they replied. 'They chase us round the square and call us horrible people, but they're lovely men. The drill's the best part of training.

Anyway, it's like ballet, really.' 'If brains were chocolate, you wouldn't 'ave enough to fill a Smartie – sir!' an NCO roars. The message may be blunt but for that very reason it comes across loud and clear – it is not the uniform that matters, not the person who wears it, but the skill he or she has acquired at Sandhurst which turns him or her into an officer in the finest traditions of the British Army.

What makes a good officer? Eileen Nolan has very definite views.

> A warm personality, the ability to get on with people, a sense of humour, loyalty, integrity and leadership, which is demonstrated by making quick decisions and having a sense of urgency. It has nothing to do with age, experience or education. The extremely interesting part of training cadets and studying their behaviour under all kinds of conditions – in the classroom, in the field, in the gymnasium – is that suddenly you see the most timid, the ones you never thought had it in them, taking the initiative. They're helpful to other girls who may be struggling, urging them on, proving that even the most difficult task can be performed and by their example instilling confidence in the rest of the class. Remember that an officer's main task is management and in today's Army it could mean managing men as well as women. For this reason an officer must be a good organizer of people, a carer, too, but most of all someone who demonstrates a skill at everything she does.

Bearing all that in mind, it should be remembered that the Army is service to the community, to the country and to the Queen, sometimes in the most dangerous circumstances. Ultimately an officer has the responsibility for making decisions which can mean life or death to those he or she commands.

Therefore the Sandhurst cadets and student officers are under continuous review. During each term there are two meetings at which progress is discussed. The first meeting decides whether individuals are on target, whether there is advice they can be given to alter the emphasis of their work or to improve weaknesses in behaviour or application to studies. If it is felt that someone is not doing well, he or she is put on a warning and given time to adjust their attitude. Towards the end of the term a decision is made at the second meeting whether individuals may go on to the next term or whether they are to be backsquadded, which means re-doing the first term. A few, perhaps ten per cent, either drop out voluntarily because they find the going too hard, or are told tactfully that some other form of employment might suit them better. At the first review meeting in the second term, decisions are made either to take individuals off warnings or to put others on warnings. The last meeting is to decide the order of merit.

By that time the examinations are over and the girls have experienced what is known as 'First Flight' – an office exercise where they adopt a role as a platoon commander or an adjutant. Here they are individually bombarded with problems, posed either personally by instructors acting as subordinates seeking quick decisions, or on paper or by telephone, while they maintain all routine work. There is no let-up for the budding officer – the problems have been fashioned from years of experience by the staff who know all the devices, designed not to trick or muddle the unwitting but to test confidence to the limit and to demand immediate action.

Sandhurst is all this and spit and polish, too. The girls must know how to apply polish to shoes – flat shoes on parade, boots on exercise – until they shine as they have never shone before. Everything from the angle of the cap badge, to the position of the feet during drill is measured and even a millimetre out of alignment brings a reprimand. The first contingents of girls found that they could not keep marching pace with the men because their skirts were too tight and so the required length of their stride was reduced to between 27 and 28 inches compared with the regular 32 inches of the men. They are as smart as the men on parade, although their warrant officer will probably insist that they are smarter. Social graces are not overlooked either; the girls are instructed on the correct way to behave at a cocktail party, how to reply to invitations, even how to hold a knife and fork in the right manner and work their way through a complicated dinner setting of cutlery. There are social divisions at Sandhurst but they must be quickly submerged. Here the Roedean girl, who is the daughter of a major-general or even of a king, rubs shoulders with the daughter of a private born in a council house in the East End of London. At Sandhurst it is the ability to get on with everyone that counts, to develop camaraderie and *esprit de corps*. Officers, they are warned, never blaspheme, never lose their tempers and rarely raise their voices in anger or in reprimand.

And so at the end of the course, the fortunate ones appear on Sovereign's Parade, so named by King George VI on 14 July 1948. During lunch at Sandhurst the King had remarked that he wished to mark the passing-out by naming the parade in future 'The King's Parade' and the champion company 'The King's Company'. At this the then adjutant, Charles Earle, stepped forward and with due respect begged to remind His Majesty that he already had a King's Company in the Grenadier Guards. 'Then it shall be "The Sovereign's Parade" and "The Sovereign's Company",' the King replied. And so it was.

On this day the two companies of WRAC – Windsor and Edinburgh, named after the wartime OCTUs – parade with the men in front of proud parents, invited guests, senior military officers and the sovereign herself perhaps, or her representative, and frequently before foreign royalty. It is then that this piece of Old England in the rolling Berkshire countryside resounds to the stirring music of the duty band, the bark of commands, the tread of marching feet, the presentation of the Sword of Honour to the top male cadet and the Sash of Honour to his female counterpart. Then, to the tune of 'Auld Lang Syne', the cadets march up the steps of Old College, beneath the graceful six-columned arch, to begin their lives as commissioned officers from midnight. Last to leave the parade is the adjutant who follows them into the Grand Entrance riding his white horse up the steps according to the custom originated by Captain F. A. M. Browning in 1926.

'Sandhurst is the best training ground for learning to be a king,' said King Hussein of Jordan, who himself went to Sandhurst and who sent his daughter there in 1986. It is also the best training ground for learning to be a gentleman or a lady, and an officer.

Brigadier Anne Field fought successfully to save the WRAC band when she was director. Here the band plays at Sandhurst.

14

THE SAME AS THE MEN

The idea of women in army helmets charging into action with bayonets fixed, of female pilots in Lightning fighters intercepting enemy aircraft, being shot down and captured, or of girls going to sea in Polaris submarines patrolling the oceans for months at a time is a little far-fetched, even for today's liberated society. Nevertheless the question of 'Women in Combat?' has become a real issue for defence chiefs faced with the dramatic changes which have taken place in warfare during the past three decades and increasingly faced with pressure from feminist groups for more equality in the armed forces.

Although the infantry is not entirely obsolete – on the contrary, the Falklands conflict amply demonstrated that it is still an essential force – the emphasis in warfare has largely shifted from the warrior skilled in close combat to the soldier trained to operate sophisticated weapons, complex lasers and micro-processors. Computerpower now directs firepower which can be remote from the 'battle area' yet able to deliver devastating destruction, rendering unrealistic the military safeguard on the deployment of combat-support personnel who must be positioned well behind the so-called front lines.

However, the objection to women assuming an active role in killing the enemy is far more fundamental than any legal or logical grounds; it takes into account cultural traditions, psychological attitudes and to a lesser extent physical capabilities, and expresses the most basic imperative of human beings, indeed of any living creatures – the survival of the species. In almost every culture female responsibility has been confined to the hearth, where she is the bearer and the rearer of offspring, a guardian of posterity. Males were the hunters and the fighters, providing a constant supply of food and guaranteeing protection. Young males were both biologically and economically the most dispensable members of the tribe. There is also a deep evolutionary symbolism in the warrior mystique, linked to chivalry and martial skills: women motivate, inspire, admire and, afterwards, applaud the victors, soothe, comfort and care for the wounded. Quite apart from the powers that gradually accrued to men in such societies and their natural wish to preserve them, desire also to keep that warrior mystique their own must have played some part in men's stance on the question of women bearing arms.

Clear evidence exists that men are still more aggressive, competitive, risk-taking, indeed more combative, than women. This is not mere male fantasy but has been acknowledged by scholars, notably the feminists Carol Jacklin and Eleanor Maccoby of Stanford University, California. In *The Psychology of Sex Differences* they concede that males are more aggressive than females in all human societies for which evidence is available. It is not that women have not for long enough had the freedom to find their own levels of aggression. The differences in boys and girls are found early in life before adults have had an opportunity to 'shape' their lives according to social values. Significantly, similar sex differences are also found in primates, Man's closest relatives, but perhaps the most convincing proof is that aggression is directly related to male sex hormones (testosterone) and can be adjusted by experimental deprivation or administration.

Some evidence that women are against the idea of assuming a combat role appeared in the 1981 survey undertaken by *Soldier* magazine, although this small sample would not be accepted by professional opinion pollsters. Yet proportionately the views have hardly changed over the years. Of four WRAC NCOs quizzed in 1987, only one said she would have no qualms about killing an intruder. 'Even a twelve-year-old boy holding a grenade?' She never hesitated: 'Especially a twelve-year-old boy holding a grenade. He's far more irrational than a grown-up. After all it's his life or mine and I know whose life I value more.'

The views of former directors of the WRAC who opposed arming women reveal that most were thinking of combat in the conventional sense. While pressing for greater utilization of women in the Army, they stopped short of arguing in favour of tasks associated too closely with combat as they believed, quite justifiably it seemed to them at the time, that women should not be exposed to any close encounters with the enemy. Both Brigadier Sheila Heaney and Brigadier Eileen Nolan now concede that the position has changed considerably from the time when they were directors. Not only does progress in electronic technology mean that killing is done by weapons operating at a distance, but they believe that the authorities will have to take into account the sociological climate and, especially, the views of young recruits joining the WRAC in the future.

Brigadier Helen Meechie is emphatic in her views on combat.

> The whole future of the Corps revolves round 'what is combat?' You get people hedge-hopping, as it were, over the question. The Americans have done a massive study into how they identify combat roles in any unit, in any job, in any location. I think they divided it into a series of categories from one to ten, depending on the liability to combat. They have cleared their own minds on what combat is.

> We haven't. We still talk about the infantry men in the trench looking at Ivan coming over the other trench and the requirement to fire a weapon. We also still talk about firing tank weapons. But we are into new technology and you've probably read in the paper, as I have, that one of the security officers at Greenham Common is a woman. There are women there responsible for firing those weapons by pressing a button. That's the area we are talking about. There are no physical limitations required to press a button. It's purely a mental approach and the question is whether or not there is any difference in approach between male and female.

Asked if she would have any inhibitions about pressing that button, she replied:

> I think in the circumstances where that button had to be pressed I wouldn't have any inhibitions. I don't think the young generation would have either. It's far too remote. I think I would have great inhibitions in a face-to-face situation but equally I have doubts about how long those inhibitions would last if it was a question of kill or be killed.

In 1981 Britain had hardly batted an eyelid over the announcement that the WRAC were to receive weapon training. Compare this with public opinion in West Germany during the early 1980s when there was a move to enrol women in the armed forces. Brigadier Meechie recalls that Germany went out of its way to test opinion, which came out against the idea of women in the military. The result was largely influenced by the extreme sensitivity of the Germans to the part their women had played in the SS during the Second World War. When she was serving as a colonel in the BAOR, Helen was asked to send an officer to Cologne University to take part in a debate on the pros and cons of admitting women to the army. There, too, the motion in favour of recruiting women was defeated. 'It was interesting to me that there should be a university debate on the issue. At the time when it was announced the WRAC would carry arms, no university in Britain held a debate on the subject.' West Germany's police force also does not have women serving in its ranks.

Even in America, where the concept of modern-day 'combat' has been thoroughly debated, where women are now integrated in the armed forces (except, since 1982, for training) and where the feminist lobby has to a greater extent influenced military thinking, the Pentagon has ruled against assigning women to combat roles. The question was raised and fully examined during the last years of the Carter administration when Jeanne Holm was Special

Assistant for Women to the President; the main reservation was not how combat would affect women but how men might react to 'infantrywomen' alongside them. The Reagan administration firmly turned down the proposal but the issue is certainly not dead, indeed there are constant reviews because feminists argue, quite logically, that until women are clearly regarded as combat-ready there can be no true equality between the sexes.

The Dutch have been the most progressive of all nations in NATO but even they appear to hesitate when it comes to the crunch. In 1986 they sent a 23-year-old helicopter pilot, Nellie Speerstra, to the NATO combat training school at Sheppard's Air Force base near Wichita Falls in Texas. There she underwent training to fly one of the world's most advanced fighter planes, the F-16, which has air-to-air and air-to-ground laser-guided missiles, wing-tip rockets and an array of bombs. Nothing could be more combative than flying one of the world's most lethal planes where the pilot is in a one-to-one situation with an enemy aircraft or can see the destructive capability of weapons when attacking ground installations. Considerable doubts were raised about Nellie's ability to develop the ruthless killer instinct held to be an essential psychological attribute of fighter pilots. Her boyfriend Erik van Destolpe was always optimistic about Nellie's chances: 'She is prepared to kill if she has to,' he assured interviewers. Yet in survival training he admitted she had had to hit a rabbit twice because her first blow was too soft. 'She didn't like that at all,' Erik said.

There is a veil of secrecy over how Nellie actually fared in Texas although the word was that her performance met the high standards required. However, the Dutch air force announced in 1987 that Nellie had been assigned to 'other duties' after completing her training, which suggests either that she failed the final and most demanding test or simply that there were second thoughts about allowing her to assume a combat role in the NATO air force.

The biggest question mark against a woman becoming a fighter pilot concerns the ability of the slighter female frame to withstand the enormous G-forces without losing consciousness. In addition trainee pilots have to endure a punishing and brutal exercise in a flight simulator; they must operate the controls successfully while being flung around the cockpit. Nellie was said to have passed this test, which makes incredible demands on the body. So where does this leave the question of physical fitness – the final barrier, and for many the deciding one, against women in combat?

In the days of long, forced marches over rough terrain when troops carried heavy equipment, the need for physical strength might have clinched the argument for the Army, but this is largely irrelevant in the present-day concept of warfare. Dexterity in operating complex instruments, and intellect in interpreting information rapidly and

Left Lieutenant Marilyn Whitley on an army parachute course at the Rhine Army Parachute Association. *Below* Corporal Pat Heelan (*right*) and Lance-Corporal Mary Smith made history by becoming the first NCOs in the WRAC to qualify as sky divers at Larkhill, Wiltshire.

Above WRAC officers at the Joint Services Sub Aqua Club. *Right* Member of the WRAC on Exercise Dolphin in the Mediterranean. The Army provides an opportunity for girls to learn underwater diving during adventure training.

accurately, are far more important considerations in ground forces and there are few who will deny that women cannot match, sometimes exceed, the skill of men in these spheres. Testing procedures for recruits have been so refined that military authorities are able to ensure that only the best operators, irrespective of sex, are used. Even the relative physical weaknesses of women are also in dispute. In 1977 tests conducted on 875 men and 825 women at Fort Jackson in South Carolina found that women performed comparably with men on basic critical tasks and skills not requiring much physical effort, and in physical readiness training the women did as well or better in 60 per cent of the tasks.

However, while women met or exceeded the male standard in the inverted crawl, bent leg sit-up and in run, dodge or jump exercises, they did not match the men in the one-mile run or horizontal ladder. Given the gap in field and track athletics between the performances of men and women it is not surprising that the one-mile times were not comparable. On the other hand probably very few men in the Army today could beat the fastest women middle-distance runners in Britain. Also, it should be borne in mind that the horizontal ladder is geared to the physical dimensions of men and requires considerable upper body strength which women cannot be expected to develop in the ordinary course of events. Overall the women far exceeded the expectations of military authorities, and these tests led to a reassessment of physical standards for job categories in the US Army. In the end it is training which makes or breaks a soldier, and very few male officers who participated in the US experimental programmes during the late 1970s doubted that women would function effectively in combat.

Colonel Kitt MacMichael, who in 1977 was adviser on women in the US Army, said the degree of difference on male and female physical ability was not necessarily of great concern. 'What is of concern is that every individual awarded a military occupational speciality is physically able to perform to the army standard. It is not our goal to make every woman an Amazon or every man an Olympic champion.'

Apart from individual females, who were the exceptions rather than the rule, there are several historical examples of women taking on the role of warriors. Perhaps the best-known were the ancient Amazons, a legendary nation of women warriors who lived in the neighbourhood of the Euxine and established a matriarchy in which the women marched to war while the men stayed at home to do the domestic and pastoral work. The name actually means 'breastless' and it was said they removed the right breast to prevent it getting in the way of the bowstring. Although these original Amazons are considered mythical, in 1541 the Spanish explorer Francisca de Orellana claimed that in a battle with the Tapuyan tribe on the banks of the River Maranon in South America he witnessed women warriors fighting alongside the men. He accordingly renamed the river the Amazon, or River of the Amazons, but others contend the name already existed, based on the Indian word *amassona* (boat destroyer), applied to the tidal bore.

Far more relevant was the so-called Amazon army of Dahomey seen by Richard Burton and other Africa explorers in the nineteenth century. Every eighteen-year-old Dahomeyan girl was required to appear before a selection committee, presided over by the King, who chose the most physically able to become women warriors, expected to fight to the death. These female levies formed the flower of the Dahomeyan army and Europeans who saw them in action during 'manoeuvres' were astonished by their stamina and fighting qualities. The most spectacular part of their training was an obstacle race which they undertook naked. They charged at and climbed a 15-foot high by 6-foot wide barrier of thorns bordering a ditch packed with glowing embers. The next obstacle was a line of huts built of prickly pear leaves. Missionaries were appalled by the dangers but recorded only minimal injuries, such as minor burns and scratches. The corps survived until the last quarter of the century; one of the reasons for its disbandment was that, because the women were forbidden sex, the birthrate had declined dramatically.

In recent times the Russians not only had a women's regiment which fought in the front line during the Second World War but a female fighter squadron and a bomber squadron. In peacetime women do not play as active a role in the modern Soviet army and, according to NATO, they now number about 10,000. It is difficult for them to become officers because the commissioning schools are barred to women and they are unlikely to obtain commissions direct from the ranks.

If one excludes guerrillas in, for instance, southern Africa and Nicaragua, one other modern example of fighting women is Israel's army. One of the reasons for the women's withdrawal from front-line positions was said to be the reaction of Israeli soldiers to the capture of a woman by the Syrians, who mutilated her in front of them. This was to some extent confirmed by Colonel Dahlia Raz, commander of the Israeli Women's Corps, during a 1978 seminar in London on the Future of Women in the Armed Services. She said that there were two points of view on women in combat. 'One is emotional; we had some very tragic experiences during the wars, especially the last one, with prisoners . . . While it is tragic enough for men, it is much worse, much more deeply felt, for women to be captured. There is also a logical point of view. Men serve in the reserve army to the age of fifty-five . . . but women have to stay in the reserve only to the age of twenty-two. It does not make sense to invest in special training and then not to use the investment . . .'

At the same seminar Chief Superintendent G. Drinkwater of the Metropolitan Police said that for the police force the front line was the streets

Major Pepi Simpson, the first WRAC officer to command a unit of the Military Police, Aldershot.

of London. 'If I walked into an armed robbery on the way back to the Yard there would be no suggestion that I should not deal with it because I am a woman. The public do not differentiate. You are a police officer and that is that . . .' Nevertheless the public were incensed by the deaths of women police officers in the Harrods bombing and during the Libyan Embassy incident. The policy of the commissioner is not to send women officers into situations where there is obviously going to be a confrontation, such as demonstrations, but there was no way of anticipating the events which claimed the lives of those two young women.

In the final analysis the real issue is whether women themselves will want to adopt a truly combat role and whether society will permit them to do so. Major-General Jeanne Holm, before her retirement the highest ranking woman to serve in the US armed forces, has no doubts that women should be given a combat role.

> It is time to accept that modern wars are 'fought' not just by an élite class of people categorized as 'combatants' but by *all* who serve.

She points out that servicewomen are assigned in thousands to jobs that would expose them to enemy attack in the event of even a limited conflict, adding:

> Moreover, to be overly concerned about the welfare and safety of military women while at the same time accepting as inevitable the obliteration of literally millions of civilian women and children in the event of a nuclear confrontation is ludicrous. Events, not policy or law, dictate who will be exposed to war and who will be in combat.

Brigadier-General Elizabeth Hoisington, former director of the WAC, has always been firmly against women in combat. Interviewed in 1986, she had this to say on that subject and on integration:

> We must have a strong military and we do not want weak links in our armour anywhere along the line because of women. Some years ago, in response to pressure for equal rights, the US Army decided that men and women should receive their basic training together. It was soon discovered that the men were not doing as well as they should be. There was not as much bonding because the men found it simple to outperform the women physically. Since 1982 the policy has been reversed and the women take their basic training separately.

She might have been echoing the opinion of General Lewis B. Hershey, former director of the Selected Service System, who was quoted in 1978 as saying: 'There is no question but that women could do a lot of things in the military. So could men in wheelchairs. But you couldn't expect the services to want a whole company of people in wheelchairs.'

The thrust of this argument is still used by those who oppose the full integration of men and women in the British Army. They feel that the disbandment of the WAC in the United States and its integration into the US Army might have opened up more careers but at the cost of destroying the *esprit de corps* which had existed for 36 years. Brigadier-General Inez Bailey, who succeeded Hoisington as director of the WAC, is also not entirely convinced that integration in the US Army was the right step.

> Although the laws have been changed to prevent sexual discrimination, it is not so easy to change attitudes. The problem areas all revolve around the cultural and sociological aspects of integration. I think we should bear in mind that equal does not mean identical. They are trying to make women look like men and act like men . . . I think women can retain the sociological aspects of their femininity and still make a contribution to the army. If you are going to be absolutely equal, then why not make men wear skirts for three and a half days a week? That, surely, is not what equality is all about.

Brigadier-General Pat Foote, who was promoted in 1986 to deputy inspector-general for inspections in the US Army, has a different approach. She believes that she might never have achieved one-star rank under the old system: 'We now have four women serving as brigadier-generals on active duty whereas before integration there was only one. So there is no numerical limit on how many we could have because the women are as well qualified as the men.'

Britain is the only country in NATO which has not so far opted for total integration, although it has been under consideration from time to time. Brigadier Meechie recalls a recent meeting of the Committee of the Senior Service Women Officers of the [NATO] Alliance at which a Norwegian observer raised a question of whether disbandment of women's corps had not sacrificed a 'focus' for females. It was generally agreed round the table that it had, because women were no longer able to identify with a common unit. 'If a woman wears a cavalry cap badge, it is, to some extent, farcical. Everyone knows that she is unlikely to be driving a tank into action. So why should she adopt the insignia of tank or infantry regiments? After all, women are posted to the administrative side of those regiments and, strictly speaking, are not actively engaged and probably never will be.'

The British Army is headed in the same general direction as the US Army but is travelling a different route. Because of its proud regimental tradition, it is the envy of other armies and the WRAC has its place as one of those regiments:

> The WRAC has established a proud tradition. Our roots go back 71 years to 1917 and that is longer than some corps in the Army [says Brigadier Shirley Nield]. The Royal Corps of Signals was established in 1920 and the Royal Electrical and Mechanical Engineers in 1942. The Royal Tank Corps shares the same anniversary as we do, having been founded in 1917. What was lost in the US Army when the WAC disbanded was that wonderful feeling of comradeship which a corps like ours can engender . . . Women are different, our needs are not exactly the same as men's, so you need someone in authority to speak up for them.

The most obvious way forward for the WRAC, according to Brigadier Nield, is for women to follow a career which does not necessarily involve infantry or a tank group.

> It is government policy, only very recently reiterated, that women should not be employed in direct combat. This is believed to reflect the generally held view of the British public and I think it probably does. Not only that, I believe it reflects the view of most members of the armed forces, both men and women. It is simplistic to insist that women, in order to be treated equally, should become identical to men. Men have their excellencies: strength, aggression, courage and the capacity to form extremely strong, well-bonded, cohesive groups, the essential ingredients of an effective combat team. What is not often stated is that women have theirs too: loyalty, imagination, patience, single-mindedness and absolute determination to see a task, once started, to its conclusion. They have also proved themselves both resolute and relentless in defence of 'their own'. Women in the Corps since 1917 have shown precisely these qualities and I believe have earned themselves a permanent place within the Army in their own right. If it is insisted that women should be judged in male terms against essentially male criteria, they will be doomed to frustration and failure. Moreover, the Army will fail to benefit from their real and much needed talents. If we have to fight, we will, but we can make a better contribution elsewhere.
>
> To use a sporting analogy, the majority of the Army, both men and women, are not essentially belligerent combat soldiers but are engaged in ensuring that the First XV arrive on the field in the best possible

> condition to win the match. I suggest that placing a couple of women in the side on the field is not the best use of their talents. It neither benefits them nor does it enhance the team's chance of winning. The real mistake is to assume that the players make the only valid and valuable contribution. Without a good deal of accurate and careful planning and practical support, the players would probably arrive late at the wrong stadium and without their shorts and find that the clubhouse has been burnt down in their absence.
>
> There is no doubt that changes will continue to be made in the employment of women in the Army and that women will wish to make a greater contribution and to receive greater recognition for that contribution. But we ignore the differences between men and women at our peril.

However, the advocates of women in combat insist that society is in a transitional period and that by the twenty-first century sex roles will have disappeared to the extent that the present constraints on women will have faded into obscurity. They view the military not as a follower of civilian customs but as an instrument to quicken change in sociological values. They remember especially that Edwardian male chauvinists dismissed the demands of the suffragists with the argument that women played no part in the defence of the realm. Since 1917 that view has been eroded to the extent that the WRAC serves with almost every regiment and corps in the Army and in 1987 was even posted to the senior Foot Guards Regiment and the Parachute battalions, although admittedly only to posts in the adjutants' offices. The cutting edge remains a masculine preserve and is really the essence of true defence – the ability to repel an invader on the field of combat. Only when that last male bastion is breached will women achieve true equality in society, the feminists contend.

Whether or not they will succeed in their campaign is a prediction only a sociologist is qualified to make, though it is doubtful if even Dame Helen Gwynne-Vaughan would have anticipated the progress made by the WRAC in recent years. On the other hand, if they listen carefully, the echoes of her distinctive and deep-toned voice probably still resound along the corridors of the present-day Ministry of Defence in answer to questions on what is good for the women.

'The same as the men . . . the same as the men . . .'

Brigadier Shirley Nield, the present director of the WRAC.

DIRECTORS

AUXILIARY TERRITORIAL SERVICE

Chief Controller Dame Helen Gwynne-Vaughan	1938-41
Chief Controller Jean Knox	1941-3
Chief Controller Leslie Whateley	1943-6
Chief Controller Mary Tyrwhitt	1946-9

WOMEN'S ROYAL ARMY CORPS

Brigadier Mary Tyrwhitt	1949-51
Brigadier Frances Coulshed	1951-4
Brigadier Mary Railton	1954-7
Brigadier Mary Colvin	1957-61
Brigadier Jean Rivett-Drake	1961-4
Brigadier Joanna Henderson	1964-7
Brigadier the Hon. Mary Anderson	1967-70
Brigadier Sheila Heaney	1970-3
Brigadier Eileen Nolan	1973-7
Brigadier Anne Field	1977-82
Brigadier Helen Meechie	1982-6
Brigadier Shirley Nield	1986-

DEPUTY CONTROLLER COMMANDANTS: WRAC

Brigadier Dame Mary Railton	1961-7
Colonel Lucy Davies	1967-77
Brigadier Eileen Nolan	1977-84
Brigadier Anne Field	1984-

SELECT BIBLIOGRAPHY

Anderson, Agnes *'Johnnie' of QMAAC.* (Publisher unknown, printed by The Plymouth Press)

Barker, Dennis *Soldiering On.* (André Deutsch, London, 1981)

Bidwell, Shelford *The Women's Royal Army Corps.* (Leo Cooper, London, 1977)

Bond, Brian *War and Society in Europe 1870-1970.* (Fontana, London, 1984)

Braithwaite, Brian; Walsh, Noëlle and Davies, Glyn (compilers) *Ragtime to Wartime, The Best of Good Housekeeping 1922-1939.* (Ebury Press, London, 1986)

Brereton, J. M. *The British Soldier.* (The Bodley Head, London, 1986)

Costello, John *Love, Sex and War.* (Collins, London, 1985)

Cowles, Virginia *Edward VII and His Circle.* (Hamish Hamilton, London, 1956)

Cowper, J. M. *The Auxiliary Territorial Service.* (The War Office, London, 1949)

Dyer, Gwynne *War.* (The Bodley Head, London, 1986)

Ewing, Elizabeth *History of 20th Century Fashion.* (Batsford, London, 1986)

Gilbert, Adrian *World War I in Photographs.* (Orbis, London, 1986)

Greer, Germaine *The Female Eunuch.* (MacGibbon & Kee, London, 1970)

Gwynne-Vaughan, Dame Helen *Service with the Army.* (Hutchinson, London, 1941)

Holdsworth, Irene *Yes Ma'am.* (Hutchinson, London, c.1943)

Holm, Jeanne *Women in the Military – An Unfinished Revolution.* (Presidio, Novato, Calif., 1982)

Izzard, Molly *A Heroine in her Time.* (Macmillan, London, 1969)

Keegan, John and Holmes, Richard *Soldiers.* (Hamish Hamilton, London, 1985)

Krippner, Monica *The Quality of Mercy, Women at War Serbia 1915-18.* (David & Charles, London, 1980)

Lawrence, Margot *Shadow of Swords.* (Michael Joseph, London, 1971)

Lewis, Peter *A People's War.* (Thames Methuen, London, 1986)

Longmate, Norman (ed.) *The Home Front.* (Chatto & Windus, London, 1981)

Marwick, Arthur *British Society Since 1945.* (Penguin, London, 1982)

— *The Deluge, British Society and the First World War.* (Macmillan, London, 1975)

— *Women at War 1914-1918.* (Fontana, London, 1977)

McLeod, Kirsty *The Last Summer.* (Collins, London, 1983)

Mitchell, David *Women on the Warpath.* (Jonathan Cape, London, 1966)

O'Day, Alan (ed.) *The Edwardian Age – Conflict and Stability 1900-1914.* (Macmillan, London, 1979)
Playne, Caroline *The Neuroses of Nations.* (Allen & Unwin, London, 1925)
Popham, Hugh *F.A.N.Y. 1907-1984.* (Leo Cooper in association with Secker & Warburg, London, 1984)
Purdom, C. B. (ed.) *Everyman at War.* (J. M. Dent, London, 1930)
Sandes, Flora *Autobiography of a Woman Soldier.* (Witherby, London, 1927)
— *An English Woman-Sergeant in the Serbian Army.* (Hodder & Stoughton, London, 1916)
Saywell, Shelley *Women in War.* (Costello, London, 1986)
Schreiner, Olive *Woman and Labour.* (T. Fisher Unwin, London, 1911)
Shepperd, Alan *Sandhurst, The Royal Military Academy.* (Country Life, London, 1980)
Sherman, Margaret *No Time for Tears.* (Harrap, London, 1944)
Stevenson, John *British Society 1914-1945.* (Penguin, London, 1984)
Terraine, John *To Win a War – 1918, The Year of Victory.* (Macmillan, London, 1986)
Thompson, Paul *The Edwardians – The Remaking of British Society.* (Weidenfeld & Nicolson, London, 1975)
Trevelyan, G. M. *English Social History.* (Longmans, Green & Co, London, 1944)
Trollope, Joanna *Britannia's Daughters.* (Hutchinson, London, 1983)
Ward, Dame Irene *F.A.N.Y. Invicta.* (Hutchinson, London, 1955)
Whateley, Dame Leslie *As Thoughts Survive.* (Hutchinson, London, 1948)
Wilson, Trevor *Myriad Faces of War: Britain and the Great War 1914-18.* (Polity Press, London, 1986)

INDEX